Co-Production and Public Service Management

Victor Pestoff has long been one of the leading writers and thinkers about co-production. His new book provides an exciting and challenging perspective for anyone interested in this topic. Highly recommended!
—**Stephen P. Osborne**, *University of Edinburgh Business School, UK*

This volume compiles a dozen essays by one of the most prolific proponents of co-production as a solution for many of the challenges facing public services and democratic governance at the outset of the 21st century. Co-production is considered a partnership between citizens and public service providers that is essential for meeting a growing number of social challenges that neither the government nor citizens can solve on their own.

These challenges include, among other things, improving the efficiency and effectiveness of public services in times of financial strain; increasing the legitimacy of the public sector after decades of questioning its ability with the spread of New Public Management; finding viable solutions for meeting the growing needs of aging populations in many parts of the world; and finally, promoting social integration and cultural pluralism in increasingly diverse societies when millions of refugees and immigrants are on the move. This involves tackling the threat of burgeoning populism following the rise of anti-immigrant and anti-global parties in many countries in recent years.

This volume addresses issues related to the successful development and implementation of a policy shift toward greater citizen participation in the design and delivery of the services they depend on in their daily lives and greater citizen involvement in resolving these tenacious problems, facilitated by the active support of governments across the globe. Moreover, it explores participatory public service management that empowers the front-line staff providing public services. Together with users/citizens they can insure the democratic governance of public service provision.

Victor Pestoff is Professor Emeritus in Political Science and currently Guest Professor at the Department of Social Sciences at Ersta Sköndal Bräcke University College in Stockholm, Sweden and the Department of People and Technology at Roskilde University, Denmark.

Routledge Critical Studies in Public Management
Edited by Stephen P. Osborne

The study and practice of public management has undergone profound changes across the world. Over the last quarter-century, we have seen

- increasing criticism of public administration as the over-arching framework for the provision of public services,
- the rise (and critical appraisal) of the New Public Management as an emergent paradigm for the provision of public services,
- the transformation of the public sector into the cross-sectoral provision of public services, and
- the growth of the governance of inter-organizational relationships as an essential element in the provision of public services

In reality these trends have not so much replaced each other as elided or co-existed together—the public policy process has not gone away as a legitimate topic of study, intra-organizational management continues to be essential to the efficient provision of public services, whist the governance of inter-organizational and inter-sectoral relationships is now essential to the effective provision of these services.

Further, whilst the study of public management has been enriched by contribution of a range of insights from the 'mainstream' management literature, it has also contributed to this literature in such areas as networks and inter-organizational collaboration, innovation and stakeholder theory.

This series is dedicated to presenting and critiquing this important body of theory and empirical study. It will publish books that both explore and evaluate the emergent and developing nature of public administration, management and governance (in theory and practice) and examine the relationship with and contribution to the over-arching disciplines of management and organizational sociology.

Books in the series will be of interest to academics and researchers in this field, students undertaking advanced studies of it as part of their undergraduate or postgraduate degree and reflective policy makers and practitioners.

Co-Production and Co-Creation: Engaging Citizens in Public Services
Edited by Taco Brandsen, Trui Steen and Bram Verschuere

Co-Production and Public Service Management: Citizenship, Governance and Public Service Management
Victor Pestoff

For more information about this series, please visit: www.routledge.com/ Routledge-Critical-Studies-in-Public-Management/book-series/RSPM

Co-Production and Public Service Management

Citizenship, Governance and Public
Service Management

Victor Pestoff

Routledge
Taylor & Francis Group

NEW YORK AND LONDON

First published 2019
by Routledge
711 Third Avenue, New York, NY 10017

and by Routledge
2 Park Square, Milton Park, Abingdon, Oxon, OX14 4RN

Routledge is an imprint of the Taylor & Francis Group, an informa business

Library of Congress Cataloging-in-Publication Data
A catalog record for this book has been requested

ISBN: 978-0-815-39504-1 (hbk)
ISBN: 978-1-351-05967-1 (ebk)

Typeset in Sabon
by Apex CoVantage, LLC

To the legacy of Nobel Laureate Elinor Ostrom and her pioneer work in the study of citizen participation in the provision of public services

Contents

Tables and Figures

Tables

Figures

Foreword

Professor Pestoff is a founding member of global research communities both in the area of social enterprise and in the area of public administration. For three decades, these research communities have explored the link between efficient and effective public service provision, citizens' active participation and even ownership in relation to the economy and democracy. Accordingly, Professor Pestoff is a pioneer when it comes to understanding the evolution of welfare pluralism based upon a convergence from previous static welfare regimes to one where welfare is allocated along lines that are more flexible. His concept and theory of the 'Welfare Triangle' with a depiction of the third sector has found deep international recognition in the research community. His research on the transition from the old social economy, marked by amalgamations of cooperatives into big global corporations, to the new social economy, noted by a mix of social enterprises and other third sector organizations, makes a valuable contribution to a field that still lacks a sufficient research base. Perhaps even more importantly, he is among the pioneers in research on hybridity, co-production and New Public Governance that are all crucial dimensions of contemporary systems of governance, especially in relation to public services.

   With this collection of articles, we get much-needed insight into the history of co-production as an academic subject and as practical ways in which co-production can be a part of transforming a welfare state, committed to the principles of inclusion and universalism, towards a participatory state. In the participatory state, ordinary citizens, users and street-level bureaucrats co-produce public services at the local level. However, even more importantly, such patterns of co-production form a new institutional core. After World War II, universalism and redistribution was a core component for architects of welfare states not only in the Nordic countries, but across the globe. Universalism and equality was realized to such a degree in Scandinavia that the welfare state perhaps became the most important mega social innovation from this part of the world during the 20th century. However, even in the Scandinavian countries, universalism and equality have been strongly challenged, if not already removed as governing principles. In his book *A Democratic Architecture for the Welfare State*, Professor Pestoff argues that contemporary welfare states have reached a historic juncture. In today's society, citizens and policy makers have to choose between a greater role for civil society and the third sector/social economy as providers of welfare, on the one hand, or unregulated privatization, on the other hand. When the universal welfare state peaked in a country like Sweden, public spending reached as much as two-thirds of GDP, but only two decades later, public spending had dropped by almost 20% in 2013. According to *The Economist*, Sweden has reached a lower level of public spending than France, and it could even soon be lower than Britain's.

With this new volume, Professor Pestoff provides both evidence and an analytical framework for understanding how citizen participation and co-production are far from neutral instruments of service provision. Consequently, these concepts face the danger of being misused as means for cuts in public funding "under the guise of empowerment". Throughout his career, Professor Pestoff has rigorously analyzed the delicate balance of the interrelated concepts of co-production, citizen participation and social enterprise, in light of their interplay with the larger questions of what type of economy and what kind of democracy we want. Based upon a rich stock of comparative evidence and a unique ability to see crosscutting patterns, he constantly argues that such powerful and potentially emancipatory concepts interact intrinsically with changing regimes of public administration. Accordingly, co-production and citizen participation are crucial behavioral mechanisms both in systems of New Public Management and New Public Governance. In both regimes, citizens are valued as co-producers and providers of services. However, only in policy systems where public governance aims at simultaneously preserving and innovating the inclusive and universal principles of welfare can co-production serve as emancipatory tools in the hands of empowered citizens. Here they may even serve as founding principles of the participatory state, which is the label Professor Pestoff has chosen for his vision of a radical "decentralization of power and influence to the lower echelons of the administration, the workers and clients of the organization, [which] promotes participatory public management".

With this volume, Professor Pestoff has provided a solid and fruitful foundation for addressing the need to reinvent democracy in an everyday practical fashion that is more frequent and compelling than when casting votes to elect national parliaments or local councils every fourth year.

Lars Hulgård,
Professor, Roskilde University, Denmark, Co-Founder and
Former President of the EMES Network

Preface

My Ph.D. dissertation was a comparative study of voting behavior, "Voluntary Associations and Nordic Party Systems: A Study of Overlapping Memberships and Cross-Pressures in Finland, Norway and Sweden" (1977). So, I have had occasion during the past four decades to ask myself what voting really means to individuals and society. Is voting merely a symbolic action or does it make a difference in a democracy? Is voting every second, third, fourth or fifth year sufficient to make democracy work and work well? Or, do citizens perhaps need to find other channels of political engagement? How do they express their views in the years in between elections? How accurate are opinion polls? This is where and why questions about participation in other channels become interesting and important. Are citizens prepared to accept the responsibility of participating in the provision of public services that they vote for and pay for with their taxes? And, if so, how many are willing to do so? Or, do they prefer to leave such questions to the politicians that they elect and bureaucrats that they pay with their taxes? Moreover, are politicians and public servants willing to recognize the contribution of citizens to the provision of public services and facilitate their participation in a meaningful fashion? This is one reason why questions about facilitating citizen participation in the provision of public financed services takes on such a sustained interest for me.

Nobel Laureate Elinor Ostrom states that co-production attributes citizens an active role in producing public goods and services of consequence to them (1996: 1073). The present volume reflects the fact that my own introduction to the concept of co-production in the early 1990s didn't initially come from the study of public administration, but rather from business administration, where it still holds traction today. In the 1980s and 1990s I worked at the School of Business, Stockholm University, as a Research Associate with a focus on consumer issues; client/citizen participation was quite naturally at the core of my research. One of my colleagues, Professor Solveig Wikström, shared an interest in consumer issues and she introduced me to the concept co-production from a business-to-business perspective. She considers co-production as a social phenomenon where the customer is no longer a passive receiver of goods and services, but rather an active and knowledgeable participant in a common production process (Wikström, 1996). She holds that this type of social exchange is motivated in part by the perceived degree of uncertainty in the exchange relationship and the potential benefit accruing to the participants from eliminating this uncertainty (*ibid*.: 363).

This concept seemed particularly relevant for my own work on cooperative childcare, so I adopted and adapted it to my research and findings. My first conference paper on this topic, "Beyond Exit and Voice in Social Services: Citizens as Co-Producers", appeared in *Delivering Welfare: Repositioning Nonprofit and Cooperative Action in Western European Welfare States* (6 & Vidal, 1994). The concept of co-production continued to intrigue me and was used to analyze the data from the Work Environment and Cooperative Social Services (WECSS) Project. A book, *Beyond the Market and State: Social Enterprises and Civil Democracy in a Welfare Society* (1998), presented the project's main results. About the same time, I joined the staff of a new university in Stockholm, Södertörn University, returned to the discipline of political science and later became Professor of Political Science at Mid-Sweden University in Östersund. However, it was then that I read the work of Professor John Alford (2002) and became familiar with the pioneering efforts of Professor Elinor Ostrom and her colleagues. Thank you, John!

Later, I became a Guest Professor at the Institute for Civil Society Studies, Ersta Sköndal Bräcke University College in Stockholm, Sweden and more recently an Adjunct Professor at the Department of People and Technology, Roskilde University, Denmark. I have now published two dozen articles on co-production and edited two books on this topic. My own perspective on the importance of studying co-production stems from its potential to facilitate greater citizen participation in the provision and delivery of public services of all types. My research focuses on typically mainstream, enduring welfare services, like childcare in Europe. Given that such services are labor intensive, co-production has the potential to provide significant economic, political and social benefits, if properly encouraged and structured in a fashion that facilitates greater citizen/user participation in some complementary and/or essential tasks, rather than the core ones.

The study of co-production also focuses on different types of social services in other parts of the world. For example, health and eldercare in most developed countries face a complex and partly contradictory mix of financial, social and political challenges. Fiscal strains combined with New Public Management agendas have produced severe cutbacks and calls for greater efficiency in public health and eldercare, resulting in a growing concern about service quality. A project called "Co-Production in Japanese Health and Eldercare—Participation and Service Quality" explores the possibility to address these issues from the perspective of greater patient and staff participation (Pestoff, Saito *et al.*, 2016). It asks how health and eldercare services can be provided when professionals and patients/clients act as 'partners' who can co-produce the service through their mutual contributions. This study investigates if and how this can result in better service quality. Moreover, it also explores how institutions that enrich the work environment and promote a multi-stakeholder dialog between the staff and clients can help to facilitate better service quality. The empirical part of this study compares four consumer and four agricultural co-op hospitals with two public hospitals, and explores a broad database collected by questionnaires to the staff, patients and volunteers at these 10 Japanese hospitals.

Acknowledgements

A number of people have encouraged and stimulated my continued interest in co-production and the arguments presented in this book, through their interactions, writings and discussion with me, but unfortunately only a few can be mentioned here, so I'll limit myself to four. First, I would like to thank Professor Lars Svedberg, who invited me to join him and his colleagues at the Institute of Civil Society Studies at Ersta Sköndal Bräcke University College in Stockholm, Sweden. I have spent a stimulating decade there. Second, I would like to mention Stephen P. Osborne, Professor of International Management at the University of Edinburgh. He is one of the most open and creative academics imaginable and he provided a platform for publishing our initial findings on co-production in the journal he edits, *Public Management Review*. Third, my friend and colleague Professor Lars Hulgård, at Roskilde University, Denmark, who is always willing to entertain new and different perspectives on a topic that both unites and divides us: democracy. Fourth, Professor Yayoi Saito at Osaka University, Japan, whose encouragement and support provides me with some new and interesting challenges in the future. To all four of you, your support means more that you can imagine. Thank you so much!

I was assisted in the revision of these chapters by my wife, Kathleen. Without her help and support it would never have reached fruition. So, I want to thank her especially for her love and support.

I also want to acknowledge the right to reuse some of my own copyrighted materials in the preparation of this volume that have recently been moderately to heavily revised. The following chapters have been adapted from:

Ch. 2   Pestoff, V., 1998; Beyond Exit & Voice in Social Services, abridged and revised in Chapter 4, Economic Aspects of Civil Democracy; Beyond the Market & State: Social Enterprises and Civil Democracy in a Welfare Society; Aldershot, Brookfield USA, Singapore & Sydney: Ashgate. Reproduced by permission of Taylor & Francis Group, LLC, a division of informa, plc.

Ch. 3   Pestoff, V., 1998; Empowering Citizens as Co-Producers, Chapter 10 in Pestoff, V., 1998; Beyond the Market & State: Social Enterprises &

civil Democracy in a Welfare Society; Aldershot, Brookfield USA, Singapore & Sydney: Ashgate. Reproduced by permission of Taylor & Francis Group, LLC, a division of informa, plc.

Ch. 4   Pestoff, V., 2006; Citizens and the Co-Production of Welfare Services: Childcare in Eight European Countries; Co-Production: The Third Sector and the Delivery of Public Services; V. Pestoff & T. Brandsen (eds), special issue of Public Management Review, 8/4: 503–520, reprinted in 2008 as a hardback and in 2009 as a paperback by Routledge: London & New York. Reproduced by permission of Taylor & Francis Group, LLC, a division of informa, plc.

Ch. 5   Pestoff, V., 2009; Towards a Paradigm of Democratic Governance: Citizen Participation and Co-Production of Personal Social Services in Sweden; Annals of Public and Cooperative Economy; 80/2: 197–224. Reproduced by permission of John Wiley & Sons.

Ch. 6   Pestoff, V. 2012; Crucial Concepts for Understanding Co-Production in Third Sector Social Services and Health Care; abridged and modified version of Chapter 2, Co-Production and Third Sector Social Services in Europe: Some Crucial Concepts and Issues; in New Pubic Governance, the Third Sector and Co-Production; V. Pestoff, T. Brandsen & B. Verschuere (eds); London & New York: Routledge. Reproduced by permission of Taylor & Francis Group, LLC, a division of informa, plc.

Ch. 7   Pestoff, V., 2014; Collective Action and the Sustainability of Co-Production; Public Management Review, 16/3: 383–401. Reproduced by permission of Taylor & Francis Group, LLC, a division of informa, plc.

Ch. 8   Copyright 2016 by V. Pestoff as Democratic Innovations: Exploring Synergies between Three Key Posts—NPM Concepts in Public Sector Reforms; and published as Chapter 15 in Social Entrepreneurship and Social Enterprises: Nordic Perspectives; L. Lundgaard Andersen, M. Gawell & R. Spear (eds), London & New York: Routledge, eISBN: 9781315621982. Reproduced by permission of Taylor & Francis Group, LLC, a division of informa, plc.

Ch. 9   V. Pestoff, 2018, Co-Production at the Crossroads? What Role for Service Users and Providers? Revised and expanded version of Co-Production at the Crossroads of Public Administration Regimes?; copyright and published 2018 as Chapter 4 in Co-Production and Co-Creation: Engaging Citizens in Public Service Delivery; T. Brandsen, T. Steen & B. Verschuere (Eds); London & New York: Routledge. Reproduced by permission of Taylor & Francis Group, LLC, a division of informa, plc.

Ch. 10 Pestoff, V., 2018; The Impact of Public Administration Regimes and Co-Production on Hybrid Organizations; forthcoming as Chapter 4 in Handbook on Hybrid Organizations; D. Billis & C. Rochester (eds); Cheltenham, UK & Northampton, MA: Edward Elgar. Reproduced by permission of Edward Elgar Publishing.

1 Rethinking Public Service Management and Renewing Democracy

Engaging Citizens as Co-Producers of Public Services

A. Introduction: Co-Production in a Participatory State

Social and welfare services in most developed countries face a complex and partly contradictory mix of financial, social and political challenges. Fiscal constraints combined with New Public Management agendas have resulted in severe cutbacks and calls for greater efficiency in public services that provoked a growing concern about service quality. This collection of essays explores the possibility of addressing these issues from a new perspective that emphasizes greater user participation. It is based on the idea that citizens can play a more active part in the provision of their own care services. It explores how public services can be provided when professionals and service users/clients act as 'partners' and where the two parties co-produce the service through their mutual contributions. Some management scholars argue that co-production makes an important contribution to the debate on public management that goes to the heart of both effective public services delivery and the role of public services in achieving societal ends—such as social inclusion and citizen engagement (Osborne *et al.*, 2013: 145). Moreover, they state that "by taking a service-dominant approach, co-production becomes an inalienable component of public service delivery that places the experiences and knowledge of the service user at the heart of effective public service design and delivery" (*ibid.*: 146). However, this volume recognizes the potential danger of the concept being misused or misappropriated as a reason for making further cuts to public funding, requiring citizens to bear even more of the burden of an inadequate social safety net, often under the guise of empowerment.

Nobel Laureate Elinor Ostrom states that co-production attributes citizens an active role in producing public goods and services of consequence to them (1996: 1073). Co-production is considered a partnership between citizens and public service providers that is essential for meeting a growing number of economic, political and social challenges in the 21st century. Neither the government nor citizens can solve them on their own. These challenges include, among other things, improving the efficiency and effectiveness of public services in times of financial strain; increasing the legitimacy of the public sector after decades of questioning its ability with the spread of New Public Management; and finding viable solutions for meeting the growing needs of aging populations in many parts of the world. Co-production promises both greater efficiency and effectiveness in public services, as well as more citizen influence in the design and delivery of public services by facilitating their participation in the provision of these services.

Failing to understand the new trends in public service management and the demands of citizens for high quality public services they depend on in their daily lives can also pose a populist threat (Pestoff, 2008a). This alarm came on the heels of the Social Democratic defeat in the 2006 Swedish *Riksdag* election that opened the door to right-wing populism combined with anti-foreigner rhetoric, even in a staunch Scandinavian welfare state. Ignoring the growing desire of many citizens to play a more active role in the provision of important public services, like childcare, primary and secondary education, health care, eldercare, handicap care, etc. alienated many voters who previously supported high quality public services in return for high taxes. Many of them also wanted to participate in the co-production of such services for themselves and their loved-ones.

Today, 10 years later, many European countries are facing populist challenges by issues related to social inclusion and cultural pluralism, in increasingly diverse societies, at a time when millions of refugees and immigrants are on the move. Tackling the threat of burgeoning populism following the rise of anti-immigrant and anti-global parties in recent European elections underlines the urgency of considering co-production not only as a way of curtailing public expenditure for major public services, but also from the perspective of citizenship, governance and public service management. In short, active citizen participation in the provision of public services they rely on in their daily lives can also help preserve and renew democracy when it faces serious populist challenges in many advanced societies.

This volume compiles over half a dozen moderately revised articles, most published between 1994 and 2016, plus a few new ones. Most of them are stand-alone articles, but some unnecessary repetition has been eliminated to improve reading. However, some overlap remains for the consistency of the argument in the context in which they were first prepared. These chapters address issues related to the successful development and implementation of a policy shift toward greater citizen participation in the design and delivery of the public services that they depend on in their daily lives. Greater citizen involvement can facilitate the resolution of some of the most tenacious problems facing governments across the globe and help win popular support for such measures.

A seminal Organisation for Economic Cooperation and Development (OECD) report on co-production calls for rethinking traditional public service delivery in a new socio-economic environment (2011). Existing models of public service provision are not only tenuous, but they are not affordable in the long-run. This lends greater urgency to developing alternative models that focus on citizen participation in public service delivery. The OECD also notes that co-production takes place at different stages in the policy process, from planning through delivery and review. However, it warns that co-production is more than mere consultations or simply giving citizens/users a say in and/or more responsibility for the design, provision or evaluation of public services (*ibid.*: 18). It involves citizens/users in more systematic exchanges with the paid staff who create and deliver public services. Therefore, co-production transforms the relationship between service users and providers, ensuring the former greater influence and ownership. Moreover, providing citizens and users with more influence over public services, particularly about service quality, may prove crucial for evoking their participation as co-producers in the most labor-intensive and enduring services like health care and social services. Herein lies both the challenges and opportunities posed by co-production, but the devil is often in the details.

Co-production comprised one of two core research areas for Nobel Laureate Elinor Ostrom and her research team in Indiana in the 1970s and early 1980s (Parks *et al.*, 1981; Ostrom, 1996), the other being governing common pool resources. Initially, it resulted in a flurry of interest, but it was overshadowed by New Public Management (NPM), which dominated thinking about public sector reforms for the next two decades. However, in the wake of heavy criticism of NPM in recent years, the concept of co-production gained renewed interest in Europe and elsewhere and it is now used by researchers in many parts of the world (Pestoff *et al.*, 2012; Brandsen *et al.*, 2018). At the turn of the century there were two main alternatives to continued governmental growth. One alternative was the marketization of public sector activities, through privatization and contracting out, etc., known as 'managerialism' and later as New Public Management (NPM). The other alternative was based on the participation of citizens, clients, customers, volunteers and/or community organizations in producing public services, as well as consuming or otherwise benefiting from them. The latter became known as New Public Governance (NPG) (Alford, 2009; Hartley, 2005; Osborne, 2010; Pestoff *et al.*, 2012). Co-production is often motivated in the public sector by cost reductions and higher quality services (Parks *et al.*, 1981; Alford, 2009). More recently the focus has grown to include new opportunities for citizens to influence the provision of important public services (Ostrom, 1996, 2000a; Fung, 2004; Pestoff, 2009). A third alternative to government growth now seems to be coalescing around ideas of greater volunteering and community responsibility for the provision of basic public services of all types, in light of massive cutbacks in public funding. The latter is called a 'Communitarian regime' herein for lack of a better word. (See Chapters 9 and 10 for more details.)

About the same time as the renewed academic and professional interest in co-production by promoting citizen participation in public service provision, Peters (1994, 1996) discussed the emergence of four alternatives to the traditional model of public bureaucracy: the market model, the participatory state, flexible government and deregulated government. Given its affinity to co-production, we will focus on participatory public sector management. In a participatory state, groups normally excluded under more hierarchical models are permitted greater involvement. This approach concentrates power in the lower echelons of the administration, the workers as well as the clients of the organization. It recognizes that the workers and clients found closest to the actual production of goods and services in the public sector have the greatest amount of information about the programs. If the energy, talents and ideas of those groups are harnessed government will work better; i.e., it will become more efficient, effective and productive. However, it calls for greater empowerment and self-government by such groups, which has clear implications for management of the public sector as a whole. Both workers and clients become more directly involved in managerial decisions and governance of the service (*ibid*: 13), often through a greater dialog between and among them. A multi-stakeholder dialog places the experience and knowledge of the service users at the heart of effective public service design and delivery (Vidal, 2013).

Although the prescriptions of neo-liberals and those proposing a participatory state may bear some similarities, they are definitely not the same. Rather than a means of creating competition among service providers in order to facilitate the market, decentralization in the participatory model is intended primarily to channel control to a different set of bureaucrats, and/ or to the clients (Peters, 1994: 16), through new direct democratic or participatory institutions. The goal of the participatory state might, therefore, be called participatory public management. We will return to this topic in greater detail in Chapters 5 and 12.

B. Growing Interest in Co-Production in Europe

In the 1990s the concept of co-production was probably influenced more by business administration than public administration in most European countries. In Sweden, for example, the business perspective was based on changing the perception of customers as passive recipients of goods and services to one where they became active and knowledgeable participants in a common production process (Wikström, 1996). This was often motivated by the uncertainty in businesses transactions and the potential benefit accruing to them by eliminating it (*ibid.*: 363). This line of reasoning was adopted by a project on cooperative childcare at the beginning of the 1990s. First, a conference paper on co-production and the third sector was published (Pestoff, 1994). Then, it was used to analyze the main results of the Work Environment and Cooperative Social Services (WECSS) Project, in the book *Beyond the Market and State* (Pestoff, 1998). It was first a few years later that the pioneering efforts of Elinor Ostrom and her colleagues were introduced through the work of Professor John Alford (2002).

Annual meetings of workgroups focusing on co-production at the European Group on Public Administration (EGPA) and International Research Society of Public Management (IRSPM) were instrumental in promoting the comparative study of co-production during the first decade of the 21st century. The results of these workshops were brought together in a special issue of *Public Management Review*, "Co-Production, the Third Sector and the Delivery of Public Services", (Pestoff & Brandsen, 2006) that was later reprinted as an edited volume by Routledge in 2008. Continued comparative research under the auspices of the EGPA and IRSPM resulted in a second edited volume, *New Public Governance, the Third Sector and Co-Production* (Pestoff *et al.*, 2012). Due to her continued teaching responsibilities Professor Ostrom could not attend these EGPA or IRSPM meetings, but she graciously contributed a Foreword to the 2012 volume. A selection of the chapters from that volume were then published in *Voluntas* in 2012. A third volume has just appeared, *Co-Production and Co-Creation: Engaging Citizens in Public Service Delivery* (Brandsen *et al.*, 2018). Today, the IIAS Study Group on Co-Production meets annually to discuss research into this topic. These meetings provide an inspiration to scholars from many parts of the world who study this phenomenon.

Having now written two dozen published articles on co-production and edited two books on this topic, my own perspective on the importance of studying co-production stems from its potential to facilitate greater citizen participation in the provision and delivery of all types of public services. However, my research focuses on traditionally mainstream, enduring welfare services, like social services and health care. Given that they are so labor intensive, co-production has a potential to provide significant economic and social benefit, if managed in a fashion that facilitates citizens/users participation in complementary and/or essential tasks, rather than the core ones.

Furthermore, it has been argued that co-production can eventually lead to a more democratic regime of governance (Pestoff, 1998, 2008a, 2009; Becker *et al.*, 2017). But, we need to stop and ask, what is democratic governance? Hirst defines governance as "a means by which an activity or ensemble of activities is controlled or directed, such that it delivers an acceptable range of outcomes according to some established social standards" (2000: 24). He points to the need to rethink democracy and find new methods of control and regulation of the big organizations that dominate life both in the public and private sectors (*ibid.*). Can co-production potentially qualify as a new method of control and regulation of big public organizations? Does democratic governance imply greater citizen participation and influence in the provision of public services, particularly those services that directly impact their daily life and/or that of their loved-ones? The following chapters argue that it does and that co-production can, therefore, contribute to promoting democratic governance.

Research on parent participation in European childcare and preschool services helps to illustrate the development of such new methods of control

(Pestoff, 2006; Vamstad, 2007). For example, in France, Germany and Sweden, parent participation in public financed third sector childcare is manifested in their responsibility for the management and maintenance of these services. A work obligation for parents not only provides them with crucial insights into details related to the daily operation of services, but also gives them a sense of belonging and 'ownership' of the services (Pestoff, 1998, 2006). Moreover, it also comprises a new method of control. The boards of cooperative childcare facilities are comprised of parents who are responsible for hiring the staff and the facility's economic stability, as well as deciding important issues like its opening and closing hours, the availability of service on holidays and during summer vacations, etc. Such issues are no longer decided by distant politicians or bureaucrats, who are mainly interested in curtailing public expenses. So, service users can gain more control over them, particularly over service quality. Thus, co-production promotes greater citizen participation and influence in the provision of public services, and thereby can qualify as a new method of control and regulation of public organizations. This not only empowers citizens but also helps promote participatory democracy.

This book addresses a number of central topics related to the study of co-production, and it combines theoretical discussions and important conceptual issues with empirical research that can help corroborate these discussions and issues. Building on ideas of Hirschman, it maintained that co-production provides a strategy for moving beyond exit and voice, particularly in collective forms. It then confronted these ideas with unique empirical material from parents using various third sector providers of childcare in Sweden in the early 1990s, which by and large confirmed these theoretical considerations. Ten years later, employing the ideas of Ostrom, my research returned to this field in a second empirical study that compared parent participation in preschool services in eight European countries. Parents with children in third sector providers participated more actively than those in public or private for-profit services. It also illustrated different types or dimensions of participation, economic, political and social, as well as a service specific dimension. A few years later, this body of research was corroborated by a newer study that focused on different providers of these services in Sweden, parent and worker co-ops, public services and small for-profit providers (Vamstad, 2007). A 'glass ceiling' was noted for parent participation in both public and for-profit providers, while both types of co-ops facilitated their involvement in co-production to a greater or lesser degree (Pestoff, 2008a, 2009).

Public policies can either crowd-in or crowd-out desired behavior by citizens, and co-production is not an exception to this rule. The above-noted research on childcare and preschool services in Europe leads to three main conclusions. First, there are different forms of citizen participation in the provision of public financed social services, namely economic, social, political and service specific participation. Second, a higher level of citizen participation is noted for third sector providers of public financed social services, because it is based on collective action and direct client participation, as illustrated by parent co-op childcare in France, Germany and Sweden. Third, some citizen participation is also noted for public provision of childcare services, but parents are encouraged to contribute more sporadically or in a limited fashion, like the Christmas or spring parties. However, they seldom have the opportunity to play a more active or significant role in managing the services or having decision-making rights and responsibilities for the service provision. Thus, a 'glass ceiling' in public services limits citizens to playing a passive role as service users who can make demands on the public sector, but they do not participate in decisions nor take any responsibility for implementing public policy. (See Chapters 5 and 7 for more details.)

Later, my research discussed some crucial conceptual issues for understanding co-production of third sector social services and health care, particularly in relation to the facility and saliency of participating in such services. It also noted that in spite of some similarities between co-production and volunteering, there are nevertheless major differences between them. It continued by examining issues of small groups, collective action and the sustainability of co-production and noted the importance of more nuanced approaches by governments to promoting co-production. It turned to democratic innovations and underlined the synergy between the three key concepts, social enterprise, public sector innovation and co-production, for developing a more coherent post-NPM paradigm. It then argued that co-production is currently at the crossroads between four public administration regimes (PARs), i.e., traditional public administration, NPM, NPG and a Communitarian regime. The principal actors in co-production, the professional staff and citizens, play quite different roles in each of them, so citizen participation will mean different things in each of them. It continued by exploring the impact of public administration regimes and co-production on hybrid organizations. It noted that their impact will depend in part on the type of third sector organization and its internal decision-making rules. Then it examined whether enhanced co-production facilitates the study of citizenship, governance and public service management or muddies the waters. It proposed to consider three/four different approaches or schools of co-production, rather than one unifying generic definition of this phenomenon. It also called for a new configuration to study co-production that includes three main actors rather than two: the professional staff, volunteers and citizens/clients, as well as three rather than two categories of tasks performed by them: core, essential and complementary.

Finally, it reaches some conclusions about the potential contribution of co-production to rethinking the management of public services, augment the legitimacy of the public sector and renew democracy by promoting greater citizen participation. It argues that co-production and the third sector together comprise a new variety of democratic governance that can readily complement representative democracy rather than replace it by populism in the 21st century.

The articles chosen for inclusion in this volume reflect these issues and concerns and it presents them in a systematic and coherent fashion. The next section provides a short summary of each of the chapters included here. Their presentation mostly follows a chronological order, starting with the earliest ones. The first half is comprised of previously published articles, while the second half includes some that were forthcoming or in press at the time of the conception of this collection, plus a few unpublished works.

C. Synopsis of the Chapters Included in This Volume

Chapter 2, Beyond Exit and Voice in Enduring Welfare Services: Citizens as Co-Producers?

This chapter extends Hirschman's concepts 'exit and voice' to the provision of personal social services. Exit and voice can complement each other, depending upon the type of goods or services provided. Exit is an appropriate response to consumer disappointments with non-durable or rarely used durable goods, while both exit and voice provide more adequate redress for continually or regularly used durable goods. Similarly, both exit and voice comprise adequate consumer responses to disappointment with minor or occasional services, while voice is more appropriate for redressing consumer disappointment with major or continually used personal social services or enduring welfare services. The transaction cost of exiting from enduring personal social services is often prohibitive for both consumers and producers. Thus, institutions for facilitating voice deserve greater attention. Social cooperatives can institutionalize the voice of consumers by integrating them into the production of personal social services, thereby rendering them into co-producers of these services. This can lead to an improvement of the quality of the services through a dialog between the consumers and producers of welfare services.

Chapter 3, Empowering Parents as Co-Producers of Childcare Services in Sweden

This chapter presents the data from the WECSS Project on alternative provision of childcare in Sweden in the early 1990s. It describes the social background of parents in parent co-ops, voluntary organizations and worker co-ops. It examines parents' motives for choosing a particular form of childcare and satisfaction with their choice. Then it compares alternative providers with municipal services for parents with experience from both public and alternative providers. It also asks, if they could choose again, would they choose a social co-op for their childcare. The WECSS Parent

Study shows that parents value the integrative aspect of the work obligation and the possibilities for participation stemming from holding an elective or honorary office. Most parents state unequivocally that alternative or
cooperative childcare services are better than municipal services, and they
provide several reasons for this. Thus, co-production helps to eliminate the
uncertainty related to interaction between producers and consumers of such
services by involving parents directly in the service provision. Their participation is seen by many parents as the best guarantee of quality.

Chapter 4, Citizens as Co-Producers of Welfare Services: Childcare in Eight European Countries

This chapter explores the role of the state, market and third sector in providing welfare services, and what role citizens can play in producing such
services. First, it introduces the concept of co-production, inspired by the
writings of Elinor Ostrom and her colleagues. The second part ties this concept to a discussion of different kinds of participation in the provision of
childcare services in Europe. That includes the economic, political, pedagogical and social involvement of parents. The concept of co-production
appears relevant for some aspects of parent participation and some forms
of providing services, but not for all kinds of participation or forms of provision. In particular, third sector alternatives, like parent associations in
France, parent initiatives in Germany and parent cooperatives in Sweden,
promote greater participation than municipal or for-profit services. Finally,
the importance of co-production is considered for promoting the development and renewal of democracy and the welfare state. It also calls attention
to differences between co-production, co-management and co-governance
in terms of citizen participation.

Chapter 5, Citizens as Co-Producers of Personal Social Services in Sweden: Toward a Paradigm of Democratic Participation

This chapter summarizes early reflections about the potential of co-production
to contribute to the democratization of the welfare state. Many countries in
Europe are searching for new ways to engage citizens and involve the third
sector in the provision and governance of social services in order to meet
major demographical, political and economic challenges facing the welfare
state in the 21st century. Co-production provides a model for the mix of
both public service agents and citizens who contribute to the provision of
a public service. Citizen participation varies between providers of welfare
services, as too does user and staff influence. Empirical materials from a
study of Swedish childcare illustrate that third sector providers facilitate
citizen participation, while a 'glass ceiling' appears to exist in municipal
and for-profit providers. Moreover, co-production takes place in a political
context, so it can be crowded-in or crowded-out by public policy. These

findings can contribute to the development of a new paradigm of participatory democracy.

Chapter 6, Crucial Concepts for Understanding Co-Production in Third Sector Social Services and Health Care

This chapter considers some issues related to the co-production of public services and the role of the third sector. This includes definitions; levels of analysis; co-production as individual acts, collective action or a mix of both; relations between the professional staff and their clients, etc. It examines why citizens become involved in co-production and the role of the cooperative gambit. It also addresses citizen involvement in terms of the nature of the providers and the salience of the service for them or their loved-ones. Then, similarities and differences between volunteering and co-production are briefly explored. Among others, we note that both types of activities are normally based on citizens contributing their unpaid time and effort that can benefit both themselves and others. Yet, volunteers provide services for others, not for themselves, while co-producers provide services both for themselves and others.

Chapter 7, Small Groups, Collective Action and the Sustainability of Co-Production

This chapter addresses the sustainability of citizen/user participation in the provision of public services. Co-producing public services promises to limit cost, but it also requires a change in the relations and behavior of public servants and citizens/users, in order for the latter to make a long-term commitment to co-production. Olson proposes two logics of collective action, not just one. Focusing on small group interaction provides an important strategy for achieving sustainable co-production, particularly of enduring welfare services. However, Ostrom criticizes simplistic approaches for promoting social cooperation in collective action situations, based on size alone. Some of her structural variables for resolving social dilemmas prove important for facilitating sustainable citizen participation in co-production. Some additional factors are also considered, like the nature of the service itself, organizational diversity, a dialog between the staff and clients and facilitating small group interactions in large organizations. This chapter concludes that governments should develop more flexible, service specific and organization specific approaches for promoting co-production, rather than simple 'one size fits all' solutions to the challenges facing public service management today.

Chapter 8, Exploring Synergies Between Social Enterprise, Social Innovation and Co-Production: Key Post-NPM Concepts in Public Sector Reforms

This chapter examines the synergies between three key post-NPM concepts in public sector reforms. These concepts are social enterprise, social innovation and co-production. Although these separate discourses share much in common, they seldom speak to each other. They refer to highly complex phenomena that involve multiple dimensions, including an economic, political and social dimension that require a multi-disciplinary approach. Yet, the academic debate normally oversimplifies them, often from the perspective of a single discipline. This chapter examines the multi-dimensional and multi-disciplinary nature of these three concepts and explores links between them for managing public services. This chapter asks how these post-NPM concepts can contribute to rethinking public sector management. It concludes that academics should recognize how the synergies between these three post-NPM concepts can contribute to public sector reforms. Moreover, governments should facilitate social enterprises and social innovations that promote co-production, rather than looking for simple economic solutions to the challenges facing public service management today.

Chapter 9, Co-Production at the Crossroads of Public Administration Regimes: What Role for Service Users, Providers and the Third Sector?

Although co-production is often called a 'partnership between citizens and public service providers', various public administration regimes are found in different countries and operate in different sectors. Four public administration regimes are considered here: Traditional Public Administration, New Public Management, New Public Governance and a Communitarian type of regime. Their differences are most clearly seen in the role played by the citizens/users of such services, as well as the professionals who guarantee the quality of public services. Citizens are considered beneficiaries in traditional public administration, consumers of public services in NPM, co-producers in NPG or service providers in a Communitarian type of regime. The role of professionals or paid staff in guaranteeing service quality also varies between command and control in traditional public administration, competitive in NPM, collaborative in NPG or back-up agents in a Communitarian type of regime. These differences can impact the costs and benefits attributed to co-production by different public administration regimes.

Chapter 10, Co-Production and Public Administration Regimes: Their Impact on Hybrid Organizations

This chapter analyzes the impact of public administration regimes and co-production of public services on hybrid organizations, particularly third sector organizations. It briefly introduces four PARs and argues that the ascent and dominance of a new regime, like New Public Management in the 1980s, may place third sector organizations (TSOs) in an unfamiliar, turbulent or even alien environment, resulting in increased complexity and hybridity. Then, it introduces the concept of co-production and notes that it can refer to a variety of phenomena at various levels that may result in greater hybridity and complexity for TSOs and their leaders. However, co-production will probably mean different things in different PARs, so in the future the leaders of TSOs will need to orient themselves towards one of two main regimes, either New Public Management or New Public Governance. However, some TSOs will facilitate co-production more readily than others and this can pose additional challenges in terms of increased complexity and hybridity.

Chapter 11, Reframing Co-Production: More Definitions or New Schools?

This chapter reflects on the fact that co-production initially emphasized the role of citizens in the implementation of public policy. With renewed interest in this phenomenon the focus has greatly expanded in scope. Today it favors a more encompassing or 'enhanced' approach involving activities on both input and output sides of public policy-making. This invites different, sometimes conflicting, approaches to framing and understanding co-production, like public administration's input/output model, service management's value chain model or co-creation's public value model. This chapter explores the presence of three approaches or schools of co-production and then considers three issues related to citizen participation in public service and the role of TSOs: (i) volunteering and the 'who and what' of co-production, (ii) the 'where' of co-production and the role of third sector organizations, and (iii) differences between social and economic understandings of 'collective' co-production. Finally, it suggests the need to reconfigure our understanding of co-production and recognize the impact of these three schools of co-production.

Chapter 12, Co-Production and the Third Sector in the 21st Century: New Schools of Democracy and Participatory Public Service Management

This chapter notes that the academic perspective on the third sector has shifted fundamentally in recent years. TSOs were portrayed for generations as 'schools of democracy' in America and they helped to 'make democracy work' in Italy 25 years ago. Today, by contrast, they are primarily perceived as 'checkbook membership' organizations that go hand in hand with 'bowling alone' and the decline of democracy in America and elsewhere. However, the participatory features of co-production, social enterprise and democratic innovation found in third sector providers of public services can coalesce into a 'new school of democracy' in the 21st century. Moreover, decentralization of power and influence to the lower echelons of the administration, the workers and clients of the organization, promotes participatory public management. This calls for greater empowerment and self-governance by groups typically excluded in hierarchal public management models. Together, these developments can promote a 'participatory state' in the 21st century.

2 Beyond Exit and Voice in Enduring Welfare Services
Citizens as Co-Producers?

A. Exit and Voice in Relation to Goods and Services

Both exit and voice are related to the nature of goods and services. It is necessary to distinguish between durable and non-durable goods and also to differentiate between enduring and non-enduring services. Differences between various types of goods and services make exit and voice more or less relevant as a means for consumer redress if they are dissatisfied. However, the transaction costs of exiting from enduring social services have not received enough attention from scholars. This chapter attempts to rectify that shortcoming.

A.1 Exit, Voice, Loyalty and Goods

Almost 50 years ago, A. Hirschman (1970) initiated a discussion of exit and voice as alternative responses to decline in the performance of firms, organizations and states in his seminal book *Exit, Voice and Loyalty*. Exit is a typical market response, where disappointed customers quietly change their patronage to other suppliers of the goods or services they purchase. Voice is a typical political response, where customers verbally express their disappointment about poor quality, either individually or collectively (*ibid.*). Both exit and voice can be brought to bear not only to protest declining quality, but also improve the quality goods or services (Stryjan, 1989; Pestoff, 1992; Möller, 1996). In particular, voice can express both complaints and suggestions for improvements.

Exit and voice are complementary consumer reactions, rather than mutually exclusive alternatives or rival consumer reactions. They correspond to essentially different social roles in modern societies, i.e., as consumers and/or citizens. Hirschman notes that voice is more costly to individuals than exit, but also that voice is much more 'rich' in information than exit, although the latter may, at times, be more unambiguous. Voice is conditioned on the influence or bargaining power that consumers can bring to bear within a firm or an organization (1970). However, his argument fails to consider the role of organizations in amplifying the voice of individuals (Pestoff, 1984,

1988). One reason for the greater costliness of voice is related to the costs of collective action (Olson, 1965). Loyalty, by contrast, serves to mitigate between exit and voice, holding exit at bay. A loyal customer will continue to buy a product that demonstrates declining quality, in the hope that it may soon improve. Möller distinguishes between two types of loyalty, instrumental and value loyalty (1996). A combination of both results in the strongest attachment to goods or services (*ibid.*). Such varying consumer reactions depend on the type of good and the various roles played by adults in Western democracies, i.e., both as consumers and citizens, etc., and this rules out that either exit or voice becomes *the* exclusive channel of consumer redress (Hirschman, 1970).

Elsewhere (*Shifting Involvement*, 1982), Hirschman addresses consumer disappointment as the source of shifts from private interests to public action and back again. He underlines the unstable nature of consumer involvement. Furthermore, he notes that different expressions of consumer disappointment are associated with specific types of goods. It is necessary to distinguish between truly non-durable goods, different kinds of consumer durables and services. He states that disappointment is seldom permanent with everyday non-durable items, where daily learning processes can calibrate expectations downward. But, they also tend to be pleasure intensive. The contrary situation is associated with goods that are durable, unique and/or with a high value. Thus, their potential for generating disappointment is related to their inherent pleasure/comfort (p/c) ratio and the regularity with which they are used (*ibid.*).

Disappointment-prone goods are much more likely to result in the use of voice than non-disappointment-prone goods. Truly non-durable goods will facilitate the exit response in case of consumer disappointment, thereby relieving the necessity for voice. Irregularly used durable goods will only remind the user of his/her dissatisfaction occasionally, and are therefore not likely to engender the need for voice. However, durables put to continual use, used at regular intervals and/or of high value, are more disappointment prone and more likely to result in voice than exit. Such goods are not frequently purchased and, therefore, provide very few opportunities for exit. Voice is more likely where exit is restricted, so disappointed consumers of regularly used or high-value durables have, in fact, little other recourse than voice.

A.2 Type of Services: Enduring and Non-Enduring

First we want to briefly consider the distinctive characteristics of services, as opposed to goods. Grönroos maintains that most services share several basic characteristics (1990):

a) Services are more or less *intangible*,
b) Services are *activities* or a *series of activities* rather than things,

c) Services are at least to some extent *produced and consumed simultaneously,*

d) The customer *participates in the production process,* at least to some extent.

(*ibid.:* 29)

Unfortunately, Hirschman does not clearly relate the concepts of exit and voice to his discussion of consumer disappointment with different types of services. This is, however, relevant to our discussion of consumers as co-producers in the provision of social welfare services. Although he mentions services briefly in his discussion of consumer disappointment, he does not compare and contrast consumer reactions to them in the same fashion as durable and non-durable goods. He notes that services also have a high potential for generating disappointment, not because they fail to deliver pleasure, but rather because their performance tends to be uneven and unpredictable, or they have a highly variable degree of quality and efficiency (1970). But, his distinction concerning the regularity of use of goods can readily be adapted to our analysis of services, and we will distinguish between two categories of services: enduring and non-enduring services.

a) Regular or *enduring services* are regularly used major services that depend on continual interaction with, and often result in a long-term social relationship between, the consumers and producers of the services. Enduring services often include attributes of greater intimacy between the two parties and more extensive social contact than non-enduring services.

b) Irregular or *non-enduring services* are minor services that are used frequently or other services that are used irregularly, do not depend on continual interaction between the consumers and providers of the services nor do they result in a long-term relationship between them. The figure below illustrates these differences.

One problem is how to distinguish more clearly between enduring and non-enduring services. Services that cater to enduring and important physical or social needs belong to the former category, like regular childcare, education, chronic health care, handicap care, eldercare, etc. These services have attributes that are based on more enduring personal and social relations between the buyers and sellers than is normally possible in a spot-market. Such needs make it necessary to establish stable long-term relations between buyers and sellers in order to guarantee some minimum demand for the provision of such services on a continual basis. Day-to-day market fluctuations would make the minimal provision of enduring services very difficult. Services found in the second category, by contrast, can readily be bought and sold in a spot-market-like situation because they are subject to supply and demand. Often repeated and relatively inexpensive services belong to

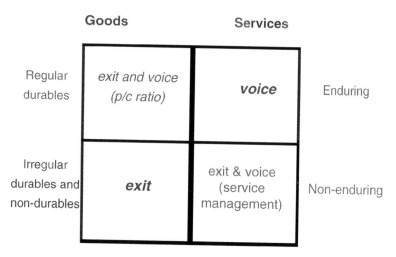

Figure 2.1 Exit, Voice and the Type of Goods or Services
Source: Pestoff, 1994.

the latter category, like hair cutting or hair dressing, getting your laundry or the car washed, occasional babysitting, eating meals out, transportation, using the telephone and fax outside home or the office, etc.

A.3 The Transaction Costs of Exit

Reflecting on the cost of exit and voice, Hirschman stated that voice was more costly than exit (1970). However, by focusing on simple consumption goods, he fails to pay close attention to the hurdles or thresholds associated with exiting from more complicated products, like social services. Möller (1996) notes that there are also some costs associated with using the exit alternative. Due to practical considerations children, sick persons and the elderly cannot change daycare centers, schools, hospitals or rest-homes very often, easily or readily. If you are dissatisfied with your current services, you need to get information about existing alternatives, systematize and analyze it, before convincing yourself that the alternative(s) would be worth investing the time and energy to change providers. Such efforts can be seen as the transaction costs for obtaining new services or changing providers (see North, 1990; Williamson, 1985, 1992).

The transaction costs of continuously shopping around for the best buy in personal social services, would soon prove prohibitive from a consumer perspective. Taken to an extreme, if each individual purchaser of childcare, elementary or higher education, chronic health care, elderly care, handicap care, etc., had to shop around once a week or even once a month in order to get information about next week's or month's service bargains or where to get the best quality for their money, there would be little time to do anything else on the weekend or at the end of the month. Endless hours would be spent comparing various offers, only to discover later that the claims of one service provider did not hold or that another provider had yet a better offer. Thus, there are significant transaction costs associated with using the exit option for enduring services.

In addition to transaction costs for the time spent with the purchase and re-purchase of social services, the individual social costs of exit and re-entry or changing from one service provider to another would also be considerable. Small children, students and sick or elderly persons would have to be moved from one service provider to another, from one week or month to another. Both parents and their small children would have to be re-socialized in a new daycare center, parents and pupils would have to be re-socialized into a new elementary or high school, the sick into new medical facilities or the elderly into new senior residences, etc. Such social costs would necessarily restrict the free flow of customers/clients from one service provider to another. So, establishing formalized or institutionalized relations between consumers and producers of enduring social services can be preferable from a consumer perspective because it helps them to reduce the transaction costs of obtaining these services.

Moreover, there are 'emotional costs' for the children or elderly persons and their guardians or relatives. The 'customer' of such services must end their old social ties and develop new ones, while the guardians or relatives must confront the staff of the old provider and motivate or explain the need to change service providers as well as meet the staff of the new provider to get to know them, etc. Thus, there are considerable costs associated with the exit alternative, and although they should not be exaggerated, neither should they be ignored. It could, of course, be argued that the clients of social services would budget their time in a fashion similar to budgeting their finances. They would not necessarily spend much more time comparing the price and quality of services than they do of goods. The important point is, however, that the amount of time required and spent is related to the type of goods or services, who it is for (a close relative or good friend) and whether the service is enduring or not.

From a firm's perspective, there would also be clear transaction costs associated with the repeated exit and entry of consumers of enduring social services. Small children, students and sick or elderly persons would have to be socialized into the receiving institution. If they leave the institution shortly after, such costs would be lost. The new clients that fill the vacancies would have to be socialized anew. Keeping order books up to date would pose another problem to managers, not to mention keeping an optimal stock of the requisite productive resources for quickly increasing or decreasing the production of services.

The manager of a school, for example, not only needs to know how many students, teachers, administrative staff, classrooms, offices, cafeteria or sports facilities, textbooks, buses, etc. are available and needed from one week or month to another. He or she must insure the availability of these and other educational resources for a longer period of time, normally one academic year, or at a minimum one scholastic term. Therefore, it is impossible for a school principal or university president simply to refer to the order books every weekend or at the end of the month to plan for next week's or next month's classes. Similarly, the manager of chronic health services not only needs to know how many administrators, doctors, surgeons, nurses, patients, rooms, beds, surgical theaters, technical equipment, ambulances, etc. are available from one week or month to another. He or she must insure the availability of medical resources over a longer period of time, at least several months, if not longer. Therefore, it is impossible for a hospital director merely to refer to the order books every weekend or at the end of the month to plan for next week's or next month's health care.

Thus, the transaction costs of a free flow of market signals for major personal social services may prove problematic, not only from a consumer, but also from a producer and a societal perspective. Unless a formal contract exists between the buyers and sellers, it would prove impossible to provide a minimum of daycare, education, health service or elderly care. The necessary resources for long-term planning of daycare, education or chronic health care would not be available if children or students and patients could freely resort to the exit alternative at any time to communicate their preferences to the managers of daycare, school or health care units. However, one way to reduce the transaction costs for the purchase of enduring social services is to remove some of the uncertainties of a spot-market by establishing formal contracts between the sellers and purchasers of personal social services for a certain period of time, i.e., either half a year or one year at a time.

B. Beyond Voice: Co-Production

B.1 Citizen Involvement as a Way of Promoting Voice

If exit and voice are not always mutually exclusive alternatives, then consumer sovereignty (exit) may sometimes need to be complemented by consumer participation (voice). The existence of the one influences the other. Exit may be necessary for augmenting consumer influence, but it is not always sufficient for doing so. Collective voice may also be necessary to achieve greater consumer influence (Pestoff, 1984). Hirschman discusses the elusive optimal mix of exit and voice points out the difficulty of combining these two consumer responses. Too much of one input diminishes the impact of the other (1970).

Reflecting on the reaction to the initial discussion of exit and voice, Hirschman notes that voice can be expected to play a greater role in relation to goods or dimensions of goods with a strong component of public interest. For example, a decline in the taste of food leads to exit, while health hazards in food leads to voice (1980). Furthermore, consumer and producer ignorance about products or services, particularly new products or services, motivate voice. Consumers often have clear preferences about their food tastes and readily use exit to express these preferences. However, expressing preferences about services, like daycare or eldercare, which are of an uncertain, and perhaps uneven, quality, both for the consumers and producers, requires voice. Similarly, voice has an important role to play for products or services where there is asymmetric information or disproportionate knowledge between sellers and buyers, such as medical care.

Ignorance about quality does not necessarily need to be limited to consumers, nor products. The demand for new services may arise more rapidly than the ability to meet it or the knowledge of how to satisfy it. Under such circumstances, it is not a question of consumer redress, but rather of educating producers and providing them with as much information as possible about their performance. Voice provides much more information about performance and is also richer in detail than exit, which remains silent about details. Moreover, services that are paid by taxes or direct charges are, in Hirschman's opinion, likely to have a high consumer disappointment potential (1982). This is not due to their failure to deliver pleasure, but rather to an uneven and unpredictable delivery and a high degree of variability in quality and efficiency. It is only through a dialog between the producers and consumers of such services that some agreement on legitimate expectations and good quality can be reached. Thus, developing techniques or institutions for promoting a dialog between consumers and producers can play a crucial role in promoting agreement about good service quality.

Customer voice is a more important component of services at the enduring end of the continuum, while exit gains greater importance at the non-enduring end of the service continuum. Consider briefly how price elasticity and quality elasticity differ. When prices increase, it is often customers with the smallest means, i.e., the marginal customers, that exit first, because they are most price sensitive. However, when quality decreases, it is often customers with the greatest means who leave first, because they are also the most quality conscious. Thus, if we want to avoid a situation where the most quality conscious and articulate consumers are the first to exit, then some means must be found to facilitate their voice and restrict their exit (Hirschman, 1970).

Therefore, developing techniques for facilitating the active and constructive voice of consumers can prove an important, if not an essential aspect of enduring services. But, just as there are two types of voice, positive and negative, so too are there two ways in which voice can be expressed, individually or collectively. Positive *individual* voice, or making suggestions for improvements, is normally the focus of service management, while positive *collective* voice, or co-production, could prove more important in certain services, especially enduring social services. Social enterprises and cooperatives can promote power sharing and a closer partnership between consumers and producers of social services. They can contribute greatly to improving the quality of social services, because they exist to promote a collective institutionalized encounter between consumers and producers in their continuous collective interaction. The institutionalized encounter and continuous interaction between clients and producers of social services is also related to the process of quality improvements stemming from such interaction. Thus, perceiving consumers as co-producers carries with it three major potential benefits, i.e., better quality products and services, shorter time required to develop new products or services and lower costs (Wikström, 1993: 8–11).

One essential way to promote greater citizen involvement as co-producers of social welfare services is to provide them with greater collective influence and bargaining power in the production process itself. Involving citizens as co-producers could result in a far-reaching form of consumer participation in the production of social services, one that goes beyond exit and voice, and facilitates active and creative consumer responses. So, what are the necessary structures or institutions that can facilitate citizen involvement? Evoking citizen participation as co-producers of welfare services requires us to rethink public service management. Greater citizen participation will not always manifest itself spontaneously among individual consumers, especially during periods of major reorganization nor curtailments of the public social and welfare services. But how can this phenomenon be understood? One answer from a business administration perspective is proposed below.

B.2 *Citizens as Co-Producers, a Conceptual Discussion*

Co-production is a phenomenon that refers to greater consumer involvement and participation in the production of goods and services. The changing patterns of interaction between firms and their consumers open new possibilities of doing business, as well as new possibilities for consumer influence. Such changes bring about a much closer relationship between consumers and producers than traditionally found in industrial society, one in which the consumer increasingly assumes the role of co-producer (Wikström, 1996). The customer is no longer a passive recipient of goods and services, but rather an active and knowledgeable participant in a common process on the marketplace. The company's role is no longer limited to providing goods or services, rather, it is a question of designing systems of activities within which customers can create their own value. The firm thereby compliments the knowledge and resources already possessed by its customers, as was normally the case in the pre-industrial period. From this interaction and cooperation in time and space, a value emerges that is the result of their cooperation.

From a business management perspective co-production is defined as "company-consumer interaction (social exchange) and adaptation for the purpose of attaining added value" (Wikström, 1996: 362). This kind of social exchange is motivated in part by the perceived degree of uncertainty in the exchange relationship and the potential benefit accruing to the participants from eliminating this uncertainty (*ibid.*: 363). An interactive way of working generates different types of values than those created by the logic of mass production (*ibid.*: 372). For our purposes, we need to specify the value or values associated with co-production of personal social services. Moreover, co-production is a multi-faceted phenomenon comprising several different aspects. It includes differing means of consumer participation in production, differing stages for their participation and varying degrees of consumer influence on that process. This research focuses on the influence of consumers on social services, in particular the influence stemming from their membership in small social enterprises that provide personal social services in Sweden.

B.3 Social Enterprises and Cooperatives as a Forum

Cooperatives have become an important alternative to the public provision of some social services in the current transformation of the welfare state and privatization of public services in Sweden. Taking daycare services as an example, the number of 'non-municipal' daycare centers more than tripled between 1988 and 1994, increasing from 538 to 1,768 centers, while the number of children attending them increased nearly five-fold during the same period, from 8,500 to 39,000. Almost two-thirds of these 'private' daycare centers are in fact run either as parent or worker cooperative day-care services (Pestoff, 1998).

   Cooperative organizations offer a unique opportunity for creating a dialog between the clients and personnel of social services, and under certain circumstances can involve the consumers as co-producers of social services. The financing of these 'privatized' social services, however, remains primarily a public responsibility. A variety of vouchers have been developed or are under development in different parts of Sweden to pay for social services, e.g., daycare vouchers, school vouchers, patient vouchers, home-help vouchers, etc. These vouchers are financed by public funds and provide access to basic social services; i.e., they constitute a quasi-market. Service vouchers are supposed to give individual consumers greater freedom of choice and to stimulate efficiency through competition, according to their proponents.

   While service vouchers may facilitate 'exit' reactions by clients, and introduce more market signals, they ignore 'voice' reactions and indirectly discourage a dialog between the consumers and providers of personal social services. Cooperatives and other nonprofit organizations can, therefore, make a unique contribution to bringing clients and personnel together and promoting an institutional dialog between them. Such a dialog could in turn help to eliminate some of the asymmetry of information and, thus, provide unusual opportunities for improving the quality of social services.

   However, such a scenario is not wholly problem free, and Hirschman (1982) warns of the excesses of involvement and of its high transaction costs. Involvement can become intoxicating, and with time may eventually lead to a reaction or withdrawal to private pursuits. It could be argued that greater consumer involvement in the production of social services could, in the long-run, be detrimental to the quality of such services. The unstable nature of consumer involvement would be reflected in the unstable quality of the services produced. Certain natural cycles might, however, mitigate the unstable nature of involvement (Stryjan, 1989). Some parents might be involved in the provision of daycare services, but not of the elementary education of their children, only to become involved again in educational matters when their children become teenagers. Other parents may opt for the opposite patterns, choosing a public or private daycare center, but then becoming involved in elementary education through a cooperative school, etc. However, Swedish experience to date suggests that there is a cumulative nature to collective action. The positive experience of participating in a parent daycare cooperative is carried over to the schools when their children grow older and results in greater parental involvement there.

Parent cooperatives and other types of nonprofit organizations providing daycare in Sweden not only facilitate a dialog between the producers and consumers of social services and enhance the meeting between them, they also encourage the direct participation of consumers in the production of such services. It is common for parent cooperatives and other nonprofit alternative forms of daycare to include a work obligation for members in their statutes. Parents are not in charge of developing the pedagogics of childcare, but they are responsible for maintenance, repairs and administration at daycare centers. This work obligation provides greater insights into the running of individual daycare centers and promotes a dialog between the personnel and parents. Parents also have a majority of the seats on the board of these daycare centers, which gives them greater influence. They are able to formulate and discuss their opinions about the quality of the service with the personnel. This leads to questions about holding service providers accountable for service quality.

Elcock (1993) distinguishes between three types of accountability: (a) 'upward' accountability to superiors and elected officials, (b) 'outward' accountability to professionals and other colleagues and (c) 'downward' accountability to those receiving the goods and services (*ibid.*: 19–20). However, it is possible to envision a fourth type of accountability, d) 'inward' accountability, found mainly in democratically controlled membership organizations, like social enterprises and service cooperatives. Here the staff is directly accountable to the consumer/members who help co-produce services.

Thus, the recent development of cooperative and nonprofit provision of social services in Sweden can facilitate the development of citizenship and citizens as co-producers of social services in several ways. The institutional involvement of members/citizens as co-producers of social services can extend their right to participate in the governmental process by facilitating their direct participation in the production of some highly relevant personal social services. It can clarify their duties as citizens and consumers of social service in terms of the obligation to contribute their time and service. It can promote a decentralization of the public sector and maintain upward accountability of the producers of social services to politicians. It can also increase the downward accountability of these same producers to their consumers or users, and it can institutionalize the inward accountability through democratic decision-making in cooperatives and social enterprises. Finally, it can strengthen the control of citizens over politicians and politicians control over the bureaucracy and the public service.

C. Conclusions

We found that it was possible to extend Hirschman's concepts of 'exit' and 'voice' to the provision of social services. In doing so, it is obvious that exit and voice are complements to each other, rather than rival or mutually exclusive alternatives. Exit is an adequate consumer response under certain circumstances and voice under others, while both can play a role under other circumstances. It is necessary to distinguish between the type of goods and/or services, in order to understand when the one or other can provide optimal redress to consumer disappointment.

In particular, voice may prove an adequate consumer response and may provide adequate consumer redress with major enduring social services. Yet, some consumers may become actively involved in the production of social welfare services and thereby become co-producers of such social services. However, in order to achieve optimal influence using voice and bargaining power in the production process, consumers may need to organize themselves. Not only do many of the market-oriented critics of the welfare state fail to recognize the complementary nature of exit and voice, they usually ignore the importance of engaged and active clients and they also underestimate both the difficulty of and the necessity for collective action and citizen involvement, as a supplement to both exit and voice.

Prohibitive transaction costs, both for consumers and for producers of major social services, not only motivate recognition of the beneficial role of voice and involvement, but, accepting them as legitimate complements to exit. This, in turn, means that we should concentrate our efforts on improving the functioning of voice and involvement, rather than merely trying to find ways to introduce market mechanisms in the production of social services. One way of doing this is to provide the third sector with a greater role in the production of social services.

Voice devoid of involvement, as seen in the Citizen's Charters in the United Kingdom (Elcock, 1993), may increase downward accountability, but it also emphasizes the role of consumers at the expense of the role of citizens. The third sector, parent cooperatives and other types of nonprofit social services can facilitate the roles of citizens and can thereby enhance the involvement of citizens as co-producers of social services. By attributing a greater role to the third sector in the production of personal social services, several socially beneficial objectives can be obtained simultaneously. First, a greater number of alternative providers of individual social services would result in greater freedom of choice for clients, where the choice would be between real alternatives, rather than merely between two or more competing service brands. Second, the third sector is the only alternative form of service production to offer consumers-cum-members-cum-citizens greater influence in the production process via their institutionalized involvement (Pestoff, 1992). Third, the third sector provides the best guarantee of achieving greater welfare pluralism in the provision of social services (*ibid.*).

The achievement of these goals, however, requires a restructuring of the relationship between the roles of consumers and citizens, the relationship between markets and politics and the relationship between the state and the third sector. This restructuring has begun in Sweden today, but the implications of it are not always clear. This process of change could be made more explicate, if the often heavily ideological terms used in the Swedish debate were replaced by more precise ones provided by Hirschman, and if his terminology were extended to include services as well as goods.

When it comes to developing new types of social services provided by the welfare state, it is not only a question of information asymmetry, opportunistic behavior and market failure, but also pure and simple lack of knowledge, both on the part of the producers and the consumers of these new social services. Both parties are ignorant of what constitutes good quality service. They need to engage in a dialog with each other in order to reach a mutual understanding of, and agreement about, what comprises good quality service. Quality is not something that can be codified, translated into numbers, nor programmed into the memory of robots. Rather, it is something that must be learned and re-learned through the repeated interaction of the providers and clients of such services (Wahlgren, 1996). Repeated encounters and discussions between the providers and clients of services helps to reduce the information asymmetries between them and eliminate some of their mutual uncertainty about the quality of the service.

Co-production facilitates the reduction of this uncertainty. By involving clients as co-producers, their expectations about the services and the values they hope to realize can be expressed and translated into practical activities. Their participation in the practical aspects of providing the enduring services they demand facilitates greater interaction with the professional providers of such services and makes more dialog between them both necessary and possible. This in turn, helps both parties to eliminate some of their uncertainty as well as to facilitate reaching an agreement about a common standard of good quality services. As a by-product, co-production provides the clients with an opportunity to observe some important aspects of the provision of social services and to control against opportunistic behavior on the part of the providers.

Thus, by involving the clients in the provision of services, co-production reduces information asymmetries between the providers and clients of social services, it facilitates a dialog between them, and it helps them to reach a mutual understanding about the capacities of the providers and the clients' expectations. It thereby helps to eliminate uncertainty about the quality of the service, it provides clients with both insights and influence, and it thereby can safeguard against opportunistic behavior.

The next chapter throws more light on these theoretical considerations about greater citizen/user participation in the provision of public financed social services. It presents the findings of the Parent Study of the project on Work Environment and Cooperative Social Services (WECSS). Overall, the findings from the Parent Study corroborate the theoretical discussion about exit, voice and co-production.

3 Empowering Parents as Co-Producers of Childcare Services in Sweden

A. Introduction

The empirical materials and data presented here stem from the Parent Study of the Swedish Project on Work Environment and Cooperative Social Services (WECSS). Nearly 600 client questionnaires were collected and analyzed in the Parent Study undertaken in the early 1990s, the results of which are reported here. We are primarily interested in exploring the value created for parents through the existence of possibilities for greater participation in some forms of cooperative daycare services as opposed to the lack of such possibilities for participation in municipal daycare facilities. Three types of social enterprises are included in our study: parent cooperatives, voluntary organizations and worker cooperatives. The WECSS Parent Study sheds light on the motives parents have for choosing one particular type of social enterprise and for becoming involved as a co-producer or not.

This chapter considers the ability of social enterprises to facilitate greater citizen participation in the production of local public services, in particular of personal social services. There are several alternative approaches to renewing the public sector. One way might be to encourage more competition, market mechanisms or exit, while another would emphasize more direct involvement by citizens or voice (Hirschman, 1970). The Swedish Power Investigation in the late 1980s discusses the perceived need for change by introducing the concept of 'service democracy'. It held that most citizens are satisfied with the services provided by the public sector and do not want to engage themselves in such matters. A comparison of childcare and eldercare in Uppsala County found "several parents with children in a parent cooperative childcare would have preferred municipal service, where they could avoid the responsibility they feel is too heavy . . . Becoming engaged in the daily activities does not attract many" (Möller, 1996: 376). "Service democracy's passive consumption is attractive to many and parents do not experience activity as a value in itself" (ibid.: 383).

Peters represents another approach to reforming the public sector and public management, under the label of a 'participatory state'. Here, various groups that are excluded under more hierarchical models should be

permitted greater organizational involvement in providing public services
(Peters, 1994). This approach concentrates on activating the lower echelons
or front-line workers and their clients, in order to enhance their role as
providers of public services. This can be seen as an attempt to induce democratic participation by means other than voting (*ibid*.: 13). The meaning
of public interest in the participatory state depends on the workers and
citizens themselves becoming more involved in making some policy choices.
It would allow citizens more consumer choice and direct control over programs, similar to the market model. But the manner in which these consumer choices would be exercised in the participatory state would be more
explicitly political. Rather than voting in the marketplace with their euros,
dollars, crowns or yen, citizens would vote through some sort of political
process. This participation might be in referenda on policy or it may take
place in local structures, like parent involvement in school committees, etc.
(*ibid*.: 15).

The concept of civil democracy was introduced in *Beyond the Market and
State: Social Enterprises and Civil Democracy in a Welfare Society* (Pestoff,
1998). It depicts this new type of citizen participation as a form of cooperative self-governance. It was defined as

> citizen empowerment through cooperative self-management of personal
> social services, where the citizens become members in social enterprises,
> where they participate directly in the production of the local services
> they demand, as users and producers of such services, and where they
> therefore become co-producers of these services.
>
> (*ibid*.: 25)

Co-production is one of the main theoretical underpinnings of *civil democracy*. Co-production bears particular importance for understanding changes
in the role of clients or consumers of personal social services. This concept is
also necessary for understanding the contribution of new social enterprises
to empowering consumers as co-producers and to the role of the new social
economy in renewing the welfare state. In particular, we are interested here
in exploring the value created for citizens as parents through the existence of
possibilities for greater participation in some forms of cooperative daycare
services contrasted with the lack of such possibilities for participating at
municipal daycare facilities. Co-production, therefore, means greater consumer involvement in production processes in general, and usually signifies
greater consumer participation in one or more aspect or phases of service
provision. For the purposes of this study, we are particularly interested in
the possibilities provided by social enterprises, like consumer cooperatives
and voluntary organizations to actively mobilize the clients of these services
as co-producers.

In Chapter 2, exit, voice and loyalty were introduced, and the costs of exit
from enduring services was discussed at length. Exit can be motivated both

by declining quality and by the expectation of better quality services. Deterioration in the quality of municipal daycare services in Sweden during the 1990s, due to severe budget cuts and the subsequent reduction in the number of staff, may provide one reason why so many parents turned to alternative childcare services in the 1990s. But many parents may also have chosen non-municipal services in expectation of being able to obtain improved services or to realize certain values not found nor feasible in municipal service, like wanting to participate in their child's daily life, without having to sacrifice the possibility of the mother having a career of her own. Not only the reasons for choosing a particular type of service, but also the subsequent support for or trust in alternative services, may express different aspects or dimensions of the services provided.

Möller distinguishes three kinds of loyalty: instrumental loyalty, value loyalty and a combination of both (1996), where the latter represents the strongest bonds between clients and a firm or organization. Parents who choose a particular type of daycare services on the basis of specific values should demonstrate greater loyalty, if they are satisfied with the services, than those parents who simply choose the services for instrumental reasons. This means that we expect parents with children in parent cooperatives or voluntary organizations that provide daycare services to be more loyal to their provider than parents with children in worker cooperative services, who mainly have instrumental motives. However, given the decline in the quality of municipal services during the 1990s, we also expect parents with children in any three types of social enterprises to be more satisfied than they were previously with municipal daycare services. The WECSS materials allow us to compare parent satisfaction with cooperative and municipal services.

B. The Social Background of Parents to Children in Social Enterprises

We will begin our presentation of the WECSS Parent Study by introducing the parents' social background and then turn to their attitudes in several relevant aspects of cooperative daycare services. Nearly one-third of the parents with children in a parent cooperative daycare center participated in the start of the cooperative daycare center, while less than one of ten parents with children in voluntary organizations or worker co-ops did so. This is a reflection of the fact that parent cooperative daycare services often had their origin in a lack of municipal services in the 1980s and parents thus took these matters in their own hands by starting daycare services of their own preference. A brief survey of the socio-economic background of the parents to children in different types of cooperative social enterprises demonstrates that they do not comprise a homogeneous group of well-off parents.

Parents with children in daycare services provided by voluntary organizations rate higher in most social respects, like mother's and father's education,

Table 3.1 The Social Background of Parents to Children in Social Enterprises Providing Daycare Services

Social Background*	Parent Co-ops	Vol. Orgs	Worker Co-ops	Average
-married	91.5	94.1	87.4	90.9
-mother's education: -gymnasium	34.7	28.9	44.8	36.9
-university	57.7	68.1	46.6	57.4
-father's education: -gymnasium	40.7	34.2	40.8	38.5
-university	50.5	61.8	47.3	52.8
-mother's occupation: -white collar	47.3	54.6	47.9	49.9
-father's occupation: -white collar	51.1	47.7	46.7	48.5
-self-employed	16.5	21.3	19.2	19.1
-housing: -tenant owner, own	15.8	10.5	17.3	14.6
home/row house	50.0	69.5	64.4	59.8
-av. monthly income: >25,000kr.	53.9	63.0	48.8	55.8
N	190	189	201	580

Source: WECSS Parent Study, Pestoff (1998)

* in percent

mother's and father's occupation, type of housing and income, than parents with children in the two other types of cooperative daycare services. Parents with children in worker cooperative daycare services often come lower than the other two, except for type housing, where parents with children in parent cooperatives come lowest. The average number of years that a child has spent in various types of cooperative daycare services is similar among different types of cooperatives. It is 2.2 years for parent cooperatives, 2.3 years for children in voluntary organizations and 1.9 years for children in worker cooperatives.

Unfortunately, comparable data for parents with children attending municipal daycare services is not available. We suspect that the averages shown above may be higher than the national average for adults with children under six or the average for parents with a child attending municipal daycare services, but there is no way to determine the exact size of such differences.

C. Parent Involvement, Motives and Satisfaction

Elsewhere we saw that the institutional differences between these three types of cooperative daycare services found a clear expression in the attitudes of the staff concerning their psycho-social work environment and possibilities for influencing their work (see Pestoff, 2000; Pestoff & Vamstad, 2014, for more details). The members of worker cooperatives were usually the most satisfied with their working conditions. Similarly, we should expect differences in attitudes between parents in different types of cooperative daycare services, as the parents also have a different institutional base in them. Parents are members of the daycare cooperative both in parent cooperatives and voluntary organizations, but not worker cooperatives. Members normally have a work obligation as well as possibilities for participating in the democratic structures of the cooperative. Does membership perhaps reflect parents' reasons for choosing one type of daycare service or another? Is membership related to the main advantages and disadvantages parents associate with each type of daycare cooperative? Does it also affect the attitudes of the parents towards their collaboration with the staff and their satisfaction with the administration of the daycare service? Finally, does it find expression in terms of parents' comparisons with municipal daycare services? We will provide answers to these and other questions below. We will begin our inquiry by considering parents' attitudes about the work obligation and holding an elective office. Following that we will consider their reasons for choosing their cooperative childcare and its advantages and disadvantages and then go on to discuss their collaboration with the staff and their satisfaction with the administration of the daycare center.

C.1 Membership, Work Obligations, Holding an Elective Office and Influence

The work obligation varies from one cooperative daycare center to another. Work obligations primarily comprise tasks related to administration and maintenance and do not normally include pedagogical activities. But, parents often function as temporary relief or substitutes for staff on sick leave or absent for participating in a course, etc., in a rotating system of 'jour' (daily) duty that eliminates the need for hiring temporary staff. The ownership structure and work obligation of parent cooperatives and voluntary organizations make for greater parent involvement in the running of such daycare services. Worker cooperatives lack both parent representation on the board and an obligation to work in the daycare center, although some of them have established an advisory body to institutionalize their contacts with parents. Such advisory bodies meet a few times per year and mainly have information functions. Given the larger average size of worker cooperative daycare services, 40–60 children compared with 15–20 children in parent co-ops and voluntary organizations, some form of parent representation in an advisory board is logical. Their size and structure seldom facilitate the informal exchange of information brought about by the work obligation in parent cooperatives and voluntary organizations, nor the formal representation of parents on the board. Table 3.2 presents data about parents' attitudes toward the work obligation.

Just over one-eighth of the parents in both these cooperative forms lack a work obligation. Negative aspects of the work obligation, such as being too demanding or unqualified, creating conflicts between parents or between parents and the staff, were seldom mentioned by parents, i.e., only between 1.3% and 5.2%, and they are not shown here for reasons of space. Moreover, only a small proportion of the parents lack an opinion altogether

Table 3.2 What Do You Think about the Work Obligation?

*work obligation**	*Parent Co-ops*	*Vol. Orgs*
-gives a feeling of participation	88.0	81.8
-gives a feeling of belonging	68.0	62.3
-gives valuable insights	63.3	54.4
-provides possibilities for influence	45.3	29.2
average/(total) no. answers	2.7/(405)	2.4/(367)

Source: WECSS Parent Study, Pestoff (1998)

*multiple options, added to more than 100% and based on eligible answers, i.e., only those who have a work obligation

about the work obligation, 7% and 5% respectively. Those aspects of the work obligation given most positive support by parents include participation, belonging, valuable insights and influence.

The parents in both these types of cooperative daycare services give similar priority to the rank order and magnitude of the positive aspects of the work obligation, except for possibilities for influence. More than four-fifths state that the work obligation gives a feeling of participation, and approximately two-thirds of them also name that it gives a feeling of belonging. In addition, the work obligation gives more than half of them valuable insights in the running of the cooperative daycare services. Thus, the work obligation is not merely, nor mainly, perceived by the parents as a chore nor in a negative sense, but rather as a positive institution for facilitating their integration into the daily activities of their daughter's or son's daycare center. The work obligation helps to eliminate uncertainty in the interaction between the parents and the staff of these two types of daycare services, as well as between parents themselves. It also helps to promote greater trust between the parents and staff of such organizations.

The work obligation itself provides fewer parents with possibilities to influence the work. However, more parents with children in parent cooperatives see opportunities for gaining influence than parents with children in voluntary organizations. This probably reflects the fact that a greater proportion of parents also hold an elective office in parent cooperatives than in voluntary organizations. They can thus combine insights gained from the work obligation to bring about changes if necessary.

More than one of four parents with children in parent co-ops or voluntary organizations provided comments to their answers concerning the work obligation, holding an elective office, etc. Their comments include several diverse topics, including both positive and negative aspects and instrumental and expressive aspects. Positive aspects comprise the necessity of keeping the costs down, contacts with other children and their parents, contacts with their own child's daily life, belonging and participating, providing greater security for the children, providing greater influence and all parents having an active responsibility. More neutral expressions underline the division between parents' responsibilities for administration, mainte-nance and occasional temporary fill in for staff on sick leave and the staff's responsibility for pedagogical matters. A few negative comments cover top-ics like only some of the parents hold an elective office, difficulties for new parents to get elected or conflicts between the parents on the board and the staff.

The question about having an elective office included parents at both par-ent cooperatives and voluntary organizations, with a seat on the board of the cooperative, as well as parents at worker cooperatives, with a seat in a parental advisory body. More than three-fifths (62.6%) of the parents with children in parent cooperatives hold an elective office in the cooperative daycare and more than two-fifths (43.2%) of parents with children in vol-untary organizations do so, while only a few parents sit on advisory boards of worker co-ops. The latter will therefore be excluded in Table 3.3. Once again the negative aspects of holding an elective office were excluded from this presentation, due to the low frequency of parents indicating negative experience with elective offices. Answers like too demanding or unqualified, creating conflicts between parents or between parents and the staff only ranged from 1.2% to 5.3%.

Those aspects of holding an elective office most often named once again include influence, participation, insights and belonging, but now in another order of importance. Unlike parents' attitudes concerning the work obliga-tion, elective office first and foremost provide parents with an opportunity to influence the work at their child(ren)'s cooperative daycare centers. For the remaining aspects of holding an elective office, we find a similar ranking, if not magnitude, by the parents of both these types of cooperative daycare services. Elective duties also provide a feeling of participation, give valuable insights and give a feeling of belonging. Nearly one-fifth of the parents do not indicate their attitude to holding an elective office, probably due to their lack of experience.

Parents also provided comments about holding an elective or honorary office. Most of their comments were positive, but some parents mentioned negative aspects. The positive comments emphasize the equality of everyone participating, while the negative aspects focus on the time demanded.

Table 3.3 What Do You Think about Your Work on the Board?

Work on the board	Parent Co-ops	Vol. Orgs
-provides possibilities for influence	66.2	53.9
-gives a feeling of participation	62.4	48.6
-gives valuable insights	54.1	44.1
-gives a feeling of belonging	40.8	34.2
-no opinion	17.4	19.6
average/(total) no. answers	2.4/(400)	2.0/(328)

Source: WECSS Parent Study, Pestoff (1998), multiple answers add to more than 100%

Through the work obligation and holding an elective office, parents in both these types of cooperative daycare services quite simply become co-producers of their own child(ren)'s daycare services. Holding an elective office provides greater influence, which helps to eliminate uncertainty in the interaction between the parents and the staff of these two types of daycare services. It also help to promote greater trust between the parents and staff of such organizations. Few, if any, of these intangible integrative aspects are available to parents with children in worker cooperatives, because they are not members, very few of them have elective positions and those who do mostly have an advisory position. Thus, their relationship with their child(ren)'s daycare services is much more marginal than the parents of the other two types of daycare cooperatives (Table 3.4).

General questions about parental influence and activity also shed more light on the differences between these three types of cooperative daycare services. More than four-fifths of parents with children in parent cooperatives and voluntary organizations claim that they can influence things in their child's daycare cooperative, while barely half of the parents in worker co-ops do so. This is a clear reflection of the differences in membership between these three types of cooperative daycare services. However, a greater proportion of parents in worker cooperatives want to be more active. This can be expressed as a parent influence/activity index or surplus. The influence/activity surplus is 65.7 for parent co-ops, 57.3 for voluntary organizations, but only 20.1 for worker cooperatives.

C.2 Choice of, Advantages and Satisfaction with Cooperative Daycare Services

Parents were asked to motivate their choice of a particular type of cooperative daycare service (Table 3.5). If they have clear motives for putting their child(ren) in one type of cooperative or another, then it should be seen in their answers. Parents' motives should reflect the values they hope to promote by choosing one form of cooperative rather than another and whether their motives were primarily value-based, instrumental or both. We should expect their answers to differ between these three types of social enterprises, and perhaps to provide us with a profile of each type of cooperative daycare service and the particular client niche they serve.

Table 3.4 Can Parents Influence Things and Want to Be More Active?

influence and activity (%)	Parent Co-ops	Vol. Orgs	Worker Co-ops
can you influence things?*	84.2	81.4	51.0
want to be more active?*	18.5	24.1	30.9
N	190	189	201

Source: WECSS Parent Study, Pestoff (1998)

* Only the positive answers are included here

Table 3.5 Why Did You Choose This Form of Daycare?

reason for choosing co-op. daycare*	Parent Co-ops	Vol. Orgs	Worker Co-ops
-possibilities for influence	52.6	42.3	**
-wanted to participate in child's daily life	45.8	31.7	6.5
-wanted a special pedagogics	15.8	50.8	17.4
-possibilities for parent collaboration	25.8	24.3	**
-no other existing alternatives	31.1	14.3	18.4
-close to home	35.3	21.2	40.8
-dissatisfied with municipal daycare	14.2	21.2	14.4
-recommended by relatives/friends	19.5	20.6	22.9
-economic advantages	28.9	9.0	7.0
average (& total) no. of answers:	2.9/(555)	2.5/(465)	1.7/(332)
N	190	189	201

Source: WECSS Parent Study, Pestoff (1998)

*   multiple answers, add to more than 100%
** these two alternatives were not available to parents with children in worker co-ops

Parents could choose from either 13 or 11 alternative motives and could provide more than one answer. Parents with children in parent co-ops provided nearly three answers each, parents with children in voluntary organizations two and a half, while parents with children in worker co-ops gave less than two answers each. The first four alternatives presented in Table 3.5 express value judgments, while the remaining five are more instrumental in their nature.

A clear profile of each type of cooperative daycare service can be seen in the motives provided by each group of parents. Parents with children in *parent cooperatives* give most importance to possibilities for influence, but they are also highly motivated by wanting to participate in their child(ren)'s daily life, as well as practical issues like closeness to home, a lack of other daycare alternatives and even economic advantages. Parents with children in *voluntary organizations* give greatest priority to special pedagogics, second priority to possibilities for influence and third priority to wanting to participate in their child(ren)'s daily life. They also refer to instrumental motives, like closeness to home, dissatisfaction with municipal services and recommendations by friends or relatives. In both these two types of cooperative daycare, parents share some values and they have value-based, as well as instrumental, motives. Parents with children in *worker cooperatives*, however, have a very different pattern of priorities and give greatest weight to practical issues like closeness to home, other unspecified motives (not shown here) and being recommended by friends. Parents with children in worker cooperatives are clearly motivated by instrumental attitudes in their choice of daycare service.

Turning to the main advantages of each form of cooperative daycare services, parents with children in parent cooperatives or voluntary organizations were provided 13 alternatives plus the option of suggesting other advantages, while those with children in worker cooperatives were only given 11 alternatives, plus an unspecified category. Once again multiple answers were possible.

The parents of children in *parent cooperatives* see the greatest advantages in more participation in their child(ren)'s daily life, the possibility to influence, an enjoyable atmosphere, an engaged staff and parent collaboration, all of which receive the support of half or more of the parents in this group. The parents of children in *voluntary organizations* find the greatest advantages in an engaged staff, a good pedagogical profile, an enjoyable atmosphere and the possibility of influence, all of which receive the support of half or more of the parents in this group. Parents with children in *worker cooperatives* give greatest priority to an engaged staff, an enjoyable atmosphere and a good pedagogical profile, which receive support from about three-fourths to one-third of the parents in this group.

Thus, once again we find different profiles for various cooperative daycare services, in terms of their advantages (Table 3.6). However, an engaged staff and an enjoyable atmosphere is given as an important advantage by parents of all three types of cooperative daycare services. The WECSS Staff Study showed a greater staff engagement among workers in all three types of cooperative daycare services than municipal facilities where they were previously employed (Pestoff, 1998).

The disadvantages associated with each type of daycare service are also typical for their organizational profile. Most or many parents in all three types of cooperative daycare services state that there is no disadvantage with their cooperative daycare service. While not minding about the work

Table 3.6 Main Advantages of This Form of Daycare?

main advantages*	Parent Co-ops	Vol. Orgs	Worker Co-ops
-more participation in my child's daily life	68.4	47.1	19.9
-enjoyable atmosphere	62.6	58.2	66.2
-possibility of influence	62.6	50.8	38.4
-engaged staff	59.5	73.5	75.6
-good pedagogical profile	35.8	64.9	38.8
-parent collaboration	50.0	37.6	**
-social network	30.0	23.8	6.5
-keep my place during pregnancy	24.7	13.8	17.9
-economic advantages	32.6	10.6	10.4
-democratically run	21.1	15.9	3.5
average (& total) no. of advantages:	4.8/(915)	4.2/(793)	1.6/(323)
N	190	189	201

Source: WECSS Parent Study, Pestoff (1998)

* multiple answers, add to more than 100%
** this alternative wasn't available to parents with children in worker co-ops

obligation *per se*, parents in both parent cooperatives and voluntary organizations are nevertheless critical of the additional time required by the cooperative form and they are also concerned with the difficulty of combining their roles as parents and employers. Parents with children in worker cooperatives name few specific disadvantages.

Parents answered several questions about their collaboration with the staff. Two-thirds or more of the parents with children in all three types of cooperatives feel that their collaboration with the staff is very good in general. They are even more positive about the staff's attitudes toward the children and clearly feel that the staff promotes the general comfort of the children. The majority of them is also very positive about the staff's attitudes toward parents. Differences between the three types of cooperative daycare services are small, suggesting that membership *per se* doesn't play an important role in forming their attitude about their collaboration with the staff. In fact, parents with children in worker co-ops are somewhat more positive about the staff's attitudes to parents.

About one of five parents with children in parent co-ops or worker co-ops provided comments to their answers about their collaboration with the staff, while more than one of eight parents with children in voluntary organizations did so. Their comments cover a wide range of topics including having good relations, a division of labor between the parents and staff, difficulties of being both a parent and an employer or having both roles as a parent and staff member, as well as mentioning some problems.

Moreover, the overwhelming majority (between 94.4% and 97.7%) of parents in all three types of cooperative daycare services feel that the staff is willing to discuss the suggestions for changes and improvements put forth by parents. About one in five parents with a child in all three kinds of cooperative daycare services also provided additional written comments to this question. Most parent comments about the staff's openness fall into one of three categories, i.e., the staff's willingness to discuss changes, the staff is willing to discuss everything but pedagogics and the staff is not willing to discuss changes. This question was followed by another asking parents to provide examples of changes that had actually been implemented at the suggestion of parents. More than one-third of them provided concrete examples of such changes.

Parents were also asked to how satisfied they were with the running and administration of their daughter's and/or son's daycare cooperative (Table 3.7). More parents with children in worker cooperatives were 'very satisfied' than parents in the two other types of cooperative daycare, while fewer of the former were 'somewhat satisfied'. However, by combining these two categories, we find that more than four-fifths of the parents in all three types of cooperative daycare services are satisfied with the running and administration of their child(ren)'s daycare service. Parents' attitudes about their collaboration with the staff and their satisfaction with the running and administration of their child(ren)'s daycare service show similar positive

Table 3.7 How Satisfied Are You with the Administration and Organization of the Daycare Center?

Satisfied with admin.*(%)	Parent Co-ops	Vol. Orgs	Worker Co-ops
-Very satisfied	42.9	44.3	55.6
-Somewhat satisfied	46.7	42.2	25.8
N	190	189	201

Source: WECSS Parent Study, Pestoff (1998)

* only those satisfied are included here

levels and they do not seem to reflect the major institutional differences between these three types of cooperative daycare services, nor the possibilities they provide for parental participation. One conclusion might be that such possibilities make little difference to parents, however, we feel that it would be both hasty and wrong.

Parents judge the performance of their child's daycare service on its own merits, not on some general or absolute merits of 'good pedagogics' or 'good childcare'. If there is a relatively good match between their own values and motives for choosing a particular type of daycare service and if the daycare service can promote such values, then parents will be satisfied. This of course may even be true for parents with children in either municipal or private daycare services. Thus, differences in work obligation and holding an elective office don't reflect these parents' satisfaction or dissatisfaction with the way the daycare services are run. Rather, their attitudes toward the work obligation and holding an elective office may reflect more fundamental differences in the attitudes and values of different groups of parents.

Some of them are more engaged in the early years of their child(ren)'s life than others, some enjoy both the integrative aspects of the work obligation and/or the influence provided by holding an elective office, while others do not. Those parents who want to participate would, however, probably not be satisfied, or not nearly as satisfied, if such possibilities did not exist. Thus, it is not a question of *the* best form of daycare services, but rather that what is good for one group of parents may not be so for another. So, greater welfare pluralism could promote numerous different forms for providing the daycare services citizens want, including municipal and private daycare services, parent cooperatives, voluntary organizations and worker cooperatives.

D. Comparisons with Municipal Daycare Services

From a parent perspective there are two main ways of comparing cooperative daycare services with those provided by municipal facilities. One is based on parallel studies of the parents in two or more types of daycare services, and by comparing the evaluation of different groups of parents with each other. The averages of each type of daycare service are obtained and compared with each other, similar to the parallel study undertaken here of the three types of cooperative daycare services. Another way is based on asking parents with experience from both types of daycare services to make such comparisons themselves. This is termed a retrospective comparison, and it is the method we chose. In the WECSS Parent Study, parents were asked if they previously had a child(ren) in municipal daycare services. If so, they were then asked whether the staff of cooperative daycare services were more open to and concerned about parents' wishes than municipal daycare facilities and how they rate cooperative daycare services in comparison with municipal daycare facilities. Tables 3.8 and 3.9 reporting the comparative questions only include those parents who have previously had a child in municipal services and can therefore make a meaningful comparative evaluation. More than one of three parents (35.0%) with children in parent co-ops had experience from both forms, more than two of five parents (42.6%) with children in voluntary organizations had such experience, while nearly half (47.6%) of the parents with children in worker co-ops did so.

Nearly three-fourths of the parents with children in all three kinds of cooperative daycare services expressed an appreciation of the openness and concern of the co-op's staff compared with that of municipal daycare services. Half or more of the parents with children in parent co-ops or voluntary organizations who were eligible also provided comments to their comparison of staff openness and concern, while three of five with children in worker co-ops did so. The overwhelming majority of their comments

Table 3.8 Is Cooperative Daycare Better Than Municipal Service?

Co-op. daycare is better than municipal	Parent Co-ops	Vol. Orgs	Worker Co-ops
-Better	81.5	85.5	77.4
n*	65	76	84

Source: WECSS Parent Study, Pestoff (1998)

*only eligible parents with experience from both forms of daycare answered this question

Table 3.9 If You Could Choose Freely Would You Choose a Parent/Worker Cooperative Again?

Would choose a co-op again?	Parent Co-ops	Vol. Orgs	Worker Co-ops
-Yes	89.5	81.0	72.1
(md*	4.7	14.8	23.9)
N	190	189	201

Source: WECSS Parent Study, Pestoff (1998)

* the figures given here are absolute percentages, i.e., they don't exclude missing data, due to the varying amount of missing data for these three categories of parents

emphasize either their dissatisfaction with municipal daycare services or the good relations they have at their present cooperative daycare center, while some say that the openness and concern of the staff is the same at both types of daycare.

When asked which form they feel is better, parents with children in voluntary organizations are slightly more positive about cooperative daycare services (Table 3.8). More than three of four of the parents in all types of social enterprises express a clear preference for the cooperative form compared to municipal daycare services. Nearly half of the parents (48.7%) with children in both parent co-ops and municipal services provided comments to this comparison, about three of four (76.9%) of the parents with children in voluntary organizations also made comments, while about three of five parents (61.9%) with children in worker co-ops did so. As such, this was the question that received the most comments from parents, indicating its saliency for them, while comparisons of staff openness and concern received the next greatest proportion of parent comments. Parent comments can be divided into three main categories. Either they stress the advantages of their cooperative, as does the overwhelming majority, the disadvantages of the municipal services and other comments, including the importance of pedagogics, that there is little difference between co-op and municipal services, etc.

Finally, parents were also asked to state, if they could choose freely, whether they would choose cooperative daycare services for their child(ren) again, given its possible disadvantages (Table 3.9). Nearly three-fourths or more of the parents in all three categories expressed a clear preference for cooperative daycare over municipal daycare facilities. Note, however, that there was much more missing data in the answers of parents with children in worker cooperative daycare services. More than one of four parents with children in parent co-ops or voluntary organizations provided comments on their preference for cooperative daycare even in the future, while more than one of five parents with children in worker co-ops did so. Once again their answers either emphasize the advantages of the cooperative form, which most of their comments mention, the disadvantages of the municipal form, special pedagogics or occasionally some disadvantages of the cooperative form.

E. Summary and Conclusions

E.1 Summary

In this chapter we explored an extension and adaptation of the concept of co-production to the area of personal social services and social enterprises providing such services. We presented data on three different forms of social enterprises providing daycare services in Sweden, i.e., parent cooperatives, voluntary organizations and worker cooperatives. However, both parent cooperatives and voluntary organizations have a work obligation associated with membership, while worker cooperatives lack this feature, as parents cannot become members. The parents of both the first two types of social enterprises express similar attitudes to the positive aspects of the work obligation. It facilitates their participation, gives a feeling of belonging and valuable insights, i.e., it enables their integration into the organization and running of cooperative daycare services. These two groups attribute less weight to gaining possibilities for influence through the work obligation. Turning to elected and honorary offices, many more parents held them in parent cooperatives than voluntary organizations, while few if any parents has such possibilities to become involved in worker cooperatives, and where so only in advisory bodies. In contrast to attitudes about the work obligation, parent attitudes about their participation on the board emphasize first and foremost the political aspect of holding an elective office in cooperative daycare services, i.e., it increases parental influence. The integrative aspects, already noted for the work obligation, are also rated highly by both groups of parents in terms of holding elective or honorary offices. The higher rate of holding elective and honorary offices in parent cooperatives than in voluntary organizations means that the parents have greater access to influence in the former than the latter type of cooperative daycare services.

Turning to reasons for choosing their preferred form of social enterprise providing daycare services, we noted a clear profile for each type of daycare service. Influence, wanting to participate more in their child(ren)'s daily life and closeness to home provide a clear profile for parents with children in parent cooperatives. Special pedagogics, wanting to influence and wanting to participate more in their child(ren)'s daily life clearly dominate the motives of parents with children in voluntary organizations. Both these sets of parents clearly motivate their choice of cooperative daycare form more in terms of expressive values than in instrumental terms. Closeness to home, a recommendation by relatives or friends and the lack of other alternatives were the main motives of parents with children in worker cooperatives, which clearly express the more instrumental attitudes of these parents.

However, having made their choice, the differences between the advantages of three types of social enterprises allow for more room for instrumental values. An enjoyable atmosphere, an engaged staff and possibility of influence are given by the parents of all three types of cooperative daycare services as one of the four main advantages, while participating in the child's daily life and pedagogics are still important for parents from the first two types of daycare services. Few disadvantages were mentioned.

Parents strongly appreciate the willingness of the staff to discuss parents' suggestions for changes and improvements Moreover, parents in all three types of social enterprises express a similar level of satisfaction with the running and administration of their child(ren)'s daycare service. However, given the clearly articulated instrumental attitude of parents with children in worker cooperatives, as opposed to the more expressive attitude of parents with children in parent cooperatives and voluntary organizations, it is an open question if parents in the latter two types of social enterprises would be as satisfied with as little influence and chance to participate as parents with children in worker cooperatives. Thus, we are suggesting that no single type of social enterprise nor organizational formula can meet the needs and requirements of all parents for daycare services. Rather, a greater welfare mix and welfare pluralism requires a greater diversity of forms for providing personal social services.

Many parents have previously had a child(ren) in municipal daycare services, and their comparisons between cooperative and municipal services are clearly to the advantage of social enterprises in terms of the openness of the staff. They also categorically feel that social enterprises providing daycare services, regardless of the type, are better than municipal services. Finally, given a free choice, they state a clear preference for social enterprises as a form, regardless of the type of social enterprise.

E.2 Conclusions

Market failure and information asymmetries make personal social services well suited for provision by third sector and nonprofit organizations, because the latter mitigates some kinds of market failure and instills more trust in the relations between the consumers and providers of such services. The enduring nature of some personal social services renders them better suited for voice than exit. Moreover, the transaction costs of providing such services via markets are prohibitive for the consumers, producers and society. All these considerations argue in favor of third sector alternatives to both markets and politics. Here co-production, social enterprises and cooperative social services can provide an alternative to markets and quasi-markets. They also contribute to the development of civil democracy and local cooperative self-management of social services.

Our findings suggest a modification of the idea of 'service democracy', where parents preferred municipal services due to the burden of responsibility and few of them saw participation in the operation of their daughter's and/or son's daycare center as a value in itself. The WECSS Parent Study clearly shows that parents with a child in a parent cooperative or voluntary organization value highly the integrative aspects of the work obligation and the possibilities for participation provided by holding an elective or honorary office. Furthermore, most parents state unequivocally that alternative or cooperative daycare services are better than municipal services, and they provide several reasons to motivate their choice, including the deterioration of municipal services. A service democracy may be the ideal for many Swedes, but a growing number of them want to reduce the uncertainty in their relation to the providers of enduring services, as seen in the rapid growth of cooperative daycare services in recent decades (Pestoff, 1998).

Co-production is motivated by the degree of uncertainty in the exchange between the producer and consumer of goods and services and the potential benefit to the participants from eliminating such uncertainty (Wikström,

1996). Social enterprises and cooperative social services with clear social goals and nonprofit motives help to generate trust between producers and consumers of such services, by minimizing or eliminating possibilities for opportunistic behavior. In the case of childcare, some types of cooperative social services eliminate uncertainty by promoting parental participation as co-producers, i.e., by the work obligation combined with their democratic procedures, where parents hold honorary offices and manage the facility. The creation of benefits related to the values of the parents is made possible by some types of cooperative daycare centers. In particular the values of parent influence, participation in their child(ren)'s daily life, special pedagogics and feelings of belonging are important values to the parents of children in parent cooperative and voluntary organizations. Co-production eliminates the uncertainty related to interaction between producers and consumers of such services because it involves parents in the production, and their participation is the best guarantee of quality, according to one parent. Co-production both enables the parents and empowers them in fulfilling their own values related to the institutional care of their children.

It is not as easy, if at all possible, to promote the same values in worker cooperatives, nor in municipal or private daycare services, but worker cooperative daycare services nevertheless promote the instrumental values of the parents. In this respect, it can be argued that parent co-ops and voluntary organizations daycare services are unique in promoting the creation of the values related to co-production. Without the existence of this form of daycare for children and without the participation and involvement of parents in the production of the cooperative daycare services, such values would not be created for these parents. Thus, these special forms of daycare service have created value for the parents by engaging them as co-producers. Both the lives and values of the parents with children in such daycare services, and most likely of their children too, would not be enriched by these possibilities, if these alternatives were curtailed for political or financial reasons. None of these values associated with co-production are available in services provided by worker co-ops, municipal or private daycare services, as parent participation and co-production are not encouraged and facilitated by them. Without such forms of daycare services, these parents would not be able to obtain such values. Thus, co-production promotes unique values for large groups of parents. It thereby enriches publicly financed personal social services and contributes to the renewal of the welfare state by turning it into a more participatory welfare society.

By providing an opportunity for the realization of the expressive values of parents social enterprises promote civil democracy and facilitate the role of citizens as co-producers. In this fashion social enterprises not only help to eliminate uncertainty in the relations between parents and the staff of daycare services, they also promote greater trust between the clients and their social enterprises.

4 Citizens as Co-Producers of Welfare Services
Childcare in Eight European Countries

A. Introduction

What role should the state and market play in the provision of welfare services? Should the state provide most welfare services, as it does today in the Scandinavian universal or Social Democratic welfare states, or should services be privatized and provided by the market, as proposed by neo-liberals? This is a hotly debated issue in all European countries and one of the main, if not the main question posed to the voters in most European elections in the last 30 to 35 years. As hotly debated as it is, it fails to consider the potential role of civil society, or the third sector and citizens. What role should the third sector play in providing welfare services, and what role should citizens play in producing such services? Answers to the latter question reflect different perspectives on citizens and different views of citizenship. Are citizens simply passive consumers of welfare services that are provided either by the state or market, or can they play an active role in producing some kinds of welfare services? Is citizenship restricted to voting in general elections, consuming goods and services, paying taxes and abiding by the laws of the land, or does it imply both rights and responsibilities that go beyond this limited view of citizenship?

Co-production or citizen involvement in the provision of public services generated a flurry of interest among American scholars of public administration in the 1970s and the 1980s (see Parks, *et al.* for a good overview). The concept was originally developed by the Workshop in Political Theory and Policy Analysis at Indiana University. During the 1970s they struggled with the dominant theories of urban governance underlying policy recommendations for massive centralization. Many scholars and public officials argued that citizens as clients would receive more effective and efficient services if they were delivered by professional staff employed by a large bureaucratic agency. But, the Indiana team found no empirical support for claims promoting centralization (Ostrom, 1996).

However, they stumbled on several myths of public production. One was the notion of a single producer being responsible for urban services within each jurisdiction. In fact, they normally found several agencies, as well as private firms, producing services. More important, they also realized that the production of a service, as contrasted to a good, was difficult without the active participation of those receiving the service. They developed the term 'co-production' to describe the potential relationship that could exist between the 'regular' producer (street-level police officers, schoolteachers or health workers) and clients who want to be transformed by the service into safer, better-educated or healthier persons. Therefore, co-production captures the synergy that can occur between what a government does and what citizens do (*ibid.*).

The concept of co-production appears very relevant to proposals for public sector reforms and could be a missing piece of the puzzle for reforming representative democracy and the welfare state. It provides insights into conditions at the micro-level or the site of production of welfare services. This perspective is often missing in many of the more macro-oriented perspectives. More than 30 years ago Barber (1984) compared weak democracy to strong democracy and proposed a more active role for citizens. Walzer (1988) argued for "more participative and decentralized forms for service provision" that make room for self-help and local initiative. He contrasted earlier decades' calls to nationalize the means of production of goods with more recent proposals to socialize the means of distribution of welfare services. This would reflect a state-sponsored democratic transformation of public service agencies at the local level and/or the transfer of authority and resources to voluntary organizations (*ibid.*: 21). In particular, he argued that it was important to increase the number of service providers who are also recipients or potential recipients of welfare services. This would allow them greater say in the management of welfare services (*ibid.*: 22).

He considered several ways of recruiting more providers of welfare services, including paying a nominal wage to volunteers and instituting a new national service for providing welfare services (*ibid.*: 22). In post-industrial societies a growing number of civil servants provide welfare services, but they do not have a natural monopoly on helping, even if they are professional helpers. The welfare state co-exists with a welfare society, even if the latter is relatively weak today and requires the continued and sustained support of the former (*ibid.*: 25). However, Walzer noted that his suggestion requires a major reform of local democracy and also an effort to extend the reach of voluntary organizations. At the same time, the state needs to be strong enough to supervise and subsidize the work of citizens and volunteers. A lively and supportive welfare society, framed, but not controlled, by a strong welfare state would represent a fundamental transformation in the relations of distribution or service provision (*ibid.*: 26) and also a reform of the relations between 'the rulers and the ruled'. In his lucid analysis of power Galbraith (1983, 1986) refers to the 'Age of Organizations' and different types and sources of power. The most germane type of power in the 20th century he calls 'conditional power'. It gains influence by persuasion and changing beliefs and it stems from organizations, i.e., big public or big private organizations, regardless of sector.

Elsewhere, Hirst (1994) argued that liberal representative democracy is overextended, stretched to its limits, due to the growth of the modern welfare state, and it cannot function as intended—to control the public administration. His solution, 'Associative Democracy', calls for a much more active role for the third sector and citizens in providing goods and services, in order to return democracy to what it once was: the will of the people. He suggested that many major policy networks should be extended to include all the governed. This could be achieved by devolving as many of the functions of the state as possible to civil society, while retaining public funding, and by democratizing as many as possible of the organizations of civil society (*ibid.*). He argues that this is not merely nostalgia or longing for a lost 'golden age', but rather as a way of developing and renewal of democracy, as well as a means for curbing the growth and dominance of big organizations in the public and private sectors, i.e., both in business and government.

Later, in his discussion of 'democracy and governance', Hirst (2002) contrasts an 'organizational society', with its large public and private bureaucracies, and the smaller organizations normally found in civil society. He calls for large-scale institutional reform of both state and social institutions. The aim of these reforms is to restore limited government by involving civil society in the functions of the state and to transform the organizations of the latter from top-down bureaucracies into constitutionally ordered, democratically self-governing associations (*ibid.*: 28). However, he recognizes that associative self-government would supplement and extend representative government, not replace it. Democracy at the national level would be strengthened and made viable by democratizing civil society. Governments' principal task would, therefore, be to raise and distribute revenue to associations and the provision of a constitutional ordering and supervision of the institutions of civil society (*ibid.*: 30).

What does greater citizen participation in the provision of welfare services, or co-production, imply for the development and renewal of democracy today? In what ways can and do citizens participate in the provision of public services? How do differences in citizen participation relate to the development and renewal of democracy? Co-production will first be considered from a theoretical perspective and then illustrated by the involvement of parents in childcare services in Europe. Thus, this chapter merges two strands of thought or two types of questions concerning citizen participation. First, it addresses the theoretical literature on co-production of public services. Second, it explores citizen participation in childcare services, based on materials collected by the TSFEPS Project, Changing Family Structures and Social Policy: Childcare Services as Sources of Social Cohesion, a comparative study between 2002 and 2005 of childcare services in eight European nations. Finally, it reaches some conclusions about the role of co-production in developing and renewing democracy and the welfare state.

B. Co-Production

There are numerous important issues related to citizen involvement in the production of public services. A review of the literature helps us to identify some of the most relevant issues. Co-production differs notably from the traditional model of public service production in which public officials are exclusively charged with responsibility for designing and providing services to citizens, who in turn only demand, consume and evaluate them. The dominant model of public service production, according to Sharp (1980), is based on two distinct spheres: one of regular (public) producers and a second sphere of goods and services consuming clients or citizens, interest groups, etc. A dialog or feedback between these spheres can be problematic. By contrast, co-production is based on the assumption of an active, participative populace of consumer producers. When the two spheres overlap to a greater or lesser degree the feedback between them is an internal process. Service delivery is a joint venture involving both citizens and government agents (Whitaker, 1980). Thus, co-production implies citizen participation in the execution or implementation of public policies.

Co-production is, therefore, noted by the mix of activities that both public service agents and citizens contribute to the provision of public services. The former are involved as professionals or 'regular producers', while 'citizen production' is based on voluntary efforts of individuals or groups to enhance the quality and/or quantity of services they receive (Parks *et al.*, 1981; Brudney & England, 1983; Ostrom, 1996). In advanced societies there is a division of labor and most persons are engaged in full-time production of goods and services as regular producers. However, individual consumers or groups of consumers may also contribute to the production of goods and services, as consumer producers. This mixing may occur directly or indirectly.

If co-production occurs, it takes place as a result of technological, economic and institutional or political influences (Parks *et al.*, 1981). Technology determines whether there are production functions for a service where both regular and consumer producer activities can contribute to the output. Economic considerations determine whether it is efficient to mix regular and consumer producer activities to produce the service. Institutional considerations determine whether an appropriate mix is permitted in situations where co-production is technically feasible and economically efficient, and whether a mix is discouraged where it is inefficient (*ibid.*: 1002).

Technical relationships between regular and consumer producers are crucial because they can either result in a situation where their inputs are substitutes for each other, or they are interdependent of each other. An appropriate mix depends on the substitutability or interdependence of producing a particular service and the relative wages and opportunity costs for regular and consumer producers. If it is a case of interdependence, there are likely to be both regular and consumer production inputs. Neither the regular nor consumer producers can supply the service alone, so inputs from both are necessary. But, institutional incentives are still necessary for co-production to exist (*ibid.*: 1002–1006).

Percy (1984) notes that co-production occurs when *both* consumers and regular producers undertake efforts to produce the *same* goods or services. However, there is no requirement that their efforts be taken through direct interactions, only that they be undertaken more or less simultaneously. In addition, Rich (1981) identifies other key dimensions of co-production. He distinguishes between the positive and negative, cooperative and compliant, active and passive as well as individual and collective dimensions of co-production. Co-production does not require the formal organization of citizens, but organizations are nevertheless a critical variable, because they can enhance the levels of co-production and facilitate coordination between citizens and public agencies necessary to achieve the desired ends (*ibid.*).

However, Warren *et al.* (1982) and Rosentraub and Warren (1987) warned against too broad a definition. They argued that by narrowing the concept one also excludes civic activities normally associated with citizenship, or 'ancillary' or auxiliary production, and actions taken totally separately from regular service agents, known as 'parallel' production. Ancillary actions are expected forms of behavior for citizens, such as obeying the law and following regulations or reporting crime. Parallel production involves services similar to those provided by public agencies, but produced by individuals without contact or cooperation with public agencies (*ibid.*).

Co-production is often seen as an approach to the enhancement of municipal productivity. Warren *et al.* (1982) maintain that co-production can lead to cost reductions, higher service quality and expanded opportunities for citizens to participate in decisions concerning public services. The latter can result in greater satisfaction with and support for public services, i.e., greater legitimacy. Thus, co-production becomes an important means of enhancing both the quality and quantity of public services, as well as helping to enrich and renew democracy at the level of service provision. However, savings to the public budget from co-production are constrained by the amount of substitution that can effectively be undertaken between citizens and service agents or public employees (Brudney, 1984). Citizens normally lack the training and experience to perform services that require specialized knowledge. Moreover, substituting paid personnel with voluntary efforts means that some of the costs are transferred to the co-producers themselves. So, the costs are not eliminated, merely shifted to the citizens (*ibid.*).

Percy (1984) maintained that the scope of the benefits resulting from co-productive efforts may affect a citizen's decision about the types and frequency of co-production undertaken. Where the benefits of the citizens' efforts are primarily to the citizen-producers themselves, co-production is likely to be greatest. However, where the benefits are more broadly scattered among the population in general, citizens' co-productive actions are less frequent (*ibid.*). Here there is a 'free-rider' problem that needs to be identified and analyzed more. So, there is a direct correspondence between resources committed and benefits received.

Rich (1981) notes that citizens may consider the net benefits of their voluntary efforts in terms of fellowship, self-esteem or other intangible benefits stemming from them. He emphasized the interface between the government and voluntary sectors and noted the importance of recognizing that voluntary action always takes place in a political context. The individual cost/benefit analysis and the decision to contribute to voluntary efforts, as well as the effectiveness of such efforts, can, therefore, be conditioned by the structure of political institutions. Centralized service delivery tends to make articulation of demands more costly for citizens and to inhibit governmental responsiveness, while citizen participation seems to fare better in decentralized service delivery (Ostrom, 1975).

Moreover, Percy (1984) also stated that organizational arrangements can facilitate or hinder co-production. Resistance to co-production strategies may be encountered in public service agencies. In particular, service workers and public administrators may see themselves as trained workers and therefore resent or resist the intrusion of untrained and inexperienced workers. Without the tacit support of public employees, the involvement of citizens in production activities might create more problems than it solves (Rosentraub & Warren, 1987). Typical examples of co-production found in the early literature on the USA include public safety and security, education, fire protection, recreation or solid waste collection and disposal (Percy, 1984).

While co-production initially attracted a lot of attention in the USA in the 1970s and 1980s, since then involving people and groups outside the government in producing public services has only received sporadic interest. However, Ostrom (1996) also analyzed co-production in developing countries, where she focused on suburban water supply in Brazil and primary education in Nigeria. She states that all public goods and services are potentially produced by the regular producer and those who are frequently referred to as the 'client'. However, she argues that the term client is a passive term, indicating that they are acted upon, or passive recipients of services. "Co-production [by contrast] implies that citizens can play an active role in producing public goods and services of consequence to them" (*ibid.*: 1073).

She points out, on the one hand, that no market can survive without extensive public goods provided by governmental agencies; but, on the other hand, that no government can be efficient and equitable without considerable input from citizens. Therefore, she concludes that "[c]o-production of many goods and services, normally considered to be public goods by government agencies and citizens organized into polycentric systems, is crucial for achieving higher levels of welfare in developing countries, particularly those that are poor" (*ibid.*: 1083). Her perspective can, of course, be extended to cover many welfare services in developed countries. Co-production is also essential for sustaining current levels of welfare service provision in many European welfare systems facing sharp budget constraints, the crunch of globalization and losing jobs to low-wage countries.

Even today academic interest in co-production recognizes that in many important areas of government activity it is impossible to deliver services without the contributions of time and effort by citizens. Today there is a renewed interest in understanding co-production or greater citizen participation in the production of public services. Alford (2002) distinguished between three sources of motivation for citizen participation in public sector services: material, solidarity and expressive incentives. He examined four cases of participation in public sector services in Australia ranging from simple to complex: the use of post codes in postal services, participation by long-term unemployed in training programs, maintenance activities by tenants in public high-rise housing complexes and taxpayer collaboration with income tax requirements (*ibid.*).

He noted that government reformers often urge the adoption of a private-sector-style 'customer focus', but critics see it as inappropriate, in particular because it diminishes citizenship. He argued that interactions between most public sector organizations and their clients differ in several fundamental ways from private sector customer transactions. From a social exchange perspective, government organizations need some things from service recipients— such as their cooperation and compliance—which are essential for effective organizational performance. Eliciting those things not only requires meeting the material needs of citizens, but also their symbolic or normative expectations. Thus, involving citizens in the co-production of public goods and services is consistent with an active model of citizenship (*ibid.*).

In addition to the basic or market exchange in which services are exchanged for money, there is also an exchange of the client's time and efforts for heightening the value the client perceives in certain situations. However, material rewards and sanctions are ineffective in eliciting the requisite client contributions in all but the most simple of tasks. Rather, many clients are motivated by more complex, nonmaterial incentives, such as intrinsic rewards, or social, solidarity and expressive values. He notes that different motivators will elicit co-production in different contextual circumstances. The more public the value consumed, the more complex the motivations necessary to co-produce. He concludes that eliciting co-production is a matter of heightening the value that clients receive from the services by making more explicit its nonmaterial aspects through intrinsic rewards, solidarity incentives or normative appeal (*ibid.*: 48).

In Sweden, the idea of enhancing the role of citizens in providing welfare services seldom gets attention from scholars and politicians. Nevertheless, citizens currently contribute much of their time and effort to the production of welfare services, both as parents in relation to childcare or youth sports activities and sports clubs, as well as relatives in terms of eldercare. They directly contribute to the realization of the final value of good quality childcare, youth sports activities and/or good quality eldercare, although such services are primarily financed by taxes. A report to the Swedish parliamentary committee, *Ansvarskommittén*, calls for a greater role for citizen participation and direct democracy in continued reforms of the Swedish welfare state (Häggroth, 2005). In order to come to grips with the growing democracy deficit and to renew the legitimacy of the welfare state and its large public sector, citizens should play a greater role in the delivery of welfare services the report concluded.

In a Scandinavian context important public services where co-production might be promoted include welfare services, like childcare, elementary and higher education, health care, eldercare, handicap care, leisure activities, etc. In universal, tax-financed welfare states found in Scandinavia, the consumer is a citizen, while the buyer or purchaser of services may be a public body, unless vouchers are used, and finally the provider of such services is often a municipal or private firm. Although the services can be financed by taxes, fees or both, they may also require that the consumer of the services contribute some of his/her time to realize the full value of the service. Many welfare services also build on enduring relations between the consumer and providers of such services rather than on one-time or intermittent relations of an *ad hoc* nature.

Chapter 3 explores parent participation in parent co-ops, worker co-ops and voluntary organizations providing childcare services for preschool children in Sweden and contrasts them with the services provided by the public sector. It shows that the motives of parents for choosing one type of childcare facility or another express the values they hope to promote by becoming co-producers. Their motives can either be instrumental or expressive, but most parents combine both, similar to the pattern noted by Alford (2002). Co-production and the work obligation associated with many alternative providers of preschool services in Sweden help to eliminate uncertainty in the relationship between producers and consumers of these services. It provides parents with greater insights into the quality of the services and gives them influence on decisions of how to run the childcare facility. Moreover, the provision of welfare services through social enterprises that facilitate co-production alters the relationship between the state and citizens in a fundamental way. Citizens are no longer passive recipients of public services. Moreover, they no longer are defined mainly by their passive roles as taxpayers who file and pay their taxes every year or voters who exercise their political rights every third or fourth year. Rather they become active participants in the production of welfare services of consequence to them that they demand themselves and pay for with their taxes (Pestoff, 1998, 2009.).

Peters (1994, 1996) discussed four emerging models of public sector provision of goods and services. He regards the participatory model as an alternative to both the old bureaucratic one and to New Public Management. A participatory state depends upon both its citizens and front-line staff becoming involved in making some choices about policy and social services.

Similar to the market model, a participatory model would also give citizens more choice and direct control over the provision of various goods and services. But the manner in which these choices would be exercised in a participatory state would be much more overtly political. Rather than voting with their feet, through vouchers or their euros, dollars, crowns or yen, citizens would vote through some sort of political process. They might participate in referenda of local policy or in local representative structures, like parent involvement in school committees (*ibid.*: 15). Alternatively, participation can take place in non-representative, but nevertheless democratic structures for providing welfare services, like public financed cooperative childcare in Sweden (Pestoff, 1998). The important point, however, is that citizens become involved in the co-production of the services that they need, pay for with their taxes and that are important for them and their loved-ones.

C. Participation in Childcare Services in Eight European Countries

Co-production will be illustrated by parents' participation in childcare services in eight European countries. Materials for this study come from the TSFEPS Project, Changing Family Structures and Social Policy: Childcare Services as Sources of Social Cohesion, a comparative European study between 2002 and 2005 of childcare services in Belgium, Bulgaria, England, France, Germany, Italy, Spain and Sweden. Case studies of different providers of childcare in two cities[1] per country contributed the empirical materials for the discussion of parent participation in childcare.

Participation in childcare services takes different forms in different countries in the TSFEPS project. It ranges from high to low and can be found at different levels of analysis, both at the aggregate or citywide level and at the individual childcare center. Participation involves different dimensions or aspects, such as economic, political, social and service specific participation. It also involves different groups or stakeholders, like the parents, staff and public authorities responsible for providing and funding preschool services, and in some cases third sector organizations (TSOs) and even a few for-profit firms that provide such services. We will begin our discussion with economic participation, then consider political, social and finally service specific participation.

Economic participation in childcare services can either involve the contribution of money, in-kind donations or time by parents. Parent fees are found in most countries and they represent one kind of economic participation. However, they are normally limited by law to a certain proportion of the total costs for providing such services, and not set by market forces related to supply and demand. Parents normally do not gain additional benefits from greater financial participation. But, parents are also expected to make contributions in-kind for the running of childcare services in some countries. This is particularly striking in the former socialist countries where the state or local authorities often lack the funds necessary to maintain reasonable material standards in childcare facilities. Here parents feel obliged to contribute both their time and various material things necessary for keeping the services running, in addition to regular parent fees. But some type of economic contribution in-kind can also be found to a lesser degree in countries with less-developed systems of childcare provision and in services arranged or initiated by parents.

By contrast, contributions of time in most EU countries are normally associated with parental participation in the running and management of childcare facilities, like those found in France, Germany and Sweden (Fraisse & Bucolo, 2003; Evers & Riedel, 2003; Strandbrink & Pestoff, 2003, 2006). In parent cooperative or parent initiative services there is often a work obligation. This excludes many parents who do not have flexible working conditions that permit them to make such contributions in time. In particular, single parent families find it difficult to meet the extra time demands of such services in most facilities included here (*ibid.*).

Political participation by parents can either take indirect, representative or corporatist forms in sector-wide municipal decision-making bodies and/or it can involve direct parental participation in decision-making bodies at the level of individual childcare centers or the site of service production. Participation can take the form of elected parental representation in the consultative committees found in public services in many countries, often stipulated by law. Small parent-run and managed childcare services often depend on the efforts of all the parents, not only a few elected representatives. Most or all parents are board members and they make most or all the decisions about the management of the childcare center, as illustrated by parent associations in France, parent initiatives in Germany or parent co-ops in Sweden.

Parent associations, initiatives and cooperatives in France, Germany and Sweden are both managed and maintained by the parents themselves. But very few examples exist of direct, systematic parent involvement in the pedagogical aspects of childcare in such facilities. Rather, parents provide a necessary complement to the professional staff. Parents can substitute for professional staff when the latter are absent due to sickness or for other reasons, such as attending training courses, etc. The presence of parents at a childcare facility can also enrich the environment of childcare facilities. In particular, the presence of fathers, in an otherwise heavily female-dominated occupation group, is positive both for young boys and girls. However, parent involvement in parent-run facilities is normally confined to performing non-professional tasks related to running and managing the facility, the maintenance and repairs, keeping the books, contacts with the authorities and occasionally even cooking. Thus, there is little risk that parents will substitute or replace the professional staff in parent associations, initiatives and cooperatives.

At the aggregate level, participation can either be *ad hoc* or it can take more corporatist forms of representation of various stakeholders in citywide consultative bodies charged with developing childcare services. The latter is normally the case when a variety of different stakeholders exist in the same geographical context, the welfare mix is accepted by most actors and no single form of production dominates the provision of childcare services. Some cities included in our eight country study demonstrated a form of corporatist representation in permanent consultative bodies for all major providers of childcare services in a given territory, while others did not. Institutions for regular citywide consultation between various service providers may be seen as the co-management of a sector. Regular consultation with most or all of the providers may also be prescribed by law, as seen in some of the TSFEPS countries (Lhuillier, 2003; Fraisse & Bucolo, 2003; Evers & Riedel, 2003). *Ad hoc* consultations may take place in a city where the municipal government normally dominates the provision of such services. Once the number of non-municipal providers grows beyond a certain level they may be consulted in an *ad hoc* fashion. This is illustrated in Sweden by the existence of such consultations in Stockholm and Gothenburg, but not Östersund. However, such consultations are not required by law (Strandbrink & Pestoff, 2003, 2006).

Social participation can take several forms. Regular meetings of parents can facilitate the creation of parent networks. Parents can be charged with helping to organize or arranging various social events, like the Christmas party, the end of the year party in June, etc. Such events can either be limited to those directly associated with the childcare facility, i.e., the staff, parents and children, or they can be open to residents of the neighborhood where the childcare center is located. In the latter case they also involve the childcare center's social relations in the neighborhood. Some country reports stress that municipal childcare services prefer to limit parties and festivals to the children, staff and parents of the facility, while parent initiatives and cooperatives prefer to see childcare as a way of integrating families into the social life of the neighborhood (Lhuillier, 2003; Fraisse & Bucolo, 2003; Evers & Riedel, 2003).

Service specific participation by parents is both natural and at the same time a highly contested phenomenon. Parents and the home are a natural part of children's growth and development and this argues for involving parents more actively in running childcare facilities. The English report in the TSFEPS Project emphasizes the pedagogical philosophy of early excellence centers (EECs) that try to involve parents in the daily activities of childcare facilities and the Belgium report refers to policies to mobilize resource-weak parents. However, these efforts seem more related to special social goals of integrating and empowering resource weak parents in these two countries.

In sum, the case studies analyzed here demonstrate a wide range of patterns of parent participation. At the level of the individual childcare services, participation took quite different forms. Most childcare services studied here fall into the top-down category in terms of style of service provision. They provide few possibilities for parents to directly influence decision-making in such services. This normally includes both municipal childcare services and for-profit firms providing childcare services in the countries studied here. Perhaps this is logical from the perspective of municipal governments. They are, after all, representative institutions, chosen by the voters in elections. They might consider direct client or user participation in the running of public services for a particular group, like parents, a threat both to the representative democracy they institutionalize and to their own power. It could be argued that direct participation for a particular group would thereby provide this group of citizens with a 'veto right' or a 'second vote' at the service level. This could provide a basis for opposing co-production. There may also be professional considerations for resisting parent involvement and participation.

The logic of direct participation is also foreign to private for-profit providers. Exit, rather than voice provide the medium of communication in markets, where parents are seen as consumers. This logic excludes both indirect and direct representation. Only the parent associations, initiatives and cooperatives noted in some countries clearly fall into the bottom-up category. Here we find the clearest examples of self-government and direct democracy. Parents are directly involved in the running of their daughter and/or son's childcare center in terms of being responsible for the maintenance, management, etc. of the childcare facility. They also participate in the decision-making of the facility, as members and owners of the facility.

D. Summary and Conclusions about Co-Production of Childcare

I will now consider the implications of these findings for the development of the concept of co-production and then discuss their implications for the contribution of co-production to the development and renewal of democracy and the welfare state. Our attempt to identify various types of citizen participation in terms of co-production resulted in examples of direct contributions in economic, political, social and service specific terms by parents to the value created by childcare facilities throughout Europe. However, some forms of participation seem more germane than others in terms of co-production. Some of the activities mentioned above could perhaps better be classified as auxiliary or ancillary activities, rather than co-production. In particular many of the social activities appear to be of this nature. They are normally part of collective childcare regardless of the country or provider. However, both the economic activities found in Bulgaria, as well as the management and decision-making activities by parents found in parent associations, initiatives and cooperatives in France, Germany and Sweden, qualify as co-production. However, we should also consider whether they might possibly be classified as parallel production.

The main reason for not classifying them as parallel production is that these childcare services are financed by public funds. Moreover, the parent associations, initiatives and cooperatives found in France, Germany and

Sweden are contributing to the fulfillment of public goals of providing child-care services to as many parents as possible and in a form that parents not only approve, but are willing to contribute to with their time and effort. In Sweden, childcare is now an entitlement for all children between the ages of 1 and 6 years old. If the parents did not make contributions of their time and effort to alternative providers or if the latter did not exist, then these same parents would need and use public services. The public authorities would, therefore, be obliged to provide them with these services, but they might be hard pressed to do so, given historical shortages in many areas. Thus, although alternative services are provided by separate organizations, they are both financed by public funds and they contribute to fulfilling public policy goals in this area.

Ostrom's discussion of co-production in terms of production functions notes that it may involve strictly substitutable or complementary processes. Substitution would imply parallel production and involve parent participation in all areas of preschool, including pedagogical activities, not just in some tasks. Parent participation, primarily in the maintenance and management of childcare facilities, comprise complementary activities that create synergies based on a clear division of labor between the professionals and parents. Here the parents take over the secondary or tertiary activities, while the professionals can concentrate on the core ones, the pedagogy of preschool learning.

Alternative provision of childcare for preschool children comprises an interesting example of co-production in France, Germany and Sweden. Public financing is available to all types of childcare providers in Sweden, e.g., public, private for-profit and third sector childcare. However, only the latter appear to facilitate extensive parent participation. Today between 10% and 15% of all preschool-aged children are enrolled in third sector childcare in Sweden.

Moreover, co-production appears to change its form with changed conditions. Initially, co-production referred to the degree of overlap between two sets of participants in the service production process: regular producers and consumers. The resulting overlap represents the joint effort of these two groups, both public professionals and citizens, in the provision of public services. It was not necessary that they be organized in the same organization. However, with today's system of contracting out and the growing welfare mix, we need to recognize that citizens can participate in various ways. They can participate on either an individual or organized basis in the provision of neighborhood safety in the USA, or in permanent organized groups of users in third sector organizations providing welfare services in Europe. The latter would include participation in parent associations, initiatives and cooperative childcare services found in France, Germany and Sweden. In the former case, users are clearly a complement to professional public providers of neighborhood safety, i.e., the police. In the latter case, citizens take over the management of welfare services, but the public sector still finances and regulates the provision of such services. This would imply an extension of the concept of co-production to include collective efforts to provide public financed services produced by third sector providers. The two main requirements for co-production are the continued public financing of such services and the participation of consumer producers or citizens in their provision.

Finally, the term co-production needs to be distinguished from similar, but different phenomena of co-management and co-governance. The growing welfare mix and diversity of providers not only implies greater citizen involvement in the provision of some public financed services, but it also becomes necessary to manage and govern this growing diversity. Co-management refers to the growing diversity or hybridization of providers of welfare services, typically found in situations where nonprofit organizations (NPOs) and/or FPOs participate in the provision of public financed services (Brandsen, 2004), with or without greater citizen involvement in terms of co-production. Co-governance refers to attempts to manage this growing diversity in a more democratic fashion through the creation of citywide, provincial and/or national bodies where various providers are represented and given a voice in governing the development of a sector. The appropriate site for co-governance structures will depend, of course, on constitutional differences between various welfare states. We found some examples of this in the childcare sector in France and Germany, but not Sweden, in spite of the growing diversity of providers of such services in all three countries. However, here we must also distinguish between consultations, no matter how frequent or structured, and decision-making. Organizational participation in consultations may or may not lead to mutual adjustment, but this differs greatly from participation in binding decisions. Co-governance requires real input and influence in the development of a sector or provision of welfare services. This may be difficult to achieve without the existence of necessary intermediate structures among various providers of welfare services. This is particularly important for small third sector providers, who may find it hard to organize themselves collectively.

In conclusion, I will turn my attention to the implications of co-production for the development and renewal of democracy and the welfare state. Co-production provides a necessary conceptual tool for understanding citizen participation at the micro-level or site of production of welfare services. It gives us a missing piece of the puzzle of democratic reform. It also underlines the importance of motivating and involving both the citizens and professionals in the process of institutional change. At the same time the political process is very important. Without the necessary political support and proper institutional structures, little progress will be made.

However, we found that some dimensions of co-production in childcare appear more germane to the development and renewal of democracy and the welfare state than others. In particular the contribution of time by parents to the political dimension, noted above, promote these goals more clearly than the economic, social or service specific dimensions. New ways need to be developed to encourage the participation of several different stakeholders in the provision of childcare services, not just a single one, as today. The staff, parents and financers of childcare services need to form multi-stakeholder organizations at the site of service production. Also, institutions should be created by the authorities to promote greater participation by alternative or third sector providers in the citywide management of childcare services. This would, of course, require a change in the laws of some European countries. However, participation in childcare services should not be seen as a 'zero-sum' game or winner-take-all situation, but rather one where various stakeholders can make a contribution to better quality childcare through dialog and cooperation with each other. Therefore, they all deserve recognition of their potential contribution to a common goal. This recognition needs to be accompanied by providing them with ways and means for gaining influence in the day-to-day decisions of a childcare facility and the overall running of such services and the management of such services, both at the site of production and citywide level.

This corresponds with calls by Barber (1984), Walzer (1988), and Hirst (1994), among others, for developing and renewing democracy and the welfare state. In particular, they call for providing welfare services through greater citizen involvement and a greater role for the third sector. The state has grown rapidly in recent decades and become part of an organizational society, where large organizations dominate both in the public and private sectors. However, these scholars do not see this as contradictory with democracy, nor do they simply call for the withdrawal of the state. Rather they see it as enhancing the role of the state, by concentrating on financing and regulation of the provision of welfare services. Walzer notes the need for a strong state that can supervise and subsidize the work of its citizens, volunteers and third sector organizations that provide welfare services. Hirst sees Associative Democracy as a means of devolving as many functions of the state as possible to the organizations of civil society in order to develop and renew democracy and curb the growth and dominance of big organizations, both in business and government.

However, without a clearer idea of how to involve citizens in these sweeping reforms, little progress can be made. Co-production provides a focus on citizen's participation at the level of local production of welfare services or the site of production. Co-production opens up possibilities for better understanding the importance of obtaining the consent and support of all three major stakeholders in such reforms, i.e., the citizens, the professional providers of welfare services and the politicians. Yet, without a clear vision of a 'good society', or at least a better society than today, it will be very difficult to promote such sweeping reforms. Thus, co-production provides a missing piece of the puzzle for developing and renewing democracy and the welfare state.

Various aspects of co-production were explored and illustrated by childcare here, but it can also be found in other areas of welfare services. It exists today in different areas like education, eldercare, handicap care and health and medical care. Parent-run and managed elementary and high schools are found in many countries, sometimes in combination with a special pedagogical approach, like Waldorf or Montessori, and sometimes when public provision fails. Third sector eldercare and other support groups provide alternatives in a rapidly growing field. Here children and relatives can become co-producers of some of the services provided to their parents and loved-ones (Dahlberg, 2004). The independent living movement is spreading in many countries and provides much greater influence for families and handicapped persons than either public or private-for-profit services (Westin, 2006). Self-help groups in areas like diabetes and HIV/AIDS are good examples of co-production in health care (Söderholm Werkö, 2008; Walden-Laing, 2001). Health care co-ops in Japan and elsewhere illustrate the possibility for informed and active members who want to maintain their health and avoid becoming passive patients in traditional public health systems (Pestoff, 2008a). Thus, the concept of co-production provides us with a better understanding of fundamental relations at the site of production of welfare services and a clearer comprehension of the dynamics of developing and renewing democracy and the welfare state.

Note

1. There were two cities per country, except for England, which only had one.

5 Citizens as Co-Producers of Personal Social Services in Sweden

Toward a Paradigm of Democratic Participation

A. Background: Democratic Governance

The concept of governance gained extensive attention recently, becoming a buzzword in the social sciences. It is used in a wide array of contexts with widely divergent meanings. Van Kersbergen and van Waarden (2004) surveyed the literature and identified no fewer than nine different definitions of the concept; while Hirst (2002) attributed it five different meanings or contexts. They include economic development, international institutions and regimes, corporate governance, private provision of public services in the wake of New Public Management and new practices for coordinating activities through networks, partnerships and deliberative forums (*ibid.*: 18–19). Hirst argued that the main reason for promoting greater governance is the growth of 'organizational society'. Big organizations on either side of the public/private divide in advanced post-industrial societies leave little room for democracy or citizen influence. This is due to the lack of local control and democratic processes for internal decision-making in most big organizations. The concept of governance points to the need to rethink democracy and find new methods of control and regulation, ones that do not rely on the state or public sector having a monopoly of such practices (*ibid.*: 21).

One of the basic controversies in political science and democratic theory is whether democracy requires active citizenship. For some, intelligent institutional design suffices to achieve the common good. Free and periodic elections combined with competitive political parties should guarantee the survival of democracy. For others, democracy and democratic governance are inconceivable without a culture of active citizenship. Calls for more active citizenship, strengthening citizen participation in service delivery and a more active role for third sector organizations have gained strength in recent years (Ostrom, 1996; Fung, 2004; Pestoff, 2008a). From the perspective of the welfare state, democratic governance, at the macro-level, can be defined as a policy or regime that promotes substantially greater citizen participation and third sector provision of welfare services, and thereby significantly greater welfare pluralism. At the micro-level, it involves significant user and staff participation and influence in the organizations providing welfare services. This could contribute to the development of a new paradigm of participative democracy (Pestoff, 2008a).

This chapter focuses on co-production and discusses the third sector and the role of citizens in the provision and governance of social services. It starts by discussing citizen participation, user influence and co-production in the provision and governance of social services. It goes on to specify major aspects of co-production in terms of the economic, social, political and service specific participation of parents in the provision of childcare. It compares four major types of providers in Sweden: parent co-ops, worker co-ops, municipal services and small for-profit firms. It also explores variations in parent and staff influence in the same four types of organizations. It considers the importance of welfare regimes and sectoral differences for co-production and third sector provision of welfare services. Finally it argues that a 'glass ceiling' exists in public and private for-profit services, both in terms of staff and user participation.

It is first when we can say who, when, where, why and how members and/ or citizens contribute to the provision of welfare services that we can take a significant step towards clarifying the importance of the democratic dimension of social enterprises in Europe. This is a timely issue, because many, if not most, European governments are searching for new ways to involve their citizens in the provision and governance of public financed welfare services. However, without further exploration of democratic and participative aspects of social enterprises, their potential will remain obscure, and proponents of market and state solutions to the current challenges facing the welfare state will retain the upper-hand.

One reason for emphasizing participation and co-production of welfare services is that we are at historic juncture where a greater role for citizen participation and the third sector provision of welfare services is fully possible. However, it remains unlikely without a concerted effort on the part of democratic forces in advanced countries to democratize the welfare state itself. Using the Swedish welfare state as a textbook example, it experienced several major changes starting in the early 1980s and is facing even greater changes in the next 12 to 20 years in terms of providing welfare services. The growing division between financing and delivering welfare services is becoming more apparent. Ideological clashes over the future of the welfare state began in the 1980s with the appearance of neo-liberalism and the renewed political activism of the Confederation of Swedish Employers (Pestoff, 1989, 2005). At that time, alternative provision of welfare services was marginal, usually found only in small specialized niches. By the year 2000 it had grown considerably (Blomqvist & Rothstein, 2000; Blomqvist, 2003), with a varying mix of for-profit firms and third sector providers in different social service areas. The economic experts in *Långtidsutredning* (2004) stated that the future of the Swedish universal, tax-financed welfare state was highly tenuous and predicted that it would be difficult to sustain in the future. So, they concluded that alternative means for producing and financing welfare services would be necessary by the year 2020.

In the late 1990s the Social Democrats attempted to stave off privatization of welfare services by adopting so-called stop laws in various service areas. This included the conversion of municipal housing into private condos and the provision of basic education and health care services. The new non-socialist government immediately removed these restrictions when it came to power in the fall of 2006 and began a new wave of privatizations. A continued public monopoly of the provision of welfare services is therefore ruled out. Thus, there appears to be two starkly different alternative scenarios for the future of the welfare state and the provision of welfare services in Sweden, either rampant privatization or greater welfare pluralism. The latter would include a major role for civil society and the third sector, as an alternative to both public and private for-profit providers of welfare services (See Figure 5.2 on page 79).

As noted, many countries in Europe are searching for new ways to engage citizens and involve the third sector in the provision and governance of social services. At a general level the reasons are similar throughout Europe. First is the challenge of an aging population, second is the growing democracy deficit at all levels, local, regional, national and European and third is the semi-permanent austerity in public finances, made more acute by the recent global economic crisis. In any given EU member state the reasons will vary and may be more specific; however, taken together they imply a major legitimacy crisis for the public sector as a provider of welfare services.

In addition to these three challenges, we can also note two major historical developments. First, the welfare state grew rapidly during the postwar period and second, parallel with this, politics became more abstract and far removed from the daily problems of ordinary citizens. The growth of the welfare state in the 1970s and 1980s provided citizens with many new social services. But it also confronted them with increasing taxes, an expanding army of civil servants to provide these new social services, and the rapid professionalization of services that previously were provided at home. The provision of such services moved from the private to the public sphere as women began to enter the labor market and no longer provided such services at home, or at least not on a full-time or 24/7 basis. Citizens thereby lost insight into and influence on the provision of many personal social services. Then in the 1980s and 1990s, as a result of political changes, many of these services were privatized to a greater or lesser degree and/or subject to increasing market management, following the ideas of New Public Management. Exit rather than voice would give citizens greater influence and competition would make social services cheaper and more efficient, it was argued. However, the transaction costs of switching providers for most long-term social services make exit prohibitive and the promised cost reductions were slow to manifest themselves. Rather, public monopolies have often been replaced by private oligopolies of welfare services.

As a reaction, many people came to feel that both public and private provision minimized their influence. With the growth of big public and private bureaucracies it became not only a question of ensuring access to good quality welfare services. Many ordinary citizens also wanted to (re)gain some limited influence on the provision of social services that comprise one of the most important aspects of their daily lives. In combination with a growing education level and reflexive individualism, this is often termed 'sub-politics' or 'life politics' (Giddens, 1998). Many citizens therefore embraced the introduction and development of new possibilities to directly engage in and influence the provision of social services that they and their loved-ones depend on today. As citizens of democratic welfare states they want to (re) claim their influence and control over the services that they both support politically and pay for with their taxes, regardless of who provides them.

The response to these three challenges will, of course, vary between countries and across sectors of service provision, but four general trends are observable. First is the growth of new and different ways to involve users of welfare services as co-producers of their own services. Second is the spread of new techniques of co-management and co-governance of social services in various European countries. A special issue of *Public Management Review* discussed these first two responses (2006, v. 8/4, reprinted in 2008). Third is the development of user councils at the local level to engage users in a dialog about public services and to facilitate user participation both in the provision and governance of such services. However, user councils remain mostly consultative and they lack decision-making powers and their own budgets. Fourth is the gradual development of functional representation of users alongside territorial channels of representative democracy in some European countries, but far from all of them (Pestoff, 2008b).

B. Co-Production: Enduring Services, User Influence and Citizen Participation

It is necessary to make a distinction between enduring and non-enduring social services. Most welfare services belong to the former category and, therefore, have an immediate impact on the life chances and quality of life of the persons and/or families receiving them. Enduring welfare services include childcare or preschool activities, basic and higher education, eldercare, handicap care and housing as well as preventive and long-term health care. Users of such services are locked into them and they cannot rely on exit to provide them with influence or redress. The transaction costs of exit are often prohibitive (Pestoff, 1998), so voice, rather than exit, provides consumers with influence and redress (*ibid.*). (See Chapter 2 for more details.) The existence of institutions that promote consumer voice are, therefore, important for enduring welfare services. Co-production facilitates consumer voice, especially when it involves collective rather than individual consumer participation in the provision of welfare services.

Why should we be concerned with the development of co-production among service users? Evers (2006) maintains that user involvement in welfare services is a general concern throughout Europe and that there are at least five different approaches to their involvement. They are partially overlapping and partially conflicting. They range from welfarism and professionalism, through consumerism and managerialism to what he calls participationalism. They are based on different values and promote different degrees of user involvement. He states that these approaches will vary among sectors and over time. Their mix will probably differ among countries. Welfarism and professionalism are closely associated with each other and neither leaves much room for user involvement. Rather clients are viewed as people with little competence of their own, who need professional help and guidance. Consumerism and managerialism call for giving users greater choice by developing more exit options and argue that the public sector needs to learn from the private sector (*ibid.*). However, that leaves little room for voice or participation.

Participationalism encourages on-site participation by users of welfare services, based on the belief that citizens should engage personally in shaping the welfare services they demand. It emphasizes multi-stakeholder organizations and requires that users become co-producers. Evers warns that a mix of these approaches may result in 'hybrid' organizations containing elements from many of them. However, some may work together better than others and they may, in fact, lead to 'mixed up' or disorganized systems where user involvement works poorly (*ibid.*).

Welfarism and professionalism are usually promoted by social democratic governments, while consumerism and managerialism are normally championed by rightist governments. However, participationalism, or more simply co-production, lacks clear political proponents today. In a service democracy of either the social democratic or rightist variety citizens are the consumers of public financed social services that are either provided by municipal authorities, private companies or perhaps both. They vote every fourth year and in the meantime they choose between various public or private service providers. By contrast, in a participatory democracy citizens would be engaged in the provision of some of their own social services, in the development of the welfare state and the renewal of democracy. By including citizens and the third sector in the provision of welfare services, the dialog between the rulers and ruled takes on a new dimension and citizens can choose between more than companies A and B providing similar services or the two ideological alternatives of more state or more market.

Co-production or citizen involvement in the provision of public services generated a flurry of interest among public administration scholars in America in the 1970s and 1980s (see Parks *et al.*, 1981 for a good overview). The concept was originally developed by the Workshop in Political Theory and Policy Analysis at Indiana University. During the 1970s they struggled with the dominant theories of urban governance underlying policy recommendations for massive centralization. Scholars and public officials argued that citizens as clients would receive more effective and efficient services if they were delivered by professional staff employed by a large bureaucratic agency. But, the Indiana University researchers found no empirical support for such claims promoting centralization (Ostrom, 1996).

They did, however, stumble on several myths of public production. One was the notion of a single producer being responsible for providing urban services within each jurisdiction. In fact, they normally found several agencies, as well as private firms, producing many services. More important, they also realized that the production of a service, in contrast to goods, was difficult without the active participation of those receiving the service. They developed the term 'co-production' to describe the potential relationship that could exist between the 'regular' producer (street-level police officers, schoolteachers or health workers) and clients who want to be transformed by the service into safer, better-educated or healthier persons (see Parks *et al.*, 1981; Ostrom, 1996).

In complex societies there is a division of labor and most persons are engaged in full-time production of goods and services as regular producers. However, individual consumers or groups of consumers may also contribute to the production of goods and services, as consumer producers. This mixing may occur directly or indirectly. Co-production is, therefore, noted by the mix of activities that both public service agents and citizens contribute to the provision of public services. The former are involved as professionals or 'regular producers', while 'citizen production' is based on voluntary efforts of individuals or groups to enhance the quality and/or quantity of services they receive (Parks *et al.*, 1981). Co-production is one way that a synergy can occur between what a government does and what citizens do (Ostrom, 1996).

Alford (2002) argues that different motives exist for co-production in different contexts. The more public the value consumed by clients, the more complex the motivations for them to co-produce. He concludes that "eliciting co-production is a matter of heightening the value that clients receive from the services by making more explicit their nonmaterial aspects through intrinsic rewards, solidarity incentives or normative appeal" (*ibid.*).

In Sweden there is little discussion of enhancing the role of citizens in providing welfare services except perhaps in terms of promoting more volunteering. However, citizens currently contribute much of their time and effort to the production of welfare services, both as parents in relation to childcare or youth sports activities in sports clubs, as well as relatives in terms of eldercare and handicap care. They directly contribute to the realization of the final value of good quality childcare, healthful youth sports activities, and/or good quality eldercare and handicap care, although such services are primarily provided by professionals and financed by taxes.

C. The Main Dimensions of Co-Production

The TSFEPS Project examined the relationship between parent participation in the provision and governance of childcare in eight EU countries (Pestoff, 2006). We found different levels of parent participation in different countries and in different forms of provision, i.e., public, private for-profit and third sector childcare. The highest levels of parent participation were found in third sector providers, like parent associations in France, parent initiatives in Germany and parent cooperatives in Sweden. We also noted different kinds of parent participation, i.e., economic, political and social. All three kinds of participation were readily evident in third sector providers of childcare services, while both economic and political participation were highly restricted in municipal and private for-profit services. Moreover, we observed variations in the patterns of participation between countries. Parents participated actively in the provision of third sector childcare at the micro-level in France, Germany and Sweden, and in their governance at the meso-level in the first two countries, but not in the latter one (*ibid.*).

Children normally attend childcare facilities between the ages of 1 and 6 years old in Sweden, when they start elementary school. During the 1990s, parent fees and other conditions for childcare varied greatly between municipalities, but with the Maxtaxa reform (the law on maximum fees for parents) at the beginning of the 21st century, they were standardized. Today they are similar between forms of providers and parents pay a very limited amount of their income per child, on a declining scale, in relation the number of children they send to a childcare facility. Thus, there are few economic incentives for parents to choose one form of provision rather than another. Previously, it was argued that parent co-ops were less expensive, probably due to lower labor costs, but there was also a work obligation for parents associated with this form of provision. Today the fee paid by parents varies slightly between municipalities, but not between the forms of provision or types of providers. All collective childcare facilities in Sweden are subsidized in a similar fashion and with a similar amount per child. Public funding covers nearly 85% of the total income for all forms of collective provision of childcare services.

Vamstad's study of the Swedish welfare state (2007) focuses on the politics of diversity, parent participation and service quality in childcare. His study was a quasi-random sample of 20 childcare providers: 6 in Östersund and 12 from selected wards in Stockholm. It included an interview with the managers of the selected facilities, and the use of questionnaires for gathering information from the staff and parents at the selected childcare centers. A total of 268 parents and 116 members of the staff at these 18 childcare centers filled in and returned such questionnaires. The response rate for the staff was 81%, while for parents it reached 50%. He compared parent and worker co-ops, municipal services and small for-profit firms providing childcare in these two regions.

His study not only confirms the existence of these three main dimensions of co-production, but it also underlines clear differences between various providers concerning the saliency of these dimensions for providing welfare services. In addition to these dimensions of co-production, a service specific dimension also exists and depends on the type of welfare service provided. In order to explore these differences in co-production further, I will consider each type of parent participation for four different types of service providers of public financed childcare in Sweden, i.e., parent co-ops, worker co-ops, municipal services and small for-profit firms.

Users participate economically in the provision of public services to insure the continued delivery of a service, to improve its quality or both. In addition to paying taxes to finance public services, financial contributions by users occur through a co-payment or user fee and/or extra payments to top it up in order to achieve better or more suitable service. Material contributions can either be donations in kind necessary to the achievement of the service or other materials that are needed to maintain the service. For example, parents may donate new or used toys to their children's childcare facility when the existing stock of toys diminishes due to loss or wear-and-tear. Parents may also contribute other items needed for repairing the premises, like paint, lumber, screws and nails, etc. Parents can also directly contribute their own time and efforts to providing services by working at the facility.

Vamstad's study included the following types of economic participation in the provision of childcare. They were asked about their willingness to pay more for better quality services or greater availability of services. They can also participate in cleaning and repairing the premises, donating materials and supplies to the facility and working at the childcare center itself. Table 5.1 presents the parents' answers about their economic participation.

There are several noteworthy, but logical differences between different types of providers of public financed childcare in Sweden, as well as some unexpected results. First, a question tapping the parents' willingness to pay more for better quality services or greater availability shows that nearly half or more of the parents, regardless of the form of service provision, are willing to do so. Parents in parent cooperatives show the greatest willingness to

Table 5.1 Parents' Economic Participation, by Type of Provider

Type of economic participation*	P-C	W-C	Mun.	F-P
Willing to pay more for better quality	73.3	65.2	48.9	54.2
Cleaning and repairs	94.6	22.7	43.7	70.8
Donate materials and supplies	36.5	13.6	6.2	0.0
Work at the childcare center	78.4	2.2	4.7	12.5
N	107	48	89	24

Source: adapted from Tables 7.6, 8.1 and 8.5, in J. Vamstad (2007); Key: P-C = parent co-op., W-C = worker co-op., Mun. = municipal, F-P = small for-profit firm

* only the percent of affirmative ('yes') answers are shown

contribute more. However, these differences should not be exaggerated, and they are less than with other forms of economic participation.

Second, nearly all parents in parent co-ops participate in cleaning and repair activities and more than two-thirds of parents in small for-profit firms do so. Similarly, nearly half of the parents in municipal childcare and nearly one-quarter of the parents in worker co-ops participate in cleaning and repair activities at their son or daughter's childcare facility. It seems safe to assume that the work obligation found at most parent co-ops guarantees more regular and frequent participation by parents in such activities. Parent participation in such activities at the other three types of providers is not only more sporadic, but is considered by some managers as a social activity, rather than economic participation, for example, if it takes place on a weekend and is combined with a social activity of some sort, like a hot-dog roast for all those involved at the end of the work.

Turning to donations of materials and supplies, more than one-third of the parents in parent co-ops participate, indicating their feelings of responsibility and 'ownership' of such services, while the level of such activities among parents in the three other types of providers is much lower and completely absent among parents with a child at a small for-profit firm. When considering work at the childcare center, the parent co-ops once again distinguish themselves from the other three forms of providing such services. More than three-fourths of parents there work at their son or daughter's facility, while less than 5% do so in municipal or worker co-op services. Nearly one of eight parents in small for-profit firms claimed that they work at their son or daughter's facility, which is an unexpected result.

Social aspects of co-production involve the contribution of materials and time to achieve the social goals of a public service or to promote its social activities. This includes contributing both time and relevant materials/ingredients for the Christmas or spring parties for the staff, parents and children, and perhaps even the surrounding community. They can also inform current and potentially new users, as well as the local community, about the benefits of a particular service provider. Vamstad's study (2007) inquired about three types of social participation, participation in parties, i.e., the Christmas or spring parties, information meetings and open house arrangements. The parents' answers are found in Table 5.2.

Table 5.2 Parents' Social Participation, by Type of Provider

Type of social participation*	P-C	W-C	Mun.	F-P
Parties	87.8	86.4	63.8	75.0
Information meetings	91.9	68.2	52.5	50.0
Open house	63.5	54.5	48.8	16.7
N	107	49	89	24

Source: adapted from Tables 8.1 and 8.5 in J. Vamstad (2007); Key: P-C = parent co-op., W-C = worker co-op.; Mun. = municipal, F-P = small for-profit firm

* only the percent of affirmative ('yes') answers are shown

Parties are the most popular social activity in all forms of provision, while open house activities are the least frequent, and may not in fact exist in all types of providers. Once again we can note a clear pattern, where parents with children in parent co-ops demonstrate higher levels of social participation than parents in the other three kinds of providers; however, we note that parents with children in worker co-ops have only marginally lower levels of participation than parent co-ops. Parents with children in either municipal services of private for-profit firms participate less frequently in social activities.

The political aspects of co-production involve the expression of users' wishes concerning the type of and way in which services are delivered. This can range from *ad hoc* discussions, regular meetings or occasionally negotiations on important matters to regular participation in decision-making and financial matters of importance for the provision of such services. Vamstad (2007) included four different aspects of this: participation in meetings with the power to decide issues, making written suggestions, attending meetings without the power to make binding decisions and engaging in informal talks with the staff, usually when leaving or getting their child(ren) from the childcare center. Table 5.3 presents the parents' answers about their political participation.

Not unexpectedly, parents with children in parent co-ops demonstrate much higher levels of participation and influence at meetings with the power to decide issues and also when making written suggestions. Nearly four of five parents in parent co-ops provide affirmative answers to the first question and two-thirds to the second question. However, nearly one-third of parents with children in municipal services claim they participate in meetings with the power to decide issues. This probably reflects the spread of 'Councils of Influence' (Inflytanderådet) in municipal childcare, however limited their factual decision-making rights (for a discussion of this see Vamstad, 2007; Pestoff, 2008a). Nearly two-thirds of the parents with children at small for-profit firms claim that making written suggestions allows them to participate, while few parents at the municipal services or worker co-ops do so.

Table 5.3 Parents' Political Participation, by Type of Provider

Type of political participation*	P-C	W-C	Mun.	F-P
Meetings with power to decide	79.7	8.9	30.2	4.2
Written suggestions	67.6	15.6	9.3	62.5
Meetings without power to decide	17.6	37.8	25.6	45.8
Informal talks	58.1	13.3	75.6	75.0
N	107	48	89	24

Source: adapted from Tables 8.1 and 8.5 in J. Vamstad (2007); Key: P-C = parent co-op., W-C = worker co-op., Mun. = municipal, F-P = small for-profit firm

* only the percent of affirmative ('yes') answers are shown

Meetings without the power to decide on issues are much more frequent at small for-profit firms, worker co-ops and municipal childcare centers than at parent co-ops, engaging from one-quarter to nearly half of the parents at such facilities. Informal talks with the staff on leaving or collecting their child are the most frequent form of participation for parents with children at municipal services and small for-profit firms. They are used by three-fourths of the parents there. Far fewer parents use them at worker co-ops. However, parents with a child at a parent co-op also appreciate this form of participation and more than half of them use it.

Membership, meetings with the power to decide and written suggestions appear to set the parent co-ops apart in terms of promoting participation from the other three forms of providing childcare. Moreover, parents in parent co-ops are members and therefore they are usually represented on the board of the daycare co-op. They make all the decisions about the management of the childcare co-op and they are ultimately responsible for its success or failure (Pestoff, 1998). Taken together, the work obligation and their responsibility for making decisions provide them with a sense of 'democratic ownership' of the childcare facility, not usually found in the other forms of childcare provision. Parents' participation in the other facilities is restricted primarily to informal talks in combination with some other channels of influence.

Turning to service specific participation, citizens can also participate in core activities on an equal footing with the professional providers, or they can be in charge of secondary or marginal activities that are necessary for the service provision, but nevertheless do not belong to its core activities. The former situation would result in substitution of professional staff by volunteers, while the latter can be termed 'complementary participation'. It is illustrated here by parents' taking responsibility for the maintenance and management of an educational facility, either at the preschool or elementary school level, but not participation in the core pedagogic activities, or at least not on a regular basis. Thus, in parent co-op preschool facilities, parents are in charge of the maintenance of the premise, the management of the facility, bookkeeping, etc. But only in case of the absence of regular staff due to illness, attending a special training course or other exceptional circumstances do they contribute to the core pedagogical activities of providing services to their own and other children. Most parent co-ops have rotating schedules that assign them responsibility to fill in for staff absences in this fashion. This division of labor tends to limit conflicts of interest between them and by the staff, as parents are not involved in the core activities. Restricting citizen participation to complementary activities can help insure both the professional provision of core services, as well as the active participation of citizens in complementary aspects of them. Their participation can also help to contain service costs as professionals are not required to provide all the complementary services, like maintenance and management, etc.

Parent co-ops in Sweden promote all four kinds of user participation: economic, social, political and complementary. They provide parents with unique possibilities for active participation in the management and running of their child(ren)'s childcare facility and for unique opportunities to become active co-producers of high quality childcare services for their own and others' children. It is also clear that other forms of childcare allow for some possibilities for co-production in public financed childcare, but parents' possibilities for influencing the management of such services remains rather limited.

D. Parent and Staff Influence

Participation and influence do not necessarily mean the same thing. So, differences noted above in the type of service provider may or may not promote greater client and/or staff influence in the provision and governance of social services. Therefore, we will now turn our attention to the perceived and desired influence for users and staff in Swedish childcare. Vamstad (2007) asked parents and staff at childcare facilities he studied how much influence they currently had and whether they wanted more. Respondents to the question about their current influence could choose between seven alternatives ranging from 'very little' and 'little' at the low end to 'large' and 'very large' at the high end. By contrast, the question about wanting more influence had a simple 'yes/no' answer. The results presented here only use some of the information about the current level of influence. Only the most frequent categories at the high end of the scale of influence are included in the tables below. Table 5.4 reports parents' influence and their desire for more, while Table 5.5 expresses the staff's influence and their desire for more.

Parent influence is greatest in parent co-ops and least in small for-profit firms. This is an expected result, and nearly nine of ten parents in parent co-ops claim much influence. However, this is twice as many as in municipal services. Half of the parents in worker co-ops also claim much influence, which is also greater than the proportion in municipal childcare. Finally, only one of eight parents claims much influence in small for-profit firms. The differences in influence between types of providers appear substantial.

Table 5.4 Perceived and Desired User Influence, by Type of Provider

Perceived influence	Much*	Av**	(n)	Want more
Parent co-op childcare	88.7	5.6	107	13.2
Worker co-op childcare	50.0	4.6	48	28.3
Municipal childcare	44.9	4.4	89	37.3
For-profit childcare	12.5	3.6	24	58.3

Source: adapted from Tables 8.6 and 8.8 in J. Vamstad (2007)

* Combines three categories: 'rather large', 'large' and 'very large'
** average score, based on a scale ranging from 1 to 7, where low scores mean little influence

Table 5.5 Perceived and Desired Staff Influence, by Type of Provider

Influence	Very large	Large	Av*	(n)	Want more
Worker co-op	72.2	16.7	6.4	18	16.7
Parent co-op	22.7	34.1	5.7	44	16.3
Sm. for-profit	12.5	37.5	5.4	8	75.0
Municipal	10.9	23.9	4.8	46	57.8

Source: adapted from Tables 8.7 and 8.8 in J. Vamstad (2007)

* average score, based on a scale ranging from 1 to 7, where low scores mean little influence

Turning to their desire for more influence, again we find the expected pattern of answers, which inversely reflect how much influence they currently experience. Very few parents in parent co-ops want more influence, while nearly three of five want more influence in small for-profit firms. In between these two types come the worker co-ops, where more than one of four wants more influence and municipal childcare where more than one of three wants more influence. With as many as one-third of the parents wanting more influence in municipal childcare, a clear desire exists for increased parent representation in decision-making. Thus, it is not merely a question of selective choice between various providers, where the more active and interested parents choose the more demanding, participative forms of childcare, while the less interested and more passive ones choose less demanding forms. There appear to be widespread expectations of being able to participate in important decisions concerning their daughter or son's childcare among parents in all types of providers. Perhaps this reflects the spread of participation to the provision of public financed welfare services, regardless of the type of provider. Certainly the Swedish reform known as 'Councils of Influence' in municipal preschools would benefit greatly by including many more of these motivated and active parents, if it were possible to offer them meaningful opportunities to participate and influence decisions. Similarly, worker co-ops would gain greater legitimacy and trust if they included the parents in a meaningful way.

Turning to the staff of childcare facilities, there were many more who answered that they had much influence, but with some notable differences in the distribution of the frequencies, so both the 'large' and 'very large' categories are included separately in Table 5.5.

Once again the logically expected pattern of influence can clearly be noted here, where the staff in worker co-ops claims the most influence and the staff in municipal facilities claims the least influence. Nearly nine of ten staff members claim large or very large influence in worker co-op childcare, while only one-third does so in municipal facilities. Nearly three of five members of staff claim much influence in parent co-ops, while half of them do so in small for-profit firms. Again, the proportions of the staff desiring more influence inversely reflect the proportion claiming much influence. Few want more influence in either the worker or parent co-ops, while the opposite is true of the staff in the other two types of childcare providers. Nearly three of five want more influence in municipal childcare and three of four do so in small for-profit firms. Thus, there appears to be significant room for greater staff influence in both the latter types of providers of childcare. Greater staff influence could also contribute significantly to improving the work environment in both these two types of childcare providers (Pestoff, 2000).

However, one interesting detail is the relatively low proportion of staff in parent co-ops wanting more influence. It is almost identical with that found for the staff in worker co-ops. The latter 'own' the childcare facility themselves, not perhaps in the sense of being able to sell it, but they make the decisions and bear the ultimate responsibility for its survival. Clearly the staff of parent co-ops is in a very different situation, as the parents 'own it': they make all the decisions and bear the ultimate responsibility. The staff normally lacks a vote, but not necessarily a voice in the management of parent co-ops. But, the striking similarity in the proportion of staff expressing a desire for more influence suggests that there must already be such a high degree of collaboration between the staff and parents in parent co-ops as to eliminate the need for more influence. It seems important to explore this matter closer in future research.

Thus, we found that neither the state nor market allows for more than marginal or *ad hoc* participation or influence by parents in the childcare services. For example, parents may be welcome to make spontaneous suggestions when leaving their child in the morning or picking her/him up in the evening from a municipal or small private for-profit childcare facility. They may also be welcome to contribute time and effort to a social event like the annual Christmas party or spring party at the end of the year. Also, discussion groups or 'Influence Councils' can be found at some municipal childcare facilities in Sweden, but they provide parents with very limited influence. More substantial participation in economic or political terms can only be achieved when parents organize themselves collectively to obtain better quality or different kinds of childcare services than either the state or market can provide. In addition, worker co-ops seem to provide parents with greater influence than either municipal childcare or small private for-profit firms can provide, and the staff at worker co-ops obtains maximum influence, resulting in more democratic workplaces. But the staff at parent co-ops does not express a desire for more influence. Thus both the parent and worker co-ops appear to maximize staff influence compared to municipal and small for-profit firms, while parent co-ops also maximize user influence.

E. Co-Production, Welfare Regimes and Sectoral Differences

A welfare regime and/or social policy can 'crowd-out' certain behaviors and 'crowd-in' others in the population. For example, a welfare reform policy that primarily emphasizes economically rational individuals who maximize their utilities and provides them with material incentives to change their behavior tends to play down values of reciprocity and solidarity, collective action, co-production and third sector provision of welfare services. Vidal (2008) argues that the lack of favorable legislation is a major obstacle for the development of social enterprises in Europe. It is impossible to isolate the development of social enterprises from decisions of government. The Italian law on social cooperatives provides a good illustration of this. It insures social cooperatives with preferential treatment in public tenders for certain social services (*ibid.*). The government alone can promote collective action, co-production and social enterprises among the different organizational options to provide welfare services.

However, it is important to remember that co-production takes different forms in different welfare regimes (Esping-Andersen, 1996) and in different policy sectors in the same country. In other words, politics and policy are important for promoting or discouraging citizen participation and co-production. For example, one welfare regime may favor a family policy based on the provision of childcare by mothers staying at home. It provides generous tax subsidies for women to remain home and generous child allowances, sometimes even beyond gymnasium and college education. Germany serves as a good example of this. Here parent participation in providing childcare is highly individual and geographically dispersed, making any forms of collective action among them very difficult. Another welfare regime may choose to invest in human capital and build extensive collective childcare facilities, something that facilitates greater collective action and citizen participation. Parents can easily interact to complain about or improve the quality of or access to collective childcare. They can collectively demand more influence in the management of the childcare and become co-producers. Sweden provides an illustration of this.

In addition, a country's social policy can promote home services in one area, while it may facilitate collective and public provision of another service. So, I will briefly contrast two different types of social services in the same welfare regime, in order to understand the importance of sectors for promoting co-production. The first service is provided by relatives to elder persons at home. They often have physical limitations or ailments and are at the end of a long life. The second welfare service is childcare for preschool children under the age of 7. These two services are provided in two very different institutional and social contexts and represent two very different types of services, but in the same country. The first comprises highly personal and individual caring tasks performed at home, 24 hours a day, seven days a week, often with little or no remuneration. It involves very intensive, geographically dispersed and isolated care services. These services are usually provided by relatives, often a female, who lack special professional training or the necessary qualifications to perform most such services. The home setting and circumstances of such care provision offer few chances for social interaction other than between the care provider and care receiver at home. Here citizen participation is highly individual and poorly organized.

Given this setting, the purpose of collective action is to provide caregivers with some social support and interaction, i.e., to help break their isolation and to help them perform their caring tasks (Dahlberg, 2004). This can take the form of voluntary organizations arranging meetings and discussion points or holding lectures and courses. Occasionally, it also involves the provision of day center services, however limited, for the elderly, so they too can have some social contacts, daytime activities, etc., and relieve the 24/7 caregivers for a few hours. In general, under these circumstances collective action is very difficult.

The second service, childcare, shares very few of the distinctive characteristics of homecare for elderly relatives. Small children are at the beginning of their lives and their parents naturally want to give them a good start in life, often better than average, in order to improve their life chances. The children and their parents are geographically concentrated in a childcare facility that can range in size from 12 to 15 children to as many as 50+ children. There is intensive social interaction. There is a professional staff, but parent involvement is very limited in public and private facilities. However, parents can join together to form a cooperative or association for managing the service and run it in a democratic fashion. Here citizen participation is collective and highly organized. Thus, both from a collective action and a co-production perspective these two services represent the opposite ends of the spectrum.

F. Crowding-In, Crowding-Out or a 'Glass Ceiling'

Co-production also implies different relations between public authorities and citizens and it facilitates different levels of citizen participation in the provision of public services. Citizen participation in public service provision needs to be distinguished along two main dimensions. To illustrate matters only three categories or levels will be considered, but there can, in fact, be greater differences between them. The first dimension relates to the intensity of relations between the provider and consumer of public services. Here, the intensity of relations between public authorities and citizens can either be sporadic and distant, intermittent and/or short-term or it can involve intensive and/or enduring welfare relations. In the former, citizen participation in providing public services involves only indirect contacts via the telephone, postal services or e-mail, etc., while in the latter it means direct, daily and repeated face-to-face interaction between providers and citizens. For example, citizen participation in crime prevention or a neighborhood watch, filing their tax forms or filling in postal codes normally only involves sporadic or indirect contacts between the citizens and authorities. Face-to-face interactions for a short duration or intermittent contacts are characteristic of participation in public job-training courses or maintenance programs for public housing that involve resident participation in some aspects (Alford, 2002). By contrast, parent participation in the management and maintenance of public financed preschool or elementary school services involves repeated long-term contacts. This places them in the position of being active subjects in the provision of such services (Pestoff, 2006, 2008a). Here they can influence the development and help decide about the future of the services provided.

Similarly, the level of citizen participation in the provision of public services can either be low, medium or high (Figure 5.1). By combining these two dimensions, we can derive a three by three table with nine cells. However, not all of them are readily evident in the real world or found in the literature on co-production. Moreover, a third dimension needs to be made explicit: the degree of civil society involvement in the provision of public services. This reflects the form of citizen participation, i.e., organized collective action, individual or group participation and individual or group compliance.

In general, we can expect to find a trend between increasing intensity of relations between public authorities and citizens in the provision of public services and increased citizen participation. Sporadic and distant relations imply low participation levels, while enduring welfare services will result in greater participation. However, when it comes to providing intensive and/ or enduring welfare services, two distinct patterns can be found in the literature. First, a high level of citizen participation is noted for third sector provision, because it is based on collective action and direct citizen participation. Parent co-op childcare in France, Germany and Sweden illustrates this. Second, more limited citizen participation is noted for public provision of enduring welfare services. It usually focuses on public interactions with individual citizen and/or user councils. Citizens are allowed to participate sporadically or in a limited fashion, like parents contributing to the Christmas or spring parties in municipal childcare. But, they are seldom given the opportunity to play a major role in service provision or to take charge of the service provision, nor are they given decision-making rights and responsibilities for the economy of the service provision.

This creates a 'glass ceiling' for citizen participation in public provision and limits citizens to playing a passive role as service users who can make demands on the public sector, but who do not make decisions nor take any responsibility in implementing public policy. The space allotted to citizens in public provision of such services is too restricted to make participation either meaningful or democratic. Thus, only when citizens are engaged in organized collective groups can they achieve any semblance of democratic control over the provision of public financed services. A similar argument can be made concerning user participation in for-profit firms providing welfare services.

It was noted earlier that participation takes quite different forms in childcare services. Most childcare services studied here fall into the top-down

Intensity of relations/Level of citizen participation	Sporadic and distant	Intermittent and/or short-term (<1 yr.)	Intensive and/or enduring welfare services (>2 yrs)	Degree of civil society involvement
High	?	?	-childcare, -basic education, -handicap care, -health care, -eldercare, -co-op housing, -work integration,	**3rd sector provision** (organized collective action or social economy organizations)
Medium	?	-job training, -tenant maintenance of public housing,	-childcare, -basic education, -handicap care, -health care, -eldercare,	**Public provision** (individual citizen - public interaction and/or user councils, either on-site or city-wide)
Low	-using postal codes, -filing personal income tax forms, -residential security	-neighborhood watch	?	**Citizen compliance** (individual & group)

Figure 5.1 Co-Production and Relations between Public Authorities and Citizens

Source: V. Pestoff (2008a)

category in terms of style of service provision. There are few possibilities for parents to directly influence decision-making in such services. This normally includes both municipal childcare services and for-profit firms providing childcare services. Perhaps this is logical from the perspective of municipal governments. They are, after all, representative institutions, chosen by the voters in elections every fourth year. They might consider direct client or user participation in the running of public services for a particular group, like parents, as a threat both to the representative democracy that they institutionalize and to their own power. It could also be argued that direct participation for a particular group would thereby provide the latter with a veto right or a 'second vote' at the service level. There may also be professional considerations for resisting parent involvement and participation.

The logic of direct user participation is also foreign to private for-profit providers. Exit, rather than voice, provides the medium of communication in markets, where parents are seen as consumers. This logic excludes any form of direct or indirect representation. Only the parent cooperatives clearly fall into the bottom-up category. Here we find the clearest examples of self-government and participative democracy. Parents are directly involved in the running of their daughter and/or son's childcare center in terms of being responsible for the maintenance, management, etc. of the childcare facility. They also participate in the decision-making of the facility, as members and 'owners' of the facility.

G. Conclusions

It was noted that co-production is the mix of activities that both public service agents and citizens contribute to the provision of public services. The former are involved as professionals or 'regular producers', while 'citizen production' is based on voluntary efforts by individuals or groups to enhance the quality and/or quantity of services they use. In complex societies there is a division of labor and most persons are engaged in full-time production of goods and services as regular producers. However, individual consumers or groups of consumers may also contribute to the production of goods and services, as consumer producers. The participation of citizens in the provision of welfare services contributes a unique dimension of democratic governance to third sector organizations not usually found in either public services or private for-profit firms.

Evers' (2006) distinction between five different approaches to user involvement in the production of social services has clear implications for citizens' possibilities to participate in the provision and governance of such services. Two of his categories for user influence are more closely associated with public production of social services, while two others are more closely related to market provision. All four of these approaches flourish in the European debate. However, his fifth approach to user influence is largely missing, i.e., greater citizen participation in the provision of social services, or co-production. The Swedish and European debate about the future of the welfare state is often highly polarized and ideologically divided between continued public provision or rapid privatization of social services, where the only options discussed are either more state or more market solutions. Citizens are normally faced with simple black/white choices between more state or more market solutions to most problems facing them. Thus, it is difficult, if not impossible, to promote a third alternative, e.g., greater welfare pluralism, more citizen participation and greater third sector provision of social services in this highly ideological context (Vamstad, 2007).

There are four kinds or dimensions of citizen participation in the provision of public financed welfare services. They are economic, social, political and service specific participation, and they were explored in greater detail in this chapter. The influence both of parents and the staff was compared in four types of service providers: parent co-ops, worker co-ops, municipal services and small private for-profit firms. Both the parents and staff of parent and worker co-ops appear to have more influence than those of municipal services and for-profit firms. Thus, we found that neither the state nor market allow for more than marginal or *ad hoc* participation by parents in the childcare services. For example, parents may be welcome to make spontaneous suggestions when leaving or picking up their child from a municipal or small private for-profit childcare facility. They may also be welcome to contribute time and effort to a social event like the annual Christmas party or spring party at the end of the year. Also, discussion groups or 'Influence Councils' can be found at some municipal childcare facilities in Sweden, but they provide parents with very limited influence. More substantial participation in economic or political terms can only be achieved when parents organize themselves collectively to obtain better quality or different kinds of childcare services than either the state or market can provide.

Both public services and small for-profit firms demonstrate the existence of a 'glass ceiling' for the participation of citizens as consumers of enduring welfare services. Evidence also suggests similar limits for staff participation in the public and private for-profit forms of providing enduring welfare services. Only social enterprises like the small consumer and worker co-ops appear to breach these limits and empower the consumers and staff with democratic rights and influence. But, it is necessary to have a realistic assessment of the range of diverse interests and varying motives for engaging in co-production from the perspective of various stakeholders, i.e., the municipal authorities, professional staff and users/citizens. The authorities and staff will have various economic, political and professional motives, while citizens' motives are based on economic, social, political and quality considerations. It is also important to understand these differences and try to bridge the gap between them in order for co-production to become sustainable. In particular, when co-production is based on enduring welfare services it requires repeated and frequent interaction between the professional staff and users/consumers, often on a daily basis. This is impossible without a dialog, something that can help both these groups to mutually adjust their expectations of each other and the service provided in a way that is beneficial for both. Their dialog also reduces the transaction costs for providing the services compared to other ways of providing it that do not require a continuous dialog between the providers and consumers of a welfare service.

These findings can contribute to the development of a policy of democratic governance, both at the macro- and micro-levels, as well as to a new paradigm of participative democracy (Pestoff, 2008a) and empowered citizenship (Fung, 2004). However, it is important to emphasize the interface between the government, citizens and the third sector and to note that co-production normally takes place in a political context. An individual's cost/benefit analysis and the decision to cooperate with voluntary efforts are conditioned by the structure of political institutions and the encouragement provided by politicians. Centralized or highly standardized service delivery tends to make articulation of demands more costly for citizens and to inhibit governmental responsiveness, while citizen participation seems to fare better in decentralized and less standardized service delivery (Ostrom, 1996).

Moreover, one-sided emphasis by many European governments either on the state maintaining most responsibility for providing welfare services or turning most of them over to the market will hamper the development of

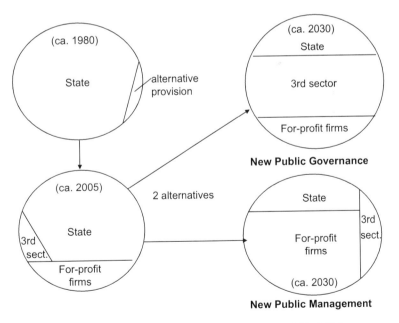

Figure 5.2 Development of the Swedish Welfare State, ca. 1980–2030

Source: V. Pestoff (2008a)

co-production and democratic governance. The state can 'crowd-out' certain behaviors and 'crowd-in' others in the population. A favorable regime and favorable legislation are necessary for promoting greater co-production and third sector provision of welfare services. Only co-production and greater welfare pluralism can promote democratic governance of welfare services.

This means that Scandinavian, and possibly other European, welfare states can follow one of two alternative trajectories in the future. They can either continue to pursue privatization of welfare services and expand the role played by for-profit firms in delivering such services. Or, they can promote a larger role for the third sector as a provider of welfare services. The latter course will promote more co-production and democratic governance of welfare services. Figure 5.2 illustrates these two alternative developments.

6 Crucial Concepts for Understanding Co-Production in Third Sector Social Services and Health Care

The relationship between the state and citizens is continually changing in post-modern societies. New forms of providing services, including public services, are emerging that challenge traditional patterns of production. In the changing relations between the government and citizens, the former sometimes attempt to involve the latter in the provision of goods and services. This is motivated by reasons of improving the efficiency of public services, the effectiveness of public policies, or to promote other important social goals, like citizen empowerment, participation and democracy, or some combination of them. Citizens in European welfare states have several different roles that represent diverse aspects of post-modern life today. They are voters, taxpayers, employees, members of a family and consumers, just to name a few, and they often belong to two or more voluntary associations. Sometimes these roles complement each other, but other times they come into conflict. Moreover, sometimes citizens play these roles as individuals, but other times they do so in close collaboration with others, i.e., in informal groups or in voluntary organizations.

Equally important, given major social and political changes in Europe and Scandinavia, particularly with the growth of the welfare state at the end of World War II, the very state they interact with has also changed significantly in nature. In the immediate post–World War II period, citizens faced a rapidly expanding, yet basically traditional public administration, with its hierarchical chain of command, where they were primarily viewed as passive clients or recipients of public services. Later, with the spread of neoliberalism and introduction of New Public Management (NPM), they were expected to become active consumers and exercise more choice between various providers of public financed services, be they public, private forprofit or nonprofit. Here, the market replaced the state as the main governing mechanism for the expression of citizens' preferences. More recently, the spread of network society (Hartley, 2005) or New Public Governance (NPG) (Osborne, 2010) implies a more plural and pluralist model of governance and provision of welfare services, based on public-private networks, where citizens are attributed an active role as co-producers of some or many of the services they expect, demand or even depend upon in order to fulfill a variety of their most important roles today (see Pestoff, 2012a, 2012b). Thus, both the shifting roles that citizens play in their daily lives and the changing context within which they play them place complex demands on the concepts and methods needed to study and understand these far-reaching changes.

A. Co-Production: Some Crucial Conceptual Issues

Co-production comprised one of the core research areas for Nobel Laureate Elinor Ostrom and her research team in Indiana in the 1970s (Parks *et al.*, 1981; Ostrom, 1996). Initially, it resulted in a flurry of interest in the late 1970s and early 1980s, but it became overshadowed by New Public Management, which dominated thinking about public sector reforms for the next two decades. However, the concept co-production gained new interest in recent years in Europe and elsewhere and it is now used by researchers in many parts of the world (Pestoff *et al.*, 2012). Co-production is often motivated in the public sector by cost reductions and higher quality services (Parks *et al.*, 1981; Alford, 2009), but more recently the focus has grown to include new opportunities for citizens to influence the provision of important public services (Ostrom, 2000a; Fung, 2004; Pestoff, 2009). (See Chapters 8 and 11 for more discussion.)

This chapter focuses on co-production of public services, particularly labor intensive ones like long-term or enduring social services. What is co-production and what are the crucial conceptual issues for better understanding its potential contribution to the renewal of the public sector and the management of public services? Five such issues are explored in the first part of this chapter, while the second part considers similarities and differences between volunteering and co-production.

A.1 Definitions of Co-Production and Levels of Analysis

Definitions of co-production range from "the mix of public service agents and citizens who contribute to the provision of public services" to "a partnership between citizens and public service providers". Variations between them can express cultural differences, differences of focus as well as different levels of analysis. We will contrast a few of them below, as there seems, at least initially, to be some discrepancy between the American, British, Canadian and European usage of the term co-production. The concept of co-production was originally developed by Elinor Ostrom and the Workshop in Political Theory and Policy Analysis at Indiana University during the 1970s to describe and delimit the involvement of ordinary citizens in the production of public services. Thus, they developed the term 'co-production' to describe the potential relationship that could exist between the 'regular producer', like street-level police officers, schoolteachers, or health workers, and their clients who want to be transformed by the service into safer, better-educated or healthier persons (see Parks *et al.*, 1981). Regular producers are the professionals or paid staff, while 'citizen production' is based on voluntary efforts of individuals or groups to enhance the quality and/or quantity of services they receive (*ibid.*).

Bovaird (2007) proposed a wider definition. According to him "[u]ser and community co-production is the provision of services through regular, long-term relationships between professionalized service providers (in any sector) and service users and or other members of the community, where all parties make substantial resource contributions" (*ibid.*: 847). His definition focuses not only on users, but also includes volunteers and community groups as co-producers, recognizing that each of these groups can have a quite different relationship to public sector organizations. I address the relationship between volunteering and co-production in more detail below and again in Chapter 11. The Blair government regarded co-production as a partnership between citizens and public service providers that was essential for meeting a number of growing social challenges, because neither the government nor citizens have the necessary resources to solve them on their own (Horne & Shirley, 2009). They argued that co-production was distinct from earlier efforts at public sector reforms like volunteerism, managerialism or paternalism (*ibid.*). However, the Cameron government that eventually replaced it put greater emphasis on volunteerism, in a policy known as Big Society. Chapters 9 and 10 explore the implications of such policy shifts for co-production.

In the UK, the term co-production has also been used to analyze the role of voluntary and community organizations (VCOs) in the provision of public services (Osborne & McLaughlin, 2004). It is sometimes contrasted with co-management or coordination between the public and third sectors in providing some public services, and with co-governance (*ibid.*) or co-construction as it is often called in Canada and Latin America (Villancourt, 2012). Such a multi-level perspective provides a more nuanced understanding than a singular focus on co-production at the individual level or using the same term for different levels. However, co-production in the UK context also appears to imply a direct, but limited, service delivery role for VCOs, i.e., they are regarded as service agents or providers. By contrast, co-management attributes a broader role to VCOs in local service management, while co-governance refers to the role of VCOs in policy formulation and community governance. The latter is best illustrated by the Voluntary Sector Compact(s) at the national and local levels and Local Strategic Partnerships designed to promote local regeneration in the UK (*ibid.*) and elsewhere in Europe.

Co-production has also recently been introduced to the continental European discussion of public sector reforms, where it refers to the growing direct and organized involvement of citizens in the production of their own social services (Pestoff, 1998, 2008a; Vamstad, 2007). The continental perspective seems to adhere more to the US than to UK usage of the term co-production. For example, parents participate in the co-production of their own childcare, both individually and collectively, by joining a parent association or cooperative preschool that provides these services in France, Germany and Sweden. We also find ample evidence of co-management and co-governance of childcare services in some European countries.

So, the term co-production has been used in different contexts and for different phenomena, however, these differences are not always made clear (Brandsen & Pestoff, 2006). Sometimes co-production is used as a general term to cover many different types of citizen participation in public service provision, where it includes various ways for citizens and/or the third sector to participate both in policy-making and policy implementation. Other times, it seems to focus on a different level or phenomena that involve citizen and/or third sector participation in policy-making and/or public service delivery. It is necessary to keep these differences in mind for the sake of clarity. So, in these chapters co-production can refer both to direct citizen participation at the site of service provision in the delivery of a public financed service, as well as to group provision of such services for themselves and others. The growing mix and diversity of service providers not only implies greater opportunities for citizen involvement in the provision of public financed services, but it also becomes necessary to manage and govern this growing diversity.

Yet, citizen participation at the site of service provision is different from the meso-level phenomenon of co-management, where the third sector participates, alongside other public and private actors, in managing the growing complexity of delivering diverse public financed services, without any direct citizen or user participation. Co-management, therefore, refers to the growing diversity or hybridization of providers of welfare services, typically found in situations where different NPOs and/or FPOs participate in the provision of public financed services (Brandsen, 2004). Elsewhere, this has been referred to as the "growing welfare mix" (Evers & Laville, 2005).

It is worth noting that both co-production and co-management take place on the output or implementation side of the political system, once a public policy has been determined. Co-governance, on the other hand, is usually found on the input side, and involves the third sector and other private actors in the determination of public policy for a given sector. Co-governance refers to attempts to manage this growing diversity in a more democratic fashion, through the creation of citywide, provincial and/or national bodies where various providers are represented and given both a voice and vote in developing and deciding the future of a sector, i.e., in its governance. The appropriate site for co-governance structures will depend, of course, on constitutional differences between various welfare states. Thus, in addition to serving as a general term for citizen and/or third sector participation in many kinds of public service, co-production can also be distinguished from co-management and co-governance. Although the above terminology will be employed to distinguish between various phenomena, it should be noted that these three concepts are not always mutually exclusive.

A.2 Co-Production: Individual Acts, Collective Action or Both?

It is often argued that the analysis of co-production needs to distinguish between individual acts and collective action and focus on one or the other. Are we mainly interested in individual or collective participation in the provision of public services? While this distinction may sometimes seem relevant or perhaps even a necessary part of a research design, in the field there is often a mix of both of them in the same service delivery. Let's look at the options available in terms of co-production.

- *Individual acts of co-production* involve *ad hoc*, spontaneous or informal acts done in public or at home. However, sometimes they are perceived as a necessary part of the service or even a mandatory activity expected of all citizens. They can involve repeated activities that take place over a long time, like students preparing for their classes and doing their homework (Porter, 2012) or mundane or seldom repeated activities, like the use of postal codes on letters and filing individual tax returns Alford (2002, 2009).
- *Collective acts of co-production* involve formally organized and institutionalized activities done together with others. They often concern the provision of enduring social services that are produced by a small group at the micro-level and they often imply as much collective interaction between participants as collective action (Pestoff, 2006).
- *A mix of both individual and collective action* is particularly relevant when it comes to social services. Many acts of co-production combine both individual and collective action(s), often in a repeated fashion over a long time. So, in addition to asking how to evoke greater individual client co-production, we also need to consider how to facilitate collective action in public service provision and the mix of both. (See Chapter 7 for more details.)

A.3 Relations between the Professional Staff and Their Clients

Co-production clearly implies different kinds of relationships between professional service providers and their clients. In some cases both parties are physically present and the production and delivery of the service are inseparable. But, there is also a frequency or time dimension involved. Many services are based on a one-time or *ad hoc* meeting between service professionals and their clients, while others can involve more frequent meetings and a long-term relationship between them. In particular, many social services are long-term and involve repeated interactions between the professional staff and their clients. In addition to these temporal aspects, different types of relations can exist between the professional staff and their clients, i.e., they can be interdependent, supplementary or complementary.

When an organization cannot produce the service without some customer input, they are considered interdependent (Parks *et al.*, 1981; Percy, 1984). Some public services are based on this. Examples of this are found in various types of educational or vocational training programs for the long-term unemployed (Alford, 2002, 2009). Without client input, no learning can take place (Porter, 2012). In addition, customers or clients can supplement or substitute the professional service provider, at least in some activities. Examples of this include properly filling in postal codes on letters and accurately filing tax forms in a timely and truthful fashion. This depends both on the clients' willingness and ability to do so, but it can be facilitated by the design of the tasks clients are expected to perform and the motives used to facilitate their co-production (Alford, 2002, 2009).

Alternatively, client inputs can complement the tasks performed by the professional staff. In spite of the clients' contributions, the staff continues to perform all or most of the key or core activities of the organization, while the clients mostly perform secondary or peripheral tasks. Parent participation in cooperative or associative preschool services provides a good example. The staff retains full pedagogical responsibility for the content and development of the preschool services, while parents are normally in charge of tasks like maintenance, management, bookkeeping and sometimes even cooking at a preschool facility (Brandsen & Pestoff, 2006). A clear division of labor in a complementary co-production situation can help avoid, or at least mitigate, some potential conflicts of interest between the staff and their clients.

A.4 *Why Citizens Become Involved in the Co-Production of Social Services*

Alford (2009) compares the engagement of public sector clients in Australia, the UK and the USA. He notes that it is often assumed that most individuals' cost-benefit analysis will only lead them to seek extrinsic self-interest rewards. However, he argues that different motives exist for co-production in different contexts. He notes that "eliciting co-production is a matter of heightening the value that clients receive from the services by making more explicit their nonmaterial aspects through intrinsic rewards, solidarity incentives or normative appeal" (*ibid.*: 187). He concluded that intrinsic rewards can also be powerful motivators, because people are not solely motivated by self-interest, but also by social values. The latter includes the enjoyment associated with interacting with other people, gaining their approval or avoiding their disapproval. Normative purposes, like participation, influence and democracy, can also be important for motivating co-production (*ibid.*).

However, in addition to these extrinsic and intrinsic motives, we also need to consider two other closely related aspects of co-production of public services: the ease of involvement and the personal motivation of individuals to participate in co-production. How easy is it for citizens to become involved in the provision of public services and why do they become active in the service provision process? The ease or facility of citizens becoming involved will depend on several things, like the distance to the service provider, the information available to them about the service and their role in its provision, etc. This reflects the time and effort required for citizens to become involved and might, therefore, be seen as the transaction costs of participation. If motivated citizens want to participate actively in the co-production of a social service, lowering the transaction costs will make it easier for them to do so. So, from this perspective we can distinguish two types of service providers: traditional and collaborative. Traditional providers are often high transaction cost providers in the eyes of service users, because there are many bureaucratic hurdles in the way of their participation, even for highly motivated citizens. Low transaction cost providers are considered 'collaborative', because they encourage and facilitate user participation. Thus, the greater the effort required of citizens to become involved, the less likely they will do so.

Citizens' motivation to become involved as a co-producer will, in turn, depend on the importance or salience of the service provided. Is the service very important for them, their family, loved-ones, a relative or a close friend? This reflects how the service affects them, their life and life chances. Does it make a direct impact on their life and/or life chances, or does it merely have an indirect or modest effect? If and when a person feels that a service is very important for them and/or their loved-ones or vital to their life chances, they will be more highly motivated to become involved in the co-production of public services, if and when they can. Here we can distinguish between greater and less salience of the service for potential co-producers.

It is also important to differentiate between enduring and non-enduring public services. Many social services belong to the former category, and therefore have an immediate impact on the life, life chances and quality of life of the persons and/or families receiving them. The importance and impact of these services guarantees high citizen/user interest in the development of such services, especially in their quality. Enduring social services include childcare or preschool, basic and higher education, eldercare, handicap care and housing, as well as preventive and long-term health care. Users of such services are locked into them for the duration of a service and can therefore not rely on exit to provide them with influence or redress. (See Chapter 2 for more details.) The transaction costs of exit are often prohibitive in enduring services, so voice, rather than exit, provides clients with influence and redress. Combining these two dimensions, the type of provider and the salience of the service, results in a classical four-fold table with the following patterns of citizen involvement, seen in Figure 6.1.

It suggests that there are different types of citizen involvement in public service provision that range from passive clients to active co-producers, with

Type of service provider/ Salience of the service:	*Traditional*	*Collaborative*
Greater	Active consumer	Active co-producer
Less	Passive client	Ad-hoc participant

Figure 6.1 Citizen Involvement in Services Provision: Nature of Providers and Salience of Service

Source: Pestoff (2012b: 25)

active consumers and *ad hoc* participants in between. In traditional or non-participatory modes of service provision, where the hurdles to participation are high, we expect either to find active consumers or passive clients. The former are the ideal type for New Public Management, while the latter are the typical mode associated with traditional public administration. In more participatory forms of service provision, where client participation is encouraged, facilitated or even required, we can expect to find both active co-producers and *ad hoc* participants. The former are the ideal type for New Public Governance (NPG), while the latter occasionally participate in some important matters, but not others, depending on a variety of factors. Thus, by combining ease of participation with the salience of the service we get a more mixed or nuanced picture of client motivation than if we only considered extrinsic and intrinsic motives.

The above distinction is illustrated by Ostrom's seminal article, "Crossing the Great Divide" (1996), which contrasts the conditions for promoting co-production in two developing countries, e.g., condominial water systems in suburban areas in Brazil and elementary education in rural Nigeria. In the latter country she notes that villagers traditionally engaged in several community projects, like building roads, the maintenance of school buildings, etc. However, she notes the detrimental effects of centralization and frequent changes in government policy concerning primary education. She compared four Nigerian villages, two where parents valued primary education highly, with good results in terms of pupils passing their school exams (85%). In the two other villages, parents valued education less and contributed very little to the local primary schools. Without parental support the teachers were incapacitated and demoralized and the children only obtained a scattered education. Moreover, she notes that co-production was discouraged by government taking over schools that villagers earlier perceived as their own, by creating chaotic changes in who is responsible for financing and maintaining them, or by top-down command type administration. She concluded that "in such situations, only the most determined citizens will persist in co-production activities" (*ibid.*: 357).

A.5 The Cooperative Gambit: Why Citizens Engage in Collective Action

As noted earlier, the pursuit of self-interest can either be individual or collective. In the latter instance there is an element of common benefit not found in the former. Collective action and even more so collective interaction have the ability to transform the pursuit of self-interest into something more than just the sum of individual self-interest. It makes possible the achievement of common goals that would otherwise be impossible for isolated, unorganized individuals. Such goals can include good quality elementary education, good quality preschool services, good quality health care, eldercare, etc., at a reasonable cost both to individuals and society.

Collective action can help solve some social and personal dilemmas created either by the lack of important social services on the market or by the variable quality of public services. If the market cannot provide an adequate amount of the service at affordable prices for most citizens or if the quality of standardized public services is not acceptable to some citizens, they can join hands to form an association to provide it for themselves and others who lack such services. Without collective action, a particular service would not be made readily available, or it would not be available in the quality desired by some groups. The lack of good quality childcare services is a prime example in many countries today. The local authorities don't provide them, or enough of them in many countries, and the market simply prices them out of reach of most parents. Thus, many families struggle to combine their professional career demands with family needs, particularly for high quality childcare. Some of them, however, can reason that if they don't join hands with other like-minded persons to form an association that provides such service for themselves and others, it simply won't be available. They recognize that without joining together no suitable childcare service will be provided for themselves and a number of concerned families.

Olson (1965) discussed the failure of large groups to form voluntary organizations in the pursuit of public interest. This is primarily due to the costs of collective action and problems of 'free-riding'. However, he refers to "the privileged position of small groups" and argues that they are subject to the second logic of collective action (*ibid.*). A small-scale group or organization allows individual members to survey and control the efforts and contributions of others, thereby avoiding or limiting problems of 'free-riding'. Thus, it is easier for small groups to organize themselves than larger ones due to greater possibilities for social controls.

A cooperative gambit is the willingness of individuals to sacrifice their short-term personal interest for the sake of the long-term individual and group benefits stemming from collective action in order to achieve a group goal to provide a social service. A social cooperative or social enterprise can create trust that helps to surmount the limits of the short-term personal interest of group members or help curb 'free-riding'. This encourages them to contribute their time, effort and other resources to achieve the fruits of their collective efforts that cannot be achieved by isolated individuals. Of course, not everyone participates in collective action, but there may be enough of them to make it worth considering why some do.

Extensive research in experimental psychology repeatedly and clearly shows that in real-world collective action situations there are two other types of norm-using players in addition to rational egoists (Ostrom, 2000b). The first group is comprised of 'conditional cooperators', who are willing to initiate or join collective action when they estimate that others will reciprocate, so they will contribute to such actions as long as others demonstrate similar behavior. The second group of cooperators is called 'willing punishers'. They rely more heavily on social control and punishment as the basis for collective action. Yet, research shows that many people combine both these traits. Both groups are prone to pursue the cooperative gambit, especially when certain institutional forms exist (*ibid.*).

Ostrom also develops six design principles for the emergence of self-governing common pool resources (CPR) (2009a). Several of them are relevant for understanding other forms of collective action, but only two of them will be considered closer here. The first is setting clear group boundaries to determine who uses a resource or service and who does not. The second principle concerns the right of members to influence decisions concerning the management of a resource or service, i.e., are they a self-governing group? Thus, a social cooperative or social enterprise created to provide a particular service for its members must establish clear boundaries and they must establish internal democratic channels to influence decisions. These two aspects are, of course, mutually reinforcing, and taken together they help to make a cooperative gambit more viable. Thus, Ostrom's research establishes that the rate of contribution to a public good is affected by various contextual factors and that these design principles make self-organized collective action more robust.

These two phenomena, small group control and the cooperative gambit, can help to explain the growth and success of co-production and third sector provision of social services in some parts of Europe. The cooperative gambit not only represents a 'quantum leap' in terms of the presumed maximization of individual short-term utilities, it also recognizes that individuals have different dispositions toward cooperation. Some persons appear more favorably disposed to cooperate than others. Moreover, it also suggests that 'methodological individualism' is biased toward short-term utility maximizing individuals and also ignores, or perhaps overlooks, the existence of other dispositions, like 'conditional cooperators' and 'willing punishers'. Thus, collective action is possible not only when 'selective incentives' are present, as Olson once argued, but also when some institutions help remove the hurdles facing collective action by 'conditional cooperators' and 'willing punishers'. This topic will be explored in greater detail in Chapter 7.

B. Volunteering and Co-Production

The turn of the century saw the development of two main alternatives to continued governmental growth in the wake of heavy criticism of the public sector. One alternative was the marketization of public sector activities, through privatization and contracting out, etc., that became known as 'managerialism' and later as New Public Management (NPM). The alternative that later became known as New Public Governance (NPG) was based on the participation of citizens, clients, customers, volunteers and/or community organizations in producing public services, as well as consuming or otherwise benefiting from them (Alford, 2009: 5; Osborne, 2010; Pestoff *et al.*, 2012). A third alternative now seems to be coalescing around ideas of greater volunteering and community responsibility for the provision of basic public services of all types, often in light of massive cutbacks in public funding. The latter is called a Communitarian regime herein, for lack of a better word.

Because two or more of these approaches employ similar concepts and refer to similar organizational forms, but expect them to play different roles and result in different outcomes, it is necessary to pause and consider their relationship briefly. In particular, we want to explore the relationship between volunteering and co-production a bit closer. Some authors suggest they are more or less the same, use them interchangeably, and consider the recent expansion of volunteers in the provision of public services as an example of the growth of co-production. Others argue that there are nevertheless some basic differences between them in terms of providing inputs to and/or consuming outputs from public goods and services. We will consider the similarities and differences between volunteering and co-production, beginning with the similarities.

Ilmonen (2005) analyzed gift giving in contemporary society. Only in modern society are self-interest and other motives somehow seen as contrary or opposed to each other, but previously this was not the case, he argued. It is important to pay attention to motives other than self-interest that provide the basis for giving a gift, including the goal of maintaining social bonds. Generosity is often not so 'pure' or altruistic as it may appear to be, and both 'pure' and 'calculative' gifts are merely ideal types. In everyday activities, generosity and the promotion of self-interest are often intertwined and difficult to distinguish. Moreover, he reminded us that whether gift giving aims at promoting self-interest or not, it clearly differs in one key respect from economic transactions in a market economy. In the end, gift giving always aims at the creation and maintenance of social bonds, while in a market economy the sale of a good promotes individual wealth accumulation with little or no consideration to social bonds (*ibid.*; Donati, 2011, 2014).

Volunteering and co-production often have a similar organizational base and their members may share similar values, although with a different emphasis.

Both volunteering and co-production can either involve informal or formal activities, so their organizational base is either individual or collective. In addition, the value orientation of volunteers and co-producers can either be oriented primarily toward benefiting persons other than themselves or can be mostly self-oriented. Contributions of time, effort and perhaps even money by volunteers and/or co-producers to producing public services can, therefore, take different organizational forms, individual or collective. Also, persons making such contributions can have different motives for doing so. However, in addition to individual and collective ways of contributing to the provision of public services, there is a mixed category that combines both individual and collective efforts, as often is the case in the real world (Pestoff, 2012a, 2012b). Moreover, in addition to self-oriented or other-oriented motives for citizens to contribute their time and effort to the provision of public services, volunteers and co-producers often have mixed motives that combine both these values to a greater or lesser degree (Pestoff, 1998, 2008a).

Often, citizen participation both in volunteering and co-producing public services appears to fall in the middle category of these two dimensions. They both require individual and collective efforts to be realized or fully achieved. They both involve a mix of promoting other-oriented social values, as well as the realization of self-interest. This implies that co-production as depicted here, may, in practice, not be all that different from activities classified as voluntary in other perspectives, approaches or institutional contexts. Thus, the perceived differences between these two phenomena may be more a question of degree than kind (*ibid.*).

In spite of sharing these common traits, they also demonstrate some fundamental differences. First, volunteers and volunteering are usually celebrated, gain social recognition and receive public attention,[1] which helps to generate research funds and spreads greater awareness about this phenomena (Gross, 2008). Until recently, co-production was a less well-known phenomenon, causing a leading British public management scholar to lament that co-production is often a hidden or ignored phenomenon, and its potential to raise the effectiveness of public policy is usually underestimated (Bovaird, 2007).

More important for the discussion at hand are the different roles that volunteers and co-producers play in providing and/or consuming public services. A major reason for the earlier loss of interest in co-production was the perception that it was about *volunteering* and *volunteers*. It appeared to depend heavily on altruism, because co-producers don't receive any financial benefits from contributing their unpaid time and efforts to improving service quality. In a climate dominated by market incentives, it seemed too risky and unreliable a motivation on which to base important public functions, like care, health, safety, etc., or major public sector reforms. However, Alford argues that this represents a misunderstanding of co-production by clients, because volunteers are analogous to the suppliers of inputs to a firm or an organization, while its clients are analogous to its buyers (2009: 6). There are, he notes, some important differences between the function of consumers and volunteers. Volunteers are not the direct beneficiaries of the service being provided, and they are logically different from consumers, because they provide input to the organization, without necessarily consuming them or gaining direct personal benefit from them (*ibid.*: 24). Co-producers, by contrast, provide necessary inputs to the provision and distribution of public services, and they also benefit personally from consuming them, both as individuals and groups.

So, there are some clear similarities between volunteering and co-production, on the one hand, yet there are also some major differences between them, on the other hand. This results in growing confusion among practitioners and scholars about what role either or both of these phenomenon play in public service delivery. Can both these phenomenon be present at the same time and can both perspectives be valid in the same country and/or same service sector? Some authors document the expanding role of volunteers in government-promoted or even government-regulated co-production (Tönurist & Srurva, 2017; Schlappa & Imani, 2016), while others caution that more analysis is necessary, because their roles seem quite different at times (Alford, 2009).

In brief, how can these different, seemingly contrary perspectives on the relationship between volunteering and co-production be reconciled? One possible explanation for both volunteering and co-production being present at the same time and being relevant phenomena in public service provision is gleaned from the early findings of research on public administrations regimes (PARs). Volunteering and co-production play quite different roles in different PARs (Pestoff, 2018a). Volunteering and co-production play a marginal role in traditional public administration and New Public Management (NPM). By contrast, New Public Governance (NPG) relies more heavily on citizen participation in the provision of public services and co-production is considered a key component or aspect of this PAR. Here it corresponds well with the idea of dual roles of citizens that make unpaid inputs to public service provision by contributing their time and efforts to improve the quality of public services and, at the same time, by consuming these public services as service users. In addition, a Communitarian regime also calls for much greater citizen inputs to public service provision, primarily to compensate for public budget cutbacks, but here their role is mainly as volunteers, rather than as service users. (See Chapter 9 for more details.)

So, much of the lack of clarity about the different roles played by volunteers and co-producers stems from the institutional context of public sector reform, failing to distinguish between PARs and the roles attributed to actors like volunteers and co-producers by different PARs. Both NPG and a Communitarian regime call for more citizen participation in the provision of public services, but citizens participate in quite different ways. They participate as co-producers in NPG, while in a Communitarian regime they participate more as volunteers.

C. Summary and Conclusions: Capacity to Embrace Co-Production

The relationship between the state and citizens is continually changing in post-modern societies. New forms of providing services, including public services, are emerging that challenge traditional patterns of production. In the changing relations between the government and citizens, the former sometimes attempt to involve the latter in the provision of goods and services. This is motivated either by reasons of improving the efficiency of public services or the effectiveness of public policies, or to promote other important social goals, like citizen empowerment, participation and democracy.

Numerous aspects of co-production have been considered in this chapter. They are crucial for understanding the potential and limits of co-production and distinguishing it from volunteering. In brief, the first part of this article explored several crucial conceptual issues related to co-production. Various definitions of co-production were considered and a generic one, stemming from the early writings of Ostrom and her colleagues, was adopted. It focuses on the mix of activities that both public service agents and citizens contribute to the provision of public services. The former are involved as professionals or 'regular producers', while 'citizen production' is based on voluntary efforts by individuals or groups to enhance the quality and/or quantity of services they use. It was expanded to include both individual and group participation in co-production.

After considering several definitions of co-production, we noted that the term has been used in different contexts and for different phenomena, however, these differences are not always made clear. They can express cultural differences, differences of focus, as well as different levels of analysis. Sometimes co-production is used as a general term to cover many different types of citizen participation in public service provision, where it includes various ways for citizens and/or the third sector to participate in both policy-making and policy implementation. Other times, it seems to focus on a different level or phenomena that involve citizen and/or third sector participation in policy-making and/or public service delivery. However, it is necessary to keep these differences in mind for the sake of clarity.

Citizen participation at the site of service provision is different from the meso-level phenomenon of co-management, where the third sector participates, alongside other public and private actors, in managing the growing complexity of delivering various public financed services, without any direct citizen or user participation. Co-management refers to the growing diversity or mix of providers of welfare services, typically found in fields where different NPOs and/or FPOs participate in the provision of public financed services. It is worth noting that both co-production and co-management and civil society organizations (CSOs), in order to innovate and deliver improved public services. Fiscal pressures, new demands and changing political priorities in the light of aging and more diverse societies make it necessary to explore new alternatives to traditional models. The OECD notes that, in terms of the share of resources devoted to ten standard public services, some, like general services, have decreased in importance over the past 10 years, while others have increased significantly, especially health care and social protection (2011: 33). This makes existing models of service provision both tenuous and unaffordable in the long-run, and lends greater urgency to developing alternative models, particularly co-production. Thus, the search for more efficient, effective and sustainable ways to organize and deliver public services offers both challenges and opportunities to rethink traditional models of public sector management.

The OECD report also notes that co-production takes place at different stages in the policy process, from planning through delivery and review. Patterns of interaction between service users and providers are different in different services, with the greatest user involvement in the delivery stage of personal services, such as health and social services, while participation in monitoring and review plays a more central role in general services, like environmental protection (2011: 13). Moreover, the OECD (2011) notes that most governments engage in co-production for a variety of reasons, but economic considerations seldom dominate. Rather, strengthening user and citizen involvement *per se*, improving service quality and improving effectiveness and service outcome are considered more important by most governments than increasing productivity or cutting costs (2011: 48).

Most OECD countries have developed different approaches to involve citizens and users in public services, ranging from simple interactions to more active consultation in decision-making. However, co-production is more than mere consultations; it involves citizens/users in more systematic exchanges to create and deliver public services (2011: 18). Co-production transforms the relationship between service users and providers, ensuring greater user influence and ownership. Thus, it should be more than simply giving citizens/users a say in and/or more responsibility for the design, provision, or evaluation of public services. The old adage 'no rights without responsibilities' can be turned around to read 'no new responsibilities without additional rights'. Providing citizens and users with more influence over public services, particularly service quality of enduring social services, may prove important for evoking their participation as co-producers. Otherwise, there is clearly a risk of turning the provision of social services into an IKEA-like do-it-yourself regime (Alcock, 2010; Taylor, 2011) that provides users and citizens with too little influence to motivate their sustained participation in co-producing welfare services. Rather, it might be interpreted as a new form of social dumping or a race to the bottom, where 'everyone does

take place on the output side of the political system, implementing public policy once it has been determined. Co-governance, on the other hand, is usually found on the input side, and involves the third sector and other private actors in the determination of public policy for a given sector. So, co-production is both a generic or umbrella term for all types and forms of greater citizen participation, as well as citizen participation at the micro-level or site of service provision. Co-management is found at the meso-level, while co-governance is a macro-level phenomenon. It was also noted that co-production is often a mix of both individual and collective action, often in a repeated fashion over a long time. So in addition to asking how to evoke greater individual client co-production, we also need to consider how to facilitate collective action in public service provision and the mix of both.

When an organization cannot produce the service without some customer input, it is considered interdependent. Some public services are based on this interdependency, for example, various types of educational or vocational training programs for the long-term unemployed. Without client input, no learning can take place. In addition, customer or client inputs can supplement or substitute those of the professional service provider, at least in some activities and to some extent. Alternatively, client inputs can complement the tasks performed by the professional staff. Here the staff continues to perform all or most of the key or core activities of the organization, while the clients mostly perform secondary or peripheral tasks. Parent participation in cooperative or associative preschool services provides a good example.

Alford (2009) argues that citizens have different motives for co-production in different contexts. In addition to self-interest or extrinsic motives, there are nonmaterial or intrinsic rewards. The latter can provide powerful motives, because people are not solely motivated by self-interest, but also by social values. Beyond the extrinsic and intrinsic motives, we also considered two other closely related aspects of co-production of public services, the ease of involvement and the personal motivation of individuals to participate in co-production. This allowed us to identify two types of service providers, traditional and collaborative. Citizens' motivations to become involved as co-producers also depends on the importance or salience of the service provided. This reflects how the service affects them, their life and life chances. The importance and impact of these services guarantees high citizen/user interest in the development of such services, especially in their quality. By combining ease of participation with the salience of the service, we get a more nuanced picture of citizen/user motivation than if we only considered extrinsic and intrinsic motives. It also suggested the existence of four types of citizen involvement in the provision and delivery of public services. It also helps shift the focus from individual users to structures that can facilitate or hinder greater citizen participation in the provision of public services.

The pursuit of self-interest can either be individual or collective. In the latter instance, there is an element of common benefit not found in the former. Collective action and even more so small group collective interaction have the ability to transform the pursuit of self-interest into something more than the sum of individual self-interest. It makes possible the achievement of common goals that would otherwise be impossible for isolated, unorganized individuals. The cooperative gambit reflects the willingness of individuals to sacrifice their short-term personal interest for the sake of the long-term individual and group benefits stemming from collective action in order to achieve a group goal to provide a social service. However, it also recognizes that individuals have different dispositions toward cooperation. Some persons appear more favorably disposed to cooperate than others. In addition to self-interested, short-term utility maximizing individuals, Ostrom's research documented the existence of other relevant dispositions, like 'conditional cooperators' and 'willing punishers', both of whom make the cooperative gambit more feasible.

Turning to the difference and similarity between volunteering and co-production, we noted that volunteering and co-production often have a similar organizational base and their members may share similar values, although with a different emphasis. However, there are also some important differences in the roles that volunteers and co-producers play in providing and/or consuming public services (Alford, 2009: 6). Volunteers are not the direct beneficiaries of the service being provided and, therefore, they are logically different from consumers. Volunteers provide inputs to a service organization, without necessarily consuming them or gaining direct personal benefit from them (*ibid.*: 24). Co-producers, by contrast, provide necessary inputs to the provision and distribution of public services and they also personally benefit from consuming them, both as individuals and groups (*ibid.*). We will return to this issue in greater detail in Chapter 11.

However, this distinction may result in growing confusion among practitioners and scholars about and what role either or both volunteers and co-producers can play in public service delivery. We asked how these different perspectives on the relationship between volunteering and co-production might be reconciled. One possible explanation for both volunteering and co-production being present at the same time and being relevant phenomena in public service provision is gleaned from the early findings of research on public administrations regimes (PARs), because they play quite different roles in different PARs. Chapter 9 addresses issues related to co-production and PARs in greater detail.

Note

1. See for example the European Commission's recent study of volunteering, initiated by the Directorate General Education & Culture, DG EAC. Its final report is over 325 pages, plus a national report on volunteering for each EU member country of about 30 pages each. Contact http://ec.europa.eu/citizenship/news/news1015 _en.htm.

7   Small Groups, Collective Action and the Sustainability of Co-Production

A. Background

The relationship between the state and its citizens is subject to co[n]change in post-modern societies. New forms of providing services, inc[luding] public services, are emerging that challenge traditional patterns of pr[ovision]tion. Co-production is a social innovation that promotes a mix of [public] service agents and citizens/users who contribute to the provision of a [public] service (Parks *et al.*, 1981). It creates a synergy between the activit[ies of] citizens and the government and implies a partnership between the se[rvice] users, on the one hand, and the providers on the other, or between the cl[ients] and professional staff in public services (Ostrom, 1996).

Osborne *et al.* (2013) recently argued that co-production is an esse[ntial] part of a broader framework to provide a new theory for public ser[vice] management—a service-dominant approach, in contrast to the manufactur[ing]dominant approach of New Public Management (NPM). The latter is ba[sed] on a 'fatal flaw' in public management theory that views public services [as] manufacturing, rather than as service processes. However, public serv[ice] needs to be understood from a broader framework called New Public Gov[er]nance (NPG). Services, in contrast to manufacturing, demonstrate three ma[jor] differences: (a) they are intangible, (b) there are different product logics f[or] manufacturing and delivering services and, most important for the discussi[on] here, (c) the role of the user is qualitatively different for manufacturing an[d] services, since services are co-produced by the service providers and consume[rs] of the services (Osborne *et al.*, 2013). Co-production makes an importan[t] contribution to the debate on public management. It goes to the heart of bot[h] effective public services delivery and the role of public services in achieving societal ends, such as social inclusion and citizen engagement (Osborne *et al.*, 2013: 145). Thus, they propose that "by taking a service-dominant approach, co-production becomes an inalienable component of public service delivery that places the experiences and knowledge of the service user at the heart of effective public service design and delivery" (Osborne *et al.*, 2013: 146).

A recent OECD (2011) report on co-production calls for rethinking traditional public service delivery in a new socio-economic environment. It also analyzes the partnership formed by governments with citizens

their own thing'. However, this risk is probably less in an NPG than in an NPM regime, because collective or group co-production comes into clearer focus in the former.

Information technology can also play an important role in co-producing public services by facilitating greater interaction between public agencies and citizens (Bauwens, 2005; Meijer, 2012). The promise of new Internet Computer Technology (ICT) make it very popular, but it often has a heavy emphasis on technical solutions that tend to ignore the human and social aspects. Therefore, ICT solutions fall outside the scope of this chapter. Also, it uses terms like 'citizen', 'user' and 'client' interchangeably. We are fully aware of the potential differences between these roles, but for the sake of simplifying the argument, we prefer to ignore them, at least temporarily. However, they are discussed in greater detail in Chapter 9.

B. Introduction: Collective Action, Co-Production and Size

Some of the pioneers who helped develop co-production argued that collective action is important for making co-production more viable and sustainable. Many of the scholars at the Workshop in Political Theory and Policy Analysis at the University of Indiana during the 1970s based their research on methodological individualism. They noted co-production does not require citizens to join an organization, but that organizations were a crucial variable, because they could enhance the levels of co-production and facilitate coordination between citizens and public agencies (Rich, 1981). However, the relationship between collective action and co-production has still not been systematically explored. This chapter highlights the potential contribution of collective action in making co-production more sustainable in the provision of public services, particularly of enduring welfare services. However, it does not ignore the importance of individual co-production, because many acts of co-production are a mix of both individual acts and collective action.

B.1 Co-Production: Individual Acts, Collective Action or Both?

It is often argued that the analysis of co-production needs to distinguish between individual acts and collective action and should focus on one or the other. While this may seem relevant or sometimes even necessary as part of a research design in this new field, in practice there is often a mix of both of them in public service delivery.

Individual acts of co-production involve *ad hoc*, spontaneous acts done in public or at home. However, they are sometimes perceived as a necessary part of the service or even a mandatory activity expected of all citizens. The use of postal codes on letters and filing individual tax returns illustrates this type of co-production (Alford, 2002). Alford (2009) recently explored how best to engage clients as co-producers of these public services.

Collective acts of co-production involve formally organized and institutionalized activities done together with others and often concern the provision of enduring welfare services. Such services are usually produced by a small group and may often imply more collective interaction than collective action. The former can promote the development of social capital, mutualism and reciprocity (Pestoff, 2006).

Many acts of co-production involve a *mix of both* individual and collective action, often in a repeated fashion for a long time. This mix of individual and collective action is highly relevant when it comes to social services, particularly enduring social services. So, the relevant question is not only how to evoke greater individual client co-production, but also how to facilitate more collective action in public service provision and a greater mix of both (Pestoff, 2012a, 2012b).

B.2 Collective Action

Hudson (2012) argued that it is important to distinguish between individual and collective co-production, particularly with reference to developments in the health care sector in the United Kingdom. His argument appears equally valid for other enduring social services and other OECD countries. He sketches three phases in the shift from mass production to mass collaboration or participatory health care in the National Health Service (NHS). First, in mass production, professionals design and deliver services to their patients, who are passive recipients of the same. Then, in today's mass customization and personalization of services, professionals and patients jointly design them, but professionals still lead the implementation. When patients can become individual co-producers of customized and personalized services, this results in a patient-consumer model. Finally, mass collaboration and participatory health care rely on sustained patient engagement to deal with complex chronic conditions. Thus, patients and communities are central both to the design and delivery of services and support in the latter model. In addition to the design of services, they also influence services' commissioning, delivery, assessment and continuous development (Bovaird, 2007). This assumes that better service quality can be achieved through collective co-production, because it also promotes greater transparency and accountability than 'consumer' choice and individual co-production found in mass customization and personalization (Hudson, 2012).

If collective action is a key question for understanding how to make co-production more sustainable, then we need to ask if and how the type of provider impacts on citizen/user participation in public services. Unfortunately, very few empirical studies compare citizen/user participation in the provision of public financed services across providers, sectors or countries. Some provisional insights can, however, be gleaned from two empirical studies of parent participation in public financed childcare and preschool services in Europe. The first study noted that co-production in the eight EU countries involved different dimensions of participation: economic, political, social and service specific (Pestoff, 2006). It also found higher levels of participation in third sector and nonprofit providers on most of these dimensions than in public and private for-profit services (Pestoff, 2008a).

The second study confirmed that parents' participation in preschool services clearly varies between providers, again with the third sector providers facilitating much greater involvement, both by parents and the staff in Sweden (Vamstad, 2007). Both these studies suggest the existence of a 'glass ceiling' for participation in public and private for-profit sector services, but show that the third sector helps breach this barrier (Pestoff, 2009). While further research is clearly necessary, these results suggest focusing on the potential contribution of the third sector to the sustainability of citizen/user participation in the provision of public services.

However, both academics and practitioners agree that the third sector is difficult to define (Kendall & Knapp, 1995) and delimit (Brandsen *et al.*, 2003). It comprises many different and diverse types of organizations, ranging from small, local self-help groups to huge, international non-governmental organizations (INGOs) and from activity-oriented to passive checkbook organizations. Moreover, the third sector often overlaps with other major social institutions, like the market, state and community, resulting in various degrees of hybridity (Pestoff, 2014b, 2018b). Given the wide range and diversity of third sector organizations (TSOs), some may be better suited for promoting co-production than others and some may facilitate more sustainable co-production than others. We will return to the topic of organizational diversity in greater detail later in this chapter.

B.3 Group Size

Organizational size has long been recognized as an important aspect of participation (Dahl & Tufte, 1973). Individuals often feel anonymous in large organizations and can easily lose their way or focus, but they feel more at home in smaller ones. Group size is also important for understanding collective action. Mancur Olson spelled out two logics in his seminal book *The Logic of Collective Action* (1965), one for small groups and another for large, mass groups. Much of his book was devoted to explaining how and why large groups are different from small ones, in terms of their potential for collective action. He proposed certain techniques or methods, like 'selective incentives', to overcome the hurdles facing their organization. In brief, he argued that small groups have a privileged position by virtue of their size, because their members can easily monitor each other's behavior and contribution to a common project. This becomes more difficult once a group grows beyond a certain size. Thus, selective incentives will serve little purpose in small groups, but they may prove important, if not essential, in larger ones.

Olson's distinction based on group size has some obvious ramifications for the study of co-production and implications for citizen participation in the provision of public services. It can provide us with a better idea of when and where co-production might prove sustainable and when it will not. Citizen participation in a small, self-governing group that provides public financed and enduring welfare services for itself will differ significantly from a large amorphous group that rarely meets each other or the public authorities who finance many of the welfare services they use. Moreover, the relations and interactions among users in a small group will result in stronger and more durable bonds than among those only engaged occasionally, if at all, in face-to-face interactions with each other or the public authorities. Small groups can also promote the growth of social capital. Thus, size appears important for several reasons, not only in terms of resources, influence, etc., but also bureaucracy. Small size means fewer resources and perhaps less influence, but it also means smaller bureaucracies and usually more engaged members (Pestoff, 1991, 2012b).

B.4 *Interaction with Other Structural Variables*

Size is one of several structural variables that Elinor Ostrom (2009a) deemed important for overcoming collective action problems. However, the impact of size has been strongly contested. Whether and how size affects the likelihood of cooperation depends on the other variables, on how they are affected by group size and how it affects them in turn (*ibid.*: 54). The other structural variables considered important in the governance of common pool resources (CPR) are whether the benefits are subtractive, the heterogeneity of a group, face-to-face communications, information about past actions, network relations and whether a player decides to participate or not (*ibid.*: 54–56). Several of them are deemed relevant for facilitating citizen participation in co-production. They are discussed below. Moreover, a few additional variables are important for evoking citizen participation in co-production and for making it more sustainable. They are also discussed and presented and discussed below.

We will briefly consider each of the seven structural variables Ostrom identified as important for resolving social dilemmas and promoting cooperation (*ibid.*). Size, as already mentioned, is an important consideration for co-production, although far from the only one. *Subtractive benefits* are clearly related to CPR, like water, fishing, forests and other natural resources, where there is a risk of overexploitation. Here, one individual's use of a resource impacts on its availability to other potential users. However, this condition does not necessarily hold for the provision of public services, especially social services. For example, public education is no more or less available if one person decides to send his/her children to school or not. In addition, in most post-industrial countries, a minimal mandatory education level is prescribed by law, in combination with an obligation for parents to send their children to school. Active parent co-production in education is therefore not a subtractive benefit. *Heterogeneity of a group* is equally as relevant for co-production as for CPR. This would be particularly so where all clients participate on a similar level, but get very different results or benefits from their efforts. *Face-to-face communication* is also equally as relevant for co-production, as it is for CPR. *Information about past actions* is also relevant, but may be filtered through the proximity of the services provided. Here, neighbors know each other and interact at different levels and in different contexts. *Network relations* are probably a natural result of the long-term interactions stemming from participation in enduring services of 3 to 10 years or more, which can also contribute to reciprocity and social capital. Finally, *choosing whether to cooperate or not* is often a non-issue in collective co-production, especially if there is a work obligation connected with the service provided. If an individual or family wants to avail themselves of a service, they must comply with the work obligation and contribute to achieving or improving the service together.

Thus, several of Ostrom's structural variables for promoting cooperation with CPR are also relevant for co-production. These variables can interact with each other in both positive and negative ways to facilitate or discourage citizen participation and co-production. The term 'small group interaction' will be used herein to distinguish a situation in which several of these structural variables interact in a positive fashion to facilitate co-production. Clearly, a small group of citizens that meets on a daily basis over several years in order to provide a particular service for itself, with public financial support, is quite different from a large amorphous group that may share some common interests, but never meets face-to-face. The former members have quite different possibilities to get to know each other, observe each other's behavior and note and correct any deviations from expectations in order to prevent 'free-riding'. Thus, we can expect a small group with regular face-to-face communications that has a homogeneous interest in achieving better service quality by working together will meet several of the criteria suggested by Ostrom. By contrast, a large heterogeneous group that never meets face-to-face will have major problems in agreeing to cooperate for a collective goal. That does not mean it is impossible, but clearly it is less likely and less sustainable. Thus, the structural variables identified by Ostrom can form a positive or negative cluster in terms of facilitating citizen participation and collective co-production.

C. Additional Structural Variables for Co-Production

There are some additional structural variables identified by research as relevant for co-production, but not necessarily so for CPR. We will now turn our attention to them. They include the nature of the service, organizational diversity, group dynamics in self-help groups and a dialog between the staff and clients. Finally, we also consider small group models for promoting sustainable co-production in larger organizations.

C.1 The Nature of the Service, Co-Production and Sustainability

How sustainable is citizen participation in the provision of public services and co-production? The answer depends, at least in part, on the types of services and how they are organized. Broad amorphous groups or broad amorphous needs among citizens are harder to organize in a sustainable fashion than narrow, better-defined groups and needs. Take, for example, the need for open recreation spaces among the general public in cities compared with the need of parents with small children for childcare services. It will probably prove much more difficult to engage local residents in the maintenance of a park or public recreation area than parents in the maintenance and management of their child(ren)'s childcare or preschool facility. The former case poses a typical 'logic of collective action' situation, where selective incentives may prove necessary to enlist some minimal citizen participation in the maintenance of a local park or outdoor recreation facility, while in the latter case some parents may be highly motivated to participate regularly in the management and maintenance of the preschool facility until their child(ren) reach school age. The motivated ones can join together and form a parent co-op if they are dissatisfied with existing public services. By contrast, *ad hoc* or more sporadic levels of citizen participation may not prove reliable or sustainable in more intensive or enduring welfare services. For example, if parent interaction with the staff is limited, parents are only allowed to make spontaneous suggestions for the children's activities when leaving or getting their own child from a daycare facility, or they are only expected to contribute cookies, or a cake to the Christmas or spring party, then they might feel their contribution is trivial and may eventually curtail their engagement or direct it somewhere else, where it might be more needed and/or appreciated. Thus, sustainability not only has to do with the nature of the group, but also with the nature of the service and how it is organized. Many public services can be (re)organized to make citizen participation more meaningful, if and when they are willing to engage in co-production.

In particular, some services are of such a nature that the users or clients are locked into them for several years, anywhere from 3 to 10 years or more. They are referred to as enduring services. Such long-term services usually include childcare and preschool services, elementary and secondary education, handicap care, eldercare, housing and preventive and long-term health care. Clients of such services are therefore in a more stable, long-term demand situation, but they cannot easily switch providers if they are dissatisfied with the service or want to improve it. The transaction costs of changing providers are often prohibitive (Pestoff, 1998), making exit very difficult. Voice, therefore, provides a more stable medium for communicating about service quality than exit. Moreover, their collective interaction can provide them with amplified voice. Thus, some form of client organization can facilitate their regular participation in co-production and can also impose collective controls on potential 'free-riding'. (See Chapter 2 for more details.)

C.2 *Organizational Diversity and Sustainable Co-Production*

If small group interaction is an important consideration for promoting sustainable user participation in welfare services, then more careful attention should be given to putting Olson's insights into small group dynamics to use when designing such services. Small group solutions can occur by chance, when the right conditions just seem to happen, or such conditions can be enabled, facilitated or designed. Can some lessons be learned from successful examples of sustainable co-production of welfare services, and if so, which examples? The 1991 Italian Law (#381) on Social Cooperatives provides a classical example of promoting collective interaction in social enterprises. By 2005 there were 7,300 social co-ops in Italy that provided various social services and employed nearly 250,000 people (Galera & Borzaga, 2009: 219). Given this success, several EU countries attempted to copy the Italian law on social co-ops, including Portugal, Spain, France and Poland. Another example of sustainable co-production that has featured in the international literature is childcare and preschool services, which provides a good starting point for our discussion.

Parent associations, initiatives and cooperatives in France, Germany and Sweden provide childcare and preschool services to are based on parent participation in the maintenance and management of the services, or sustainable co-production. There is normally a work obligation coupled with membership in such services that makes parents' participation highly regular and sustainable as long as they avail themselves of such services, which is usually until their child(ren) start school. Depending on the number of children each family has enrolled in the services, it makes a commitment to participate in the maintenance and management of the children's preschool for 5–9 or more years. Here too, co-production becomes more predictable and sustainable.

A third example of sustainable co-production is found in the growing number of self-help, mutual aid, and patient groups in many OECD countries. Karlsson's study illustrates this for groups with problems like alcohol abuse, illness and physical disorder, grief and parenthood (2002). Group members emphasized the importance of mutual understanding in the group, the spirit of community and the information gained from the group. Their understanding of such problems is based on their own experience and it often differs notably from that of the professionals. Sometimes, it led to new and innovative treatment models not found in the public sector (*ibid*). Moreover, an in-depth study of two regional diabetes groups in Sweden underlined the importance of information and mutual support for coping with the symptoms of diabetes (Söderholm Werkö, 2008), that allows members to become co-producers of their own health care. All of these sustainable efforts were made possible by organizations that promoted small group interactions.

However, organizational diversity also has important implications for the question about what role the third sector can play in promoting sustainable co-production. Clearly not all TSOs are equally prepared for this, because not all of them are membership organizations that can promote greater client participation. Issues like organizational goals and purpose, type of members, governance structures, etc., are important to take into account when attempting to assess the potential of the third sector for promoting sustainable co-production. This depends, in part, on their own internal decision-making rules. Many nonprofit organizations are not governed in a fashion that promotes or even permits participation by their members, volunteers or clients. Most charities and foundations are run by a board of executives that is appointed by key stakeholders, rather than elected by their members or clients. However, social enterprises in Europe usually include representatives of most or all major stakeholder groups in their internal decision-making structures, and they are often governed as multi-stakeholder organizations, allowing for input from all major stakeholders. In fact, participation by key stakeholders and democratic decision-making are two of the core governance criteria applied by the European EMES Research Network to define and delimit social enterprises (Defourny *et al.*, 2014). Thus, if governments intend to facilitate greater citizen co-production in the provision of enduring welfare services, they need to devise ways of promoting self-help groups, social service co-ops and other forms of third sector provision of such services that tend to be small-scale and facilitate formal, collective interaction among well-defined groups of service users in a democratic fashion.

There is, of course, a difference between institutional frameworks that promote social co-ops, like Italian Law 381/1991, and other attempts to replicate many of the good examples or best practices found in numerous small-scale experiments in various parts of Europe (Brandsen & Honingh, 2015). This harbors some important implications about recommendations of 'scaling-up' these small-scale social experiments and innovations in order to make them more economically viable and feasible. However, economies of scale can often prove elusive, particularly in public service delivery. If politicians want to promote greater citizen participation and more co-production in the public sector, they must avoid the trap of thinking that 'big is beautiful' and that they can simply promote larger and larger units of the same type of citizen participation and co-production. The idea of scaling-up or replicating successful social innovations and social enterprises represents a mechanistic, mass production perspective of service provision. Hartley and Benington (2006) discuss three phases in the development of successful innovations in public services: first comes imitation, then adaptation and finally innovation. Genuine innovation normally needs to develop and take root. Scaling-up often implies some kind of shallow imitation that, with time, can perhaps result in adaptation to the new environment. However, only after serious efforts to adapt the good example to its new environment, allowing it to grow into and with the new environment, allowing it to tap into the specific conditions and tacit knowledge found in that new environment, can we expect innovation to develop and take root (Hartley & Benington, 2006).

C.3 *Small Group Dynamics in Self-Help Groups*

Karlsson's (2002) study of self-help groups in Sweden provides additional insights into the advantages of small groups in relation to sustainable co-production. This study focused on small, autonomous groups that met regularly to cope with a mutual problem they faced and provide each other with mutual support. It concentrated on groups working with problems of a physical, mental or social nature. It identifies the main characteristic of these small self-help groups in terms of developing or creating a common understanding of their mutual problem and providing mutual support to resolve it. A self-help group is made up of persons who experience various aspects of such problems in their daily life. Regular meetings between people with the same experience facilitate reaching a common understanding of their problem. Rather than being regarded as deviant or different, as they commonly are by professionals in the public sector, in a self-help group they discover that there are other people like themselves. The knowledge developed in self-help groups is different from professional knowledge, because it is based on their own personal experiences, and it is more comprehensive than a narrowly focused professional perspective. So, they naturally have a more complete understanding of their own problem and they can therefore develop more holistic and often viable solutions to them (*ibid.*).

The group is not only where knowledge about their problems is developed or created, but also where various solutions are tested when participants apply this knowledge to their own lives; self-help groups therefore take on a double meaning for participants (*ibid.*). So, small group dynamics can prove very important for facilitating the participation of persons with serious physical, mental or social problems and for retaining their participation over time, i.e., turning them into sustainable co-producers of their own care.

C.4 *Promoting a Dialog between the Staff and Clients*

How can client input be facilitated by the design of the task clients are expected to perform and the motives used to evoke their co-production? In the public sector, limiting client input to tasks that do not require advanced professional skills is one way to facilitate co-production and to evoke greater user/citizen participation, in exchange for more and/or better services (Alford, 2002, 2009). In social services, complementary co-production means that clients undertake secondary or tertiary tasks that do not require core professional skills, while the staff can focus on the core functions (Pestoff, 2012a, 2012b). Moreover, a clear division of labor in a complementary co-production situation can help avoid or at least mitigate some potential conflicts of interest between the staff and their clients. This is particularly true for job security, because clients do not substitute the professional staff; rather, they work together with them for a common goal of better and/or more services (*ibid.*).

Vidal (2013) explores how multi-stakeholder techniques can promote cooperation between key stakeholders providing public services, in particular, collaboration between professional providers and users of public services. Their cooperation is both voluntary and it lasts over a period of time. She argues that a multi-stakeholder dialog and multi-stakeholder governance are two techniques that can help promote cooperation and a strategic partnership between them (*ibid.*). The concept of multi-stakeholder governance assumes that an organization's decision-making bodies include different stakeholders. So, they must engage in a dialog with each other and reach a compromise on many issues in order to survive and fulfill their expectations. Such an organization does not promote the expectation of a single stakeholder, but rather it defends various stakeholders' interests (*ibid.*). This is particularly important in the provision of social services, because users or clients are locked into such services, often for the life of the service from the user's perspective.

Multi-stakeholder governance implies a system of formal representation that provides both a voice and vote to all major stakeholders, while a multi-stakeholder dialog insures informal representation and a voice, but not necessarily a vote to all major stakeholders (*ibid.*). For example, in most parent co-op preschools in Sweden, the teachers attend the board meetings and they have a say, but not a vote, on important issues. Parents do, of course, listen closely to the staff and weigh their arguments carefully before deciding. Vamstad (2012) shows that parent cooperative preschool services in Sweden promote a dialog between the parents and teachers that leads to higher quality services than those available in the public sector. However, in traditional public preschool services, there is little dialog or collaboration between the parents and staff. Parents can, of course, make spontaneous, *ad hoc* suggestions for activities and contribute to the Christmas or spring party, but little else; that is not sustainable co-production. (See Chapter 5 for details.)

In addition to promoting a dialog between the staff and clients, both these techniques can also help to avoid some of the negative consequences of asymmetric information and power relations between providers and users of social services. Asymmetric information stifles communication between users and producers of services, or between the parents and teachers of preschool services. The lack of information also results in frustration among service users and inefficiencies. One classical way to reduce such inefficiencies would be for clients to use the exit option (Vidal, 2013). But, as already noted, exit is not feasible in many enduring social services. So, in the absence of exit, voice becomes a more realistic or at least a second best option. If the main stakeholders involved in the provision of a social service can be brought together and enter into a continuous and systematic dialog with each other about issues important for all of them, then steps can be taken to alleviate some of the asymmetric information and power relations between them (*ibid.*)

A closer look at Vamstad's (2007, 2012) comparative study of parent co-op and municipal preschool services in Sweden helps shed a bit more light on this topic. He shows that parents in parent co-ops felt much more informed about the activities and operation of the preschool than parents in municipal services. Nearly three-fourths of parents in parent co-ops claimed 'much' or 'very much' insight into the activities, while barely one-quarter of parents in municipal services did so (*ibid.*). Moreover, concerning the asymmetry of power, his study also shows that nearly nine-tenths of the parents claim that they have 'much' or 'very much' influence in parent co-ops, while less than half of the parents do so in municipal services (*ibid.*). These differences even hold for the staff. Nearly three-fifths of the staff in parent co-ops make a similar claim to having much influence, while barely one-third of the staff do so in municipal services. Moreover, more than one-third of the parents and nearly three of five staff members in municipal services claim they want more influence, while barely one-eighth of parents and notably less than one-fifth and staff do so in parent co-ops (*ibid.*). Thus, the high level of communication between the parents and staff that characterizes parent co-ops facilitates a mutual understanding of diverse problems, ranging from service quality to work environment, and also allows for such problems to be addressed swiftly and in close collaboration (*ibid.*). (See Chapter 5 for more details.)

C.5 *Small Group Models to Promote Sustainable Co-Production in Large Organizations*

Sustainable co-production can also be found in some large-scale providers of health care, under certain circumstances. A good example is found in cooperative health care in Japan, which depends in part on co-production. The Japanese Consumer Cooperative Union runs 76 hospitals, with an average bed count of just over 175 beds, making it a medium-scale operation. In this unique system, members are encouraged to actively take part in their own health care. Active health co-op members are divided into small discussion groups (*hans*) of five to seven members each and led by a trained leader. Members monitor their own blood pressure and heart rate, test the salt content of their urine, etc., and relate them to facts about their diet, exercise and lifestyle. These small cooperative groups meet regularly to discuss their health. The meetings cover a variety of items as food and diet plus exercise and lifestyle, with the aim of bringing them more in balance with each other. Small group dynamics and discussion can contribute to actively promoting a more healthy lifestyle and preventative health care. Moreover, the boards of directors of cooperative hospitals are organized as multi-stakeholder organizations with representatives of the various stakeholders, including the doctors, the other medical staff, the patients/members, etc. (Pestoff, 2008a, Chapter 7; Pestoff, Saito *et al.*, 2016). This provides patients with a clear channel for their voice in the cooperative hospital's decision-making.

D. Conclusions and Recommendations

Co-production promotes a mix of public service agents and citizens/users who contribute to the provision of public service. It is an essential part of a broader framework to provide a new theory for public service management: NPG. In contrast to the manufacturing-dominant approach of NPM, NPG comprises a service-dominant approach, where co-production becomes a central aspect of public service delivery. It places the experience and knowledge of the service user at the center of effective public service design and delivery. The OECD states that citizen participation is more important in the service delivery phase of social services than in general services. This also has some clear economic implications, because social services are often more labor intensive than general services. However, the OECD noted that considerations of strengthening user and citizen involvement *per se*, improving service quality and improving effectiveness and service outcome clearly weigh more heavily for most governments than increasing productivity or cutting cost.

This chapter explored factors that contribute to making citizen participation in public service delivery more sustainable, particularly in enduring welfare services. The early research on co-production felt that organizations were crucial because they could enhance the levels of co-production and facilitate the coordination between citizens and public authorities (Rich, 1981). This chapter argues that collective action can facilitate co-production and help make it more sustainable in several different ways. However, we noted that co-production is often a mix of individual and collective action. Therefore, we began by considering Olson's emphasis on the importance of group size for collective action. However, size is only one of seven structural variables that Ostrom maintained were important for overcoming collective action problems and she warned against giving size too much weight. The likelihood of cooperation depends on other variables and how they interact with size. Several of the structural variables she discusses for resolving dilemmas related to common pool resources also bear relevance for co-production. However, not all the structural variables that contribute to cooperation in a CPR situation are equally relevant for co-production. Some of them nevertheless seem to cluster into 'small group interactions' that facilitate citizen participation in the provision of public services. It was, therefore, necessary to consider some additional variables that can contribute to making co-production sustainable. They included the nature of the service itself, organizational diversity, small group dynamics in self-help groups and promoting a dialog between the staff and clients.

Moreover, services that only involve short-term or sporadic interactions between the professional providers and their clients cannot be expected to result in the same pattern of interaction between them nor the same degree of client participation as those found in more long-term or enduring welfare services. When it comes to long-term services, clients are in a more stable, long-term demand situation. They cannot easily switch providers if they are dissatisfied with the service, want different service or want to improve it, because the transaction costs of changing providers are prohibitive (Pestoff, 1998). Voice provides a more suitable medium of communication between them, and their collective interaction can help to amplify their voice. Thus, some form of client organization can facilitate their regular participation and can also impose collective control on 'free-riding'.

Governments will, therefore, need to weigh both the advantages and disadvantages of individual and collective co-production in different types of services and phases of service design and delivery. They also need to realize that co-production is often a mix of individual acts and collective action. Both can facilitate citizen participation in the delivery of public services, but they are often intertwined in a mix of individual and collective efforts. Governments should, therefore, not solely emphasize the benefits of one form, while ignoring those of the other, nor their mix. Government policies can both crowd-in and crowd-out citizen participation (Ostrom, 2000a). They can also promote individual and/or collective co-production. Failing to recognize the benefits of both and their natural mix in enduring welfare services can result in major hurdles to the development of co-production and citizen participation in the delivery of public services.

Given the implications of the 'logic of small group interaction' discussed earlier, governments should carefully weigh the benefits and costs of a policy that encourages and facilitates small groups to provide enduring welfare services for themselves with public funds. Thus, if they intend to facilitate more citizen co-production in the provision of enduring welfare services, they need to devise ways of promoting self-help groups, social service co-ops and other forms of third sector provision of enduring welfare services that tend to be small-scale and facilitate formal, collective interaction among well-defined groups of service users. In addition, given the wide range and diversity of TSOs, some may be better suited for promoting co-production than others, and some will facilitate more sustainable co-production than others. Social enterprises that conform to the EMES criteria (www.emes.net) appear to hold the most potential for sustainable co-production. Research also suggests the existence of a 'glass ceiling' for participation in public and private for-profit sector services, but shows that the third sector helps to breach this barrier. Moreover, sustainable co-production is not only a question of citizens/users assuming greater responsibilities for the provision of welfare services, but also granting them greater rights in designing, commissioning, delivering and evaluating them. In particular, small group dynamics can prove very important for facilitating the participation of persons with serious physical, mental, or social problems and for retaining their participation over time, i.e., turning them into sustainable co-producers of their own care. Furthermore, facilitating small group interaction in large organizations, like those found in Japanese co-op health care, could serve as a model for promoting co-production in other medium-sized welfare services, like eldercare, where the clients reside in domiciliary facilities. Here too, finding the right mix of individual and collective co-production is crucial.

It is also important to realize that co-production is not a panacea for the problems facing the provision of public services and that there is no 'one size fits all' solution for the great variety of services provided by governments in Europe. Therefore, it appears urgent for governments to develop the necessary policies and strategies that take differences in size, ownership and other important structural variables, like the nature of the service, into account. However, mechanistic attempts to replicate or scale-up successful small-scale experiments appear to be based on a flawed understanding of public service provision.

Finally, co-production is a new research field and little systematic comparative research is yet available (Verschuere *et al.*, 2012). In particular, there is still very little research on the mix of individual and collective co-production and how they are related to each other. Moreover, much more research is necessary in order to understand and take advantage of the potential benefits of collective action in making co-production more sustainable. Further comparative research is clearly necessary to understand citizen/user participation in various types of service providers, for different types of important welfare services and also in different countries. In particular, it would be interesting to compare small service co-ops with small and medium enterprises (SMEs) and other small social enterprises providing similar services. Moreover, efforts to facilitate a multi-stakeholder dialog between welfare providers and their clients may provide a key for promoting greater sustainability in the co-production of public financed welfare services. Both research on and policies designed to promote this should be encouraged in order to develop greater sustainability of co-production.

This brief summary suggests several important research topics related to sustainable co-production. This research would include studies that:

1. Compare the costs and benefits of individual, collective and mixed co-production for the public sector, the users or clients and citizens in order to better understand and facilitate sustainable co-production;
2. Develop new models and methods to better understand the relation between individual and collective co-production and their mix in enduring welfare services;
3. Compare co-production in different types of public services in order to discern which ones are typical or best suited for individual, collective and mixed co-production;
4. Compare citizen participation and co-production for different types of service providers, public, for-profit, nonprofit and cooperative, in order to discern how best to increase citizen participation in the forms of provision where it is lower;

5. Compare co-production and citizen participation in the delivery of public services in different countries in the same service, like preschool services, education, handicap care or eldercare, in order to discern which institutional arrangements promote greater citizen participation;

6. Compare citizen sustainable co-production in different public management regimes, like traditional public administration, NPM and NPG, in order to discern how and why one regime performs better than another in facilitating sustainable co-production; and

7. Compare different legal and institutional frameworks in order to discern if and how they facilitate sustainable citizen participation and co-production in the provision of enduring welfare services.

Taken together, they provide a robust, comparative research agenda on sustainable co-production that will promote a better understanding of individual, collective and mixed co-production and the participation of citizens in the design and delivery of public services.

8 Exploring Synergies Between Social Enterprise, Social Innovation and Co-Production

Key Post-NPM Concepts in Public Sector Reforms

The concepts of social enterprise, social innovation and co-production have much in common. They all have clear economic, political and social dimensions and they all refer to highly complex phenomena involving multiple dimensions that require a truly multi-disciplinary approach. Yet, the academic debate normally oversimplifies them, often from the perspective of a single discipline. This chapter notes their complex nature and explores potential links between them in relation to the delivery of public services. This should contribute to the conclusion from some of the earlier chapters that governments need to develop more flexible, service specific and organizational specific approaches for renewing public services. This could be achieved, at least in part, by facilitating and promoting social enterprise, social innovation and co-production, rather than looking for simple 'one size fits all' solutions to the challenges facing public service delivery.

A. A Field with Different Dimensions

The journal *Voluntas* (vol. 28/6, Dec. 2017) recently devoted a special issue to social enterprise and welfare regimes. It underlines the capacity of European social enterprises to remedy many of the welfare states' structural challenges, at core economic, political and social junctures, from the 1990s onward (Baglioni, 2017: 2325–2338). The academic debate on social enterprise in Europe emphasizes the importance of several aspects or dimensions. According to the EMES approach, social enterprises are not merely private firms that indirectly promote social values, provide social services or practice corporate social responsibility (CSR). Rather, they are organizations or firms that successfully combine different economic, social and governance functions. Similarly, the academic discourse on public sector innovations has moved beyond the traditional perspective employed by industry and manufacturing that does not fit well with the provision of public services. This debate recognizes that public sector innovations take various forms and promote a variety of goals. In addition to efficiency and effectiveness, they include both social and/or political goals. Also, the debate on co-production recognizes the existence of different kinds of citizen participation in the provision of public services, i.e., economic, social and political (Pestoff, 2006).

The concept of co-production is probably older than the other two (Ostrom, 1996), but it was notably absent from the academic and political debate in the 1980s and 1990s, in the wake of New Public Management (NPM). In the NPM era, its two cousins, social enterprise and social innovation, became key elements of alternatives to pure market solutions for the challenges facing the public sector and public services. So, co-production may appear to some as the 'new kid on the block', but in fact it has a lot in common with its cousins, social enterprise and social innovation. The aim of this chapter is to bring their common elements into clearer focus and discuss the implications of this for the study of public management.

The OECD (2011) considers co-production a major social innovation in the provision of public services, one that can provide greater user control and influence over public services. Osborne *et al.* (2013) argue that co-production is an essential part of a broader framework to provide a new theory for public service management—a service-dominant approach. It stands in sharp contrast to the manufacturing dominant approach of NPM, which caused a 'fatal flaw' in public management theory that views public services as manufacturing rather than as service processes Osborne *et al.* (2013). Services demonstrate three major differences with goods: (a) they are intangible, (b) they are subject to different production logics and, most important here, (c) the role of the user is qualitatively different in manufacturing and services. The latter are often co-produced by the professional providers and consumer of the services (Osborne *et al.*, 2013). Thus, public service needs to be understood from a broader framework called New Public Governance (NPG) (Osborne, 2010). Co-production can, therefore, make an important contribution to the debate on public management, because it is a key concept that goes to the core of both effective public services delivery and the role of public services in achieving societal ends, such as social inclusion and citizen participation (Osborne *et al.*, 2013: 145).

This chapter considers the main three dimensions of each of these post-NPM concepts. We will start by discussing the economic, political and social aspects of social enterprise, then turn to social innovation and finally to co-production. Recognizing their separate dimensions as well as understanding the similarity between them will facilitate forging links between them and also emphasize the synergy between the goals they promote. Less space is, however, given to co-production in this chapter as it has been discussed at length earlier. It briefly notes some comparative evidence from social enterprises providing childcare in Sweden, when we noted that co-production facilitates greater client and staff participation and influence than either public or for-profit services.

B. Social Enterprise

We will begin by considering the public debate on social enterprise and then turn our attention to the academic discourse.

B.1 The Public Debate

The public debate about social enterprise and social entrepreneurship suffers from a mix of the vagaries of two contrary tendencies. The first tendency is to define it in such broad terms that the rule seems to be 'anything goes'. So, almost any and every business firm, including those with only indirect or vague social goals, as well as those practicing some form of corporate social reporting or corporate philanthropy, can easily qualify as a 'social enterprise'. This is often a key part of their strategy to achieve greater sales, turnover and profit. The second tendency reflects the opposite rule; 'almost nothing qualifies' and very few organizations are able to meet the rigorous criteria necessary to gain official recognition as a social enterprise in some European countries. These two tendencies help illustrate the risk of market or bureaucratic capture of central academic concepts.

In the first case, some definitions of social enterprise are so vague or loose that a big international fast food chain might qualify as a social enterprise, because it offers many young people their first job and helps them get a foot into the labor market. In addition, it may also support or provide some important social services for a small group. However, while such activities may represent important social values, they don't comprise the main focus of such a big international food chain's business. Rather they are related to a business strategy of employing cheap unskilled labor in order to keep its costs down and/or promote its public image. So, they are a means to an end, rather than an end in themselves. Similarly, a mammoth retailer may provide jobs in many communities across the nation, which is clearly laudable in times of high unemployment, but such retailers are also notorious for their low wages and poor working conditions. But, it could perhaps qualify as a social enterprise under such vague criteria. Also, the world's largest tobacco manufacturer might qualify as a social enterprise, if it donated funds to a nonprofit to help feed the needy elderly in a major city. Or, why not consider a big European state-owned energy company that mines huge reserves of brown coal for its operations abroad and manages nuclear plants both inside and outside its national borders. Could it also be considered a social enterprise if it regularly arranged a marathon or other big sporting event in a major European capital? Could the term 'social enterprise' also be applied to a global electronics company that claims to be 'the number one social business enterprise in the world' simply because it improved the capacity of its corporate social report? Questions about the nature of social enterprise are not always easy to answer, especially without clear standards or guidelines, however these examples illustrate market capture of a central academic concept. Moreover, some neo-liberal governments in the EU also embrace a very broad definition of social enterprise in their efforts to privatize the provision of social services (Pestoff & Hulgård, 2016), which suggests political capture.

In the second case, some public bureaucrats, academics and even representatives of the social enterprise community itself can promote an agenda that employs a very narrow focus on a certain kind of social enterprise, to the exclusion of many others. For example, public bureaucrats can seize a new, popular academic term like social enterprise in an attempt to promote their own policy aims. Thus, the European Social Fund and public labor market agencies in several European countries have coupled the term social enterprise with policy aims of job creation, particularly for persons with a physical, social or psychological handicap. Understandably, public bureaucracies are interested in promoting work integration social enterprises (WISEs), because they appear to offer new and innovative ways to promote employment and job-training for their target populations. Therefore, public bureaucrats in some EU states define social enterprise so narrowly that it excludes most other types of cooperative social services, like childcare, eldercare, etc., or services of general interest and collectively managed enterprises serving a specific community. So, in the public debate in many EU countries, social enterprise has become synonymous with WISE. For example, the 2004 Finnish Act on Social Enterprises has a specific focus on WISE. A similar development can be observed in Denmark (Socialstyrelsen, 2014), Poland (Pestoff, 2011a) and Sweden (Levander, 2011). Thus, WISE has become equivalent to and sometimes even the official definition of social enterprise in certain EU countries. However, this excludes other phenomenon that fit closely with European academic approaches to the study of social enterprises. Thus, some observers even suggest that the European bureaucrats may have 'hijacked' the concept of social enterprise for their narrow policy goals, to the detriment of the public debate and development of the sector itself (Moulaert *et al.*, 2013; Pestoff & Hulgård, 2016). This is a prime example of bureaucratic capture of a central academic concept.

B.2 The Academic Debate

The terms 'social entrepreneurship' and 'social enterprise' are sometimes used interchangeably, but they should nevertheless be distinguished from each other. Academic definitions of social entrepreneurship can range from narrow to broad (Galera & Borzaga, 2009). According to the narrow definition, social entrepreneurship is clearly located in the nonprofit sector and refers to the adoption of entrepreneurial approaches by nonprofit organizations in order to earn extra income. This presumes that the social mission remains explicit and central to nonprofit organization activities. By contrast, broad definitions refer to a conception where this phenomenon can be found anywhere and in any business or setting, for-profit, nonprofit, public sector or any mix thereof (Galera & Borzaga, 2009: 212).

In continental Europe, social enterprise as an academic concept refers to an organizational unit or enterprise (Borzaga & Defourny, 2001; Defourny, 2007; Hulgård, 2014; Defourny & Nyssens, 2014). This understanding stems from strong collective traditions found in cooperatives, mutuals and associations in Europe (Defourny & Nyssens, 2006). Thus, the main feature of the European social enterprise tradition is setting up autonomous institutional structures specifically designed to pursue social goals in a stable and continuous way through the production of goods or services of general interest (Defourny & Nyssens, 2006: 213). The USA, by contrast, has shown a preference for the term social entrepreneurship and adopted a broader understanding of the term that includes the idea of "market based approaches to social issues" (Kerlin, 2006) that can be undertaken by any organization or firm in any sector of the economy. Moreover, this broad definition focuses more on the phenomenon of entrepreneurship and individual entrepreneurs than the organizations or enterprises involved in them, and more on the existence of a 'social mission' as a major or minor element of a corporate strategy than the process and governance dimension that can generate a social value (Moulaert *et al.*, 2013; Pestoff & Hulgård, 2016).

Much of the American debate on social enterprise appears dominated by economists, with little input from other disciplines, and it often promotes vaguely universal definitions. Thus, social enterprise is considered an activity that is "intended to address social goals through the operation of private organizations in the marketplace" (Young, 2008: 23) or it "involves the engagement of private sector forms of enterprise and market based activity in the achievement of social purpose" (Young, 2009: 175). However, such broad, market-oriented attempts to define social enterprise provide little guidance for understanding what to include or not to include in the term social enterprise.

B.3 Evolution of the European Perspective

In Europe, by contrast, the policy and legal context appears much more conducive to the development of social enterprises as welfare actors, and European legal frameworks reflect specific legal traditions, welfare regimes and economic issues dealt with at the national level. Thus, we find a greater diversity of approaches and solutions in Europe (Defourny & Nyssens, 2014: 218). This can take two expressions. On the one hand, in order to understand this gradual change in the third sector, the EMES scholars promoted a common definition of social enterprise, based on multiple and diverse indicators of social enterprises in various EU countries (Defourny & Nyssens, 2014). On the other hand, the EMES Network's efforts are based on an extensive dialog between and among several disciplines, including economics, sociology, political science and management. They also take into account the various national traditions present in the EU. Thus, the EMES Network emphasizes three main dimensions of social enterprises: their economic, social and governance dimensions (Pestoff & Hulgård, 2016).

According to EMES, a social enterprise's *economic project* is comprised of continuous production of a good or service, based on some paid work and it takes an economic risk. Its *social dimension* relies on pursuing an explicit social aim that is usually launched by a group of citizens or a third sector organization and that has clear limits on the distribution of its surplus or profit. Moreover, what makes the EMES approach truly unique is the existence of a third dimension, *participatory governance*. Here we find issues related to an organization's autonomy from both the state and market, its participatory nature of involving the major parties or stakeholders affected by its activities and the exercise of democratic decision-making, based on the idea of one-member/one-vote, rather than capital ownership or shareholders.

However, it is important to note that all three dimensions are necessary, yet none of them is sufficient itself. Only when they are combined or taken together can they help define and delimit social enterprise. Thus, the EMES approach clearly goes beyond the simple zero-sum perception of a continuum ranging from purely economic to purely social pursuits that dominates much of the American debate. Moreover, the interrelated nature of the EMES criteria helps reinforce them, making for a more robust sustainable phenomenon than if a single criterion was adopted or applied to the study of social enterprise. So, the more complex multi-dimensional approach of EMES has clear advantages over using a single dimension or criteria for defining social enterprises or relying on key concepts from a single discipline.

C. Public Sector Innovation: Traditional, Social and/or Governance?

Scholars define innovation in many different ways, however, most of them emphasize a newness aspect, primarily in terms of being new to the (public) organization that adopts it. However, these divergent definitions of innovation offer little consensus about what to include and how it is best achieved. For example, some authors equate innovation in public services with entrepreneurship or being proactive and taking risks in providing health care (Wood *et al.*, 2000; Salge & Vera, 2009; Hinz & Ingerfurth, 2013). Product and process innovations are commonly distinguished (Rogers, 1995). Product innovations can be understood as what is produced or, more appropriately in public sector settings, what kind of service is delivered. Process innovations pertain to how a service is provided (Walker, 2014: 23). Yet, process innovations can affect both the management and the organization, because they change relationships among organizational members and affect the rules, roles, procedures, structures, etc. (Walker, 2014).

Social innovation is an ambiguous term, with many and often contending definitions. There is, nevertheless, a growing realization of the difference between various types of innovation and the need to explore the uniqueness of social innovation. The latter is much more complex than simply applying standard business or market techniques to social issues. Social innovations neither stem from the research and development (R&D) centers of big business nor the bureaucracies of central government. The origin of social innovations can vary widely, as noted by some authors. For example, Johnson (2010) suggests that there are four different sources or environments that facilitate the creation of new ideas, processes and things. They can be divided into two main categories: market-networked and non-market-networked innovations. Fulsang and Sundbo (2009) distinguish between entrepreneurial or technology-based innovations, on the one hand, and value-based or reflexive innovations, on the other. A key objective of the WILCO Project— Welfare Innovations at the Local Level in Favor of Social Cohesion (Brandsen, 2014)—was an attempt to contextualize the social innovations and to understand them from the wider social and political context in which they originate. Brandsen, Evers *et al.* (2016) compare and contrast two main types of innovations, market or R&D innovations, like the iPhone and social innovations. The former are intentionally non-contextual and therefore designed to sell in different markets around the world. Social innovations include the numerous local solutions to homelessness, unemployment, etc. illustrated by their book (Brandsen & Honingh, 2015).

The Bureau of European Policy Advisers (BEPA), defines social innovation as "innovations that are social both in their ends and means . . . that simultaneously meet social needs (more effectively than alternatives) and create new social relationships or collaborations" (BEPA, 2010: 7). Furthermore, Beckers *et al.* (2013) argue that social innovations in public services have four distinct elements. First, they aim to achieve long-term outcomes that are relevant for society. Second, they go beyond technical changes by promoting fundamental changes in social relationships. Third, most of the important stakeholders, especially the end users, should be involved in the design, development and implementation of new goods and services. Finally, social innovation not only refers to the achievement of new outcomes, but also to the very processes of innovation. Thus, they are usually open to, but also embedded in a specific local and institutional context, something that may make it harder to replicate or scale them up (Brandsen, 2014: 3–4; Brandsen & Honingh, 2015).

Governance innovation in the public sector is a specific category or type of social innovation, because it involves changes in the relationship between service providers and their clients in ways that imply new forms of citizen engagement and new democratic institutions (Hartley, 2005). Rather than being limited to changes within a single organization, most public sector innovation takes place above the level of a given organization and transforms the social structures and processes that deal with a problem (Moore & Hartley, 2012: 55). They propose four interrelated criteria to distinguish public sector innovations from private sector product and process innovations. Governance innovation should (a) create network-based production systems; (b) mobilize new pools of resources that can extend or improve the performance of such services; (c) change the instruments that governments use to steer the production system for achieving social goals; and (d) alter the configuration of decision-making. Furthermore, this can raise important questions about the distribution of rights and responsibilities in society and how best to evaluate them (Moore & Hartley, 2012: 68–69). Thus, in addition to the economic or financial aspects, social innovations in the public sector have clear social and political implications.

Moreover, it is important to distinguish between the outcome of a social innovation achieving some or all of its goals and the very processes involved in achieving them. The latter can provide an added value in terms of promoting collaboration between various participants and generating social capital. Thus, the participation process of social innovations is very important in itself. The open participation of various stakeholders gives each of them a stake in the innovation. It also provides the glue that creates connections and relations between various stakeholders and links between the different levels of the innovations process that help them to survive and eventually succeed in the local context.

D. Co-Production

D.1 Co-Production: Some Conceptual Issues

Nobel Laureate Elinor Ostrom and her colleagues analyzed the role of citizens in the provision of public services in terms of co-production (Parks *et al.*, 1981). The concept of co-production was originally developed by Ostrom and the Workshop in Political Theory and Policy Analysis at Indiana University during the 1970s to describe and delimit the involvement of ordinary citizens in the production of public services (Ostrom, 1996). They struggled with the dominant theories of urban governance, whose underlying policies recommended massive centralization of public services, but they found no support for claims of the benefits of large bureaucracies. They also realized that the production of services, in contrast to goods, was difficult without the active participation of those persons receiving the service (*ibid.*).

Thus, they developed the term 'co-production' to describe the potential relationship that could exist between the 'regular producer', like street-level police officers, schoolteachers, or health workers, and their clients who wanted to be transformed by the service into safer, better-educated or healthier persons (see Parks *et al.*, 1981). Initially, co-production had a clear focus on the role of individuals or groups of citizens in the production of public services. Co-production is, therefore, noted by

> the mix of activities that both public service agents and citizens contribute to the provision of public services. The former are involved as professionals or 'regular producers', while 'citizen production' is based on voluntary efforts of individuals or groups to enhance the quality and/or quantity of services they receive. (*ibid.*)

More recently, Bovaird (2007) proposed another definition of co-production: "User and community co-production is the provision of services through regular, long-term relationships between professionalized service providers (in any sector) and service users and/or other members of the community, where all parties make substantial resource contributions" (*ibid.*: 847). This definition focuses not only on users, but also includes volunteers and community groups as co-producers, recognizing that each of these groups can have a quite different relationship to public sector organizations.

As noted earlier, the OECD argues that co-production is social innovation in public services, because it promotes a partnership that governments form with citizens and civil society organizations in order to innovate and deliver improved public service outcomes. Moreover, such partnerships offer creative policy responses that enable governments to provide better public services in times of fiscal constraints; thus, governments consider citizen input as a source of innovation and change (*ibid.*). Furthermore, compared with existing solutions of private sector involvement, the emerging focus on greater citizen participation transforms the relationship between service users and providers, ensuring more user control and ownership (*ibid.*). However, co-production involves more than merely consulting with clients. In addition, citizen participation is more important in the delivery phase of social services than in general services, where citizens are more active in service design. This has some major economic implications, because social services are more labor intensive than general services. However, the OECD noted that government motives for embracing co-production put greater weight on considerations of strengthening user and citizen involvement *per se*, improving service quality and improving effectiveness and service outcome than on increasing productivity or cutting cost (OECD, 2011).

D.2 The Three Main Dimensions of Co-Production

Results from two separate studies of alternative providers of public financed childcare in Europe and Sweden help illustrate the processes in social enterprises that promote more client/citizen participation in delivering public financed services, namely greater co-production. The results of these studies have been presented earlier in Chapters 4 and 5 and won't be repeated in detail here. However, they will be briefly summarized for the context of the argument about a synergy between these three key concepts.

The TSFEPS Project, described in Chapter 4, examined the relationship between parent participation in the provision and governance of childcare in eight EU countries (Pestoff, 2006). It found different levels of parent participation in different countries and in different forms of provision, such as public, private for-profit and third sector childcare. The highest levels of parent participation were found in third sector providers, like parent associations in France, parent initiatives in Germany and parent cooperatives in Sweden. It also noted the existence of different kinds of parent participation, i.e., economic, political and social. All three kinds of participation were readily evident in third sector providers of childcare services, while both economic and political participation were much more restricted in municipal and private for-profit services.

Vamstad's follow-up study (2007), reported in Chapter 5, compared parent and worker co-ops, municipal services and small for-profit firms providing childcare in two regions of Sweden: Stockholm and Östersund. His study not only confirms the existence of the three main dimensions of co-production, but also underlines the difference between various providers concerning the saliency of these dimensions. Both these studies demonstrate that parent co-ops in Sweden provide parents with unique possibilities for active participation in the management and running of their child(ren)'s childcare facility and for unique opportunities to become active co-producers of high quality childcare services for their own and others' children. It is also clear that other forms of childcare allow for some limited forms of co-production in public financed childcare, but parents' possibilities for influencing the management of such services remains rather limited.

These studies demonstrate that co-production by social enterprises promotes social and governance innovations in the provision of public services and provide a key component for rethinking public service management. Co-production of social services offers new opportunities as well as challenges for collective solutions to growing problems facing the public provision of social services in Europe. It gives citizens both more choice and more voice, as well as allowing and encouraging them to play a more active role in the decision-making processes surrounding the design and delivery of public services. Yet, co-production is a new concept that remains relatively unknown and mostly absent from the academic and political debates about reforming public services in many European countries.

Its place in the Nordic countries varies considerably, and it is not nearly as established or widely used as concepts like social enterprise and social innovation. In Denmark co-production has gained considerable traction in recent years and has become quite well established in both the political and academic debates (Thomsen & Jakobsen, 2015; Hald Larsen, 2015; Tortzen, 2016). It is also beginning to gain recognition in Finland, both in the political and academic debates (Botero *et al.*, 2012; Pekkola *et al.*, 2015; Tuurnas, 2015), and it is occasionally mentioned in the academic debate in Norway (Larsgaard *et al.*, 2015). But, it is almost absent from the Swedish debate about reforming public services, except by a few internationally oriented scholars mentioned earlier. Perhaps closer Nordic cooperation in the academic and policy fields will eventually promote a greater understanding and appreciation of this conceptual 'new kid on the block'.

E. Summary and Conclusions

The concepts of social enterprise, social innovation and co-production share much in common and comprise three related post-NPM concepts. This chapter considered their three main dimensions, i.e., their economic, political and social dimensions. We noted the importance of all three dimensions in all three of these key concepts. We argued that recognizing these separate dimensions as well as understanding the similarity between them could facilitate forging links between them and help emphasize the mutuality or synergy of the goals they promote. All three require a multi-disciplinary approach to thoroughly understand their potential contribution to renewing the public sector and public services in the 21st century.

The EMES Network developed nine ideal type criteria for defining and delimiting social enterprise that were later combined into three economic, three political and three social criteria. According to this approach, a social enterprise's *economic project* is comprised of continuous production of a good or service, based on some paid work and it takes an economic risk. Its *social dimension* relies on pursuing an explicit social aim, it is usually launched by a group of citizens or a third sector organization and has clear limits on the distribution of its surplus or profit. A truly unique aspect of the EMES approach is the third dimension, *participatory governance*. Here we find issues related to an organization's autonomy from both the state and market, its participatory nature of involving the major parties or stakeholders affected by its activities and the exercise of democratic decision-making, based on the idea of one-member/one-vote, rather than capital ownership or shareholders. However, it is important to note that all three dimensions are necessary, yet none of them is sufficient on its own. Only when combined or taken together can they help define and delimit social enterprise.

Social innovation is an ambiguous term, with many and often contending definitions. The BEPA defines it as "innovations that are social both in their ends and means . . . that simultaneously meet social needs (more effectively than alternatives) and create new social relationships or collaborations" (BEPA, 2010: 7). Brandsen (2012) suggests that social innovations in the public sector promote closer collaboration between professional providers and their clients. Moreover, governance innovation is a specific category or type of social innovation, because it involves changes in the relationship between service providers and their clients in ways that imply new forms of citizen engagement and new democratic institutions (Hartley, 2005). Thus, in addition to economic or financial aspects, social innovations in the public sector have clear social and political implications. Moreover, it is important to distinguish between the outcome of a social innovation and the very processes involved in achieving it. The latter can provide an added value in terms of promoting collaboration between various participants and generating social capital.

Co-production focuses on the collaboration between professional providers and their clients. Ostrom and her colleagues developed the term in the late 1970s to describe the potential relationship that could exist between the 'regular producer', like street-level police officers, schoolteachers, or health workers, and their clients who wanted to be transformed by the service into safer, better-educated or healthier persons (see Parks *et al.*, 1981). The

OECD (2011) regards co-production as an important social innovation in public services that promotes a partnership between governments and citizens/civil society organizations in order to deliver improved public service outcomes. Co-production implies new forms of citizen engagement and the development of new participative democratic institutions in the public sector, thereby emphasizing the potential to be a significant social and governance innovation for the public sector.

Empirical evidence from two comparative studies of childcare demonstrates the unique capacity of small social services co-ops to promote all three dimensions (economic, social and governance) of the three main concepts (social enterprise, social innovation and co-production) in the renewal of public services. This unique constellation of concepts and the clear similarity between their three central dimensions underlines their mutual contribution to renewing public service. Moreover, the empirical evidence demonstrates that they can clearly deliver on their promise to curtail costs while also promoting and developing social and democratic goals in the public sector.

Thus, we need to forge closer links between the three key post-NPM concepts, social enterprise, social innovation and co-production, in order to fully understand their potential contribution to renewing the public sector and the management of public services. We also need to make links between the multiple dimensions involved in these complex and interrelated concepts and forge closer links between the various disciplines interested in studying these phenomena. Focusing on a single dimension or employing the approach of a single academic discipline will not prove sufficient to fully understand them. We need to avoid vain searches for simple solutions to complex matters. If we want to explore ways to diminish the growing democracy deficit in most European welfare states, it is important to understand the overlap between the political dimensions of social enterprise, social innovation and co-production, particularly given their high degree of similarity. Moreover, there are clear similarities between them and democratic governance. The latter does not just refer to new voter techniques or a new internet computer technology (ICT) approach. It needs to focus on changing social relations between the professional providers of public services and its users, involving new groups in decision-making and promoting new ways of including the end users of public services in both their design and delivery.

If governments intend to facilitate citizen participation in the provision of enduring social services, they will need to devise ways of promoting self-help groups, social service co-ops and other forms of third sector provision of enduring welfare services that tend to be small-scale and facilitate formal, collective interaction among well-defined groups of service users. But, mechanistic attempts to replicate or scale-up successful small-scale experiments appear to be based on a flawed understanding of public service provision.

Finally, co-production is a new research field compared with social enterprise and social innovation, and little systematic comparative research is yet available (Verschuere *et al.*, 2012). Recognizing their common dimensions and traits could help to give co-production research a more focused role in rethinking public service management. Comparative research is necessary to understand citizen/user participation in various types of service providers for different types of welfare services and also in different countries. In particular, it would be interesting to compare small service co-ops with small and medium enterprises (SMEs) and other small social enterprises providing similar services. Research on social enterprises and social innovation should be encouraged in order to promote more sustainable co-production.

9 Co-Production at the Crossroads of Public Administration Regimes

What Role for Service Users, Providers and the Third Sector?

Citizens play numerous roles in modern, post-industrial societies and they are usually involved in several different institutions that govern these roles. Among others, they are consumers, clients of public services, members of organizations, voters in democratic elections, activists in *ad hoc* groups, family members of a household, wage earners on the labor market, etc. (Pestoff, 1998). Some of these diverse roles may come in conflict with each other, but the institutions that govern them can also provide citizens with alternative channels of influence. In addition, citizens maintain different relations with the persons, firms and/or organizations that provide them with goods and services. They are consumers of goods and products, customers of services sold on the market, clients of services provided by the public sector and citizens of the state where they were born and/or live (*ibid*.: 70). The content of these relations and roles can and does change over time, as seen with the spread of New Public Management (NPM). NPM depoliticized the relations between citizens and the state. This was achieved, in part, by introducing market mechanisms between citizens and the state that augmented their role as clients and customers of the goods and services once provided by the public sector, but diminished their rights as citizens (Pierre, 1996; Pestoff, 1998). The market, rather than the state became the chief mechanism for determining the 'will of the people'.

This example helps to illustrate that a concept can acquire new, and sometimes conflicting, meanings in different public administration regimes (PARs). In particular, new concepts like social enterprise, social innovation or co-production can be interpreted quite differently in different PARs. Similarly, the role of citizens who use goods and services and the persons who provide the same can also shift with different PARs. In this chapter we will focus on the role of the principal actors in co-production, i.e., the users and providers of public financed services, and of third sector organizations (TSOs) that sometimes deliver them.

After introducing the concept of public administration regimes, this chapter briefly presents four of them, i.e., traditional public administration, New Public Management (NPM), New Public Governance (NPG) and a Communitarian regime. Changes in public administration regimes will set limits for citizen participation and co-production of public services, as well as establish the parameters for service users and providers, and third sector organizations and their leaders. It is, therefore, important to compare PARs and understand how they differ in terms of their values and focus, particularly for service users and providers and the third sector.

A. Background

Traditional definitions of co-production range from "the mix of activities that both public service agents and citizens contribute to the provision of public services" to "a partnership between citizens and public service providers", where the service professionals collaborate with their clients, either as individuals or in groups, who want to enhance the quality and/or quantity of the services on which they depend. Therefore, Ostrom coined the term 'co-production' to capture the potential relationship between the 'regular producer', like street-level police officers, schoolteachers or health workers, and their clients who want to be transformed by the service into safer, better-educated or healthier persons (see Parks *et al.*, 1981). She also reminds us that co-production attributes citizens an active role in the provision of public goods and services of consequences to them, rather than the passive one usually assigned to public sector clients (1996: 1073).

Today, co-production appears to be at the crossroads between different public administration regimes, with a different focus on when, where, why and how citizens can and should participate in the design and delivery of public services. In particular, they have different ideas about the role of users and professionals in promoting service quality. So, we need to ask what impact do different public administrative regimes have on our perception of and the type of co-production that develops. Co-production may mean something quite different in different public administration regimes. So, our perspective on and definition of co-production will depend largely on the context in which we study the phenomenon.

B. Four Public Administration Regimes

In the immediate post–World War II period, citizens faced a rapidly expanding, yet basically traditional public administration, with its hierarchical chain of command, where they were primarily viewed as passive clients or beneficiaries of public services. Later, in the 1980s and 1990s, with the spread of New Public Management (NPM), they were expected to become active consumers and exercise more choice between various providers of public financed services, either public, private for-profit or nonprofit. Here the market replaced the state as the main mechanism for governing the expression of citizens' preferences. More recently, we find the spread of network society (Hartley, 2005) or New Public Governance (NPG) (Osborne, 2006, 2010). NPG implies a more plural and pluralist model of provision and governance of welfare services. It is based on public-private networks, where citizens are expected to play an active role as co-producers of some aspects of the services they demand and have come to depend upon in their daily life. A fourth alternative public administration regime (PAR) now appears on the horizon, called here a Communitarian regime. We need, therefore, to inquire how changes in the public sector and the development of new public administration regimes are reflected in their perspective on the role of service users and professional service providers, as well as their potential impact on the relationship between the third sector and public sector.

This presentation employs some figures that relate these four public administration regimes to each other in terms of their two main dimensions, i.e., citizen activity in and social responsibility for service provision. This allows us to compare the public administration regimes in terms of the role played by the key actors in co-production, i.e., the service users and service providers.

Figure 9.1 briefly summarizes some of the main points about different public administration regimes, but cannot cover all aspects, since that would take us far beyond the scope and purpose of this chapter. In particular, we briefly consider the theoretical roots, value base and some key concepts of each administrative regime. After, attention is given to the role of the principal actors in co-production, i.e., the service users and professionals of public financed social services. Here, we can both note some similarities and striking contrasts between different public administration regimes. Taken together these elements comprise crucial aspects of different public administration regimes, similar to the idea of different welfare regimes (Esping-Andersen, 1990) and production regimes (Kitschelt *et al.* 1999). In particular, PARs attribute quite different weight to the role of citizens and professionals in public service delivery, and their perspective differs sharply on how to guarantee service quality (Vamstad, 2012).

From a historical perspective, we will begin with traditional public administration, as seen during most of the 20th century, followed by New Public Management (NPM), starting in the 1980s, and more recently the newly emerging paradigm of New Public Governance (NPG) at the turn of the century, based on ideas of network governance. We conclude this brief overview with a potential new regime found in ideas of community and volunteering, illustrated by Big Society in the United Kingdom, integrated community care in Japan and similar phenomenon elsewhere. While these four regimes differ in some important aspects, they also share some common features. Although each public administration regime may be linked to a particular ideology or historical period, they can also be conceived as 'layered realities' that co-exist with each other (Hartley, 2005; Osborne, 2010). Thus, more than one regime may be found in any given society at any given time, operating in different service sectors. One public administration regime may dominate in one sector, while another may do so in another. Moreover, they can shift over time, through the spread and ascent of a new public administration regime.

Two variables are employed herein to analyze the relations between and among public administration regimes: (a) the degree of citizen activity in

Active

Communitarian	**Now Public Governance**
Individual responsibility. Mix of market and community ideology. Volunteering & charity. Night watchman state. Users are 'enforced' service providers.	Shared responsibility. Network theory. Service processes and outcomes. Governs through networks. Users are co-producers.

Individual ————————————————————————▶ **Collective**

New Public Managemant	**Traditional Public Admin.**
Efficiency – lowest cost. Public choice theory. Manufacturing logic. Freedom of choice. Users are customers.	Equal treatment of all citizens. Hierarchical control to implement policy. Serve the public. Public goods provided by public servants. Users are passive beneficiaries.

Passive

Figure 9.1 Public Administration Regimes: Citizen Participation and Responsibility

providing a public service and (b) the institutional arrangement or degree of public responsibility for providing basic public services. The first variable is rather straightforward and ranges from low to high. The second is more complex, but reflects the degree of public vs. private responsibility for providing services to citizens. Health care or childcare can illustrate this. Is it a universal service provided to everyone in a given territory, or is it mainly dependent on individual initiative, where access to service often depends on controlling various private assets? In the former case there is a collective responsibility for providing a service, with certain limits or restrictions based on eligibility, while the responsibility is primarily individual in the latter case. This variable ranges from individual to collective. Figure 9.1 depicts these four PARs in terms of these two analytical dimensions.

B.1 Traditional Public Administration

Traditional public administration promises equal treatment of all citizens and has its theoretical roots in sociology, political science and public policy. It is based on a hierarchical model of command and control, stemming from ideas of Max Weber, with clear lines of vertical authority and responsibility. His ideas were later developed and expanded by President Woodrow Wilson (Ostrom & Ostrom, 1971). The value base of traditional public administration is found in public sector ethos, or serving the public, and its key concept is public goods that are provided by public or civil servants. It places a heavy emphasis on professional policy implementation and bureaucratic norms that determine good service quality.

B.2 New Public Management

New Public Management (NPM) promises greater efficiency in the provision of public services and lower costs. Its theoretical roots were found in growing criticism in the 1980s of the inefficiencies of traditional public administration, that were articulated in 'public choice' theory and management studies. It promoted ideas of the marketization and commercialization of public services in order to rectify these shortcomings and improve the efficiency and productivity of public sector services. Managerialism plays a big role in NPM. Its value base stems from industry and it promotes a manufacturing logic that emphasizes service inputs and outputs, rather than a service logic that focuses on outcomes (Osborne *et al.*, 2013). Its key concepts are 'freedom of choice' for consumers and competition between various providers in order to insure good service quality.

B.3 New Public Governance

New Public Governance (NPG) is premised on a shared responsibility for the provision of public goods and services; its theoretical roots stem from sociology and network theory. Its value base is considered as 'participatory democracy' by some (Pestoff, 2009) and 'neo-corporatist' by others (Osborne, 2010). NPG is based on a service logic of production that focuses on service processes and outcomes, where public value is a key concept (Denhardt & Denhardt, 2008). It governs through networks and partnerships, where the third sector and social enterprises can play an important role and citizens are active co-producers of public services. Citizen interaction with professionals also help to determine what is considered good quality service.

B.4 Communitarian Regime

The following is an early approximation at best, although more clues are gleaned from Brudney and England (1983), Horne and Shirley (2009), and Bovaird and Löffler (2012). A Communitarian regime is premised on citizens having individual responsibility for provision of goods and services they require. Several examples help illustrate this, although some may now appear a bit dated. The Coalition Government in the UK after 2010 introduced a program called Big Society to promote community empowerment by reorganizing public services and facilitating social action (Slocock, 2015; Hudson, 2011). Its value base stems from volunteering, philanthropy and charity, accompanied by significant budget cuts for public services, while it encourages families, communities and the third sector to fill the vacuum left behind. Citizens become informal caregivers or 'enforced' co-producers who are responsible for providing much of their own welfare and care services (Fotaki, 2011). Similar policies have surfaced elsewhere: in Japan, under the guise of 'Integrated Community Care' for the elderly and disabled (Agenosono *et al.*, 2014; Tsutsui, 2014; Tabata, 2014); as NGOization in Thailand (Ungsuchaval, 2016); and in Europe, including Denmark (cf. Politiken, 2015) and the Netherlands (cf. Nederhand & Van Meerkerk, 2017), under the label of 'co-production and/or co-creation'. These diverse policy expressions are gathered herein under the heading of a 'Communitarian type of regime'. Citizens are now primarily responsible for implementing public services. However, given the patchwork nature of service provision by users and family, it is difficult to develop any standards for service delivery.

C. The Role of the Principal Actors in Determining Service Quality

We will continue by briefly contrasting PARs in terms of the role played by citizen/users and the professional staff. They are the two principal actors according to classical definitions of co-production (Parks *et al.*, 1981; Ostrom, 1996). We will explore their role in promoting service quality. Then, we will also comment on the implications for the third sector in service delivery.

C.1 The Role of Citizens and Users in Service Quality

The role of user in the provision of public financed services is central to this analysis. Thus, we can envision the role of users of public services as either beneficiaries, consumers, co-producers or informal caregivers/service providers of such services, as depicted in Figure 9.2. The figure also indicates some important attributes of these different roles. They are related to the most important dimensions of our analysis, the level of activity by service users and the degree of individual or collective action necessary to make such services available to themselves.

Traditional public administration tends to be perceived as paternalistic by many because it is achieved through the 'professional gift' model of service provision. Here citizens are considered the beneficiaries of public services, in a typically passive role as recipients of services, with few or no exit or voice options available to them. Their only recourse or channel of influence is found in the electoral system, which at best can provide indirect, intermittent representation of their interest, depending on the outcome of an election.

New Public Management often attempts to achieve its goals by using a 'carrot and stick' approach to incentives, both for providers and users of services, which can either discourage or reward different kinds of behavior.

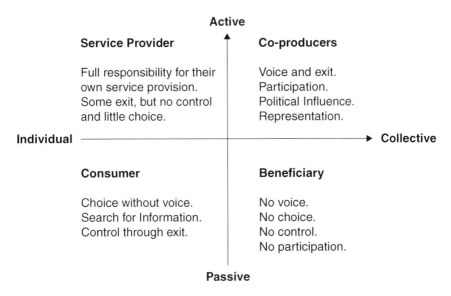

Figure 9.2 The Role of Citizens as Users of Public Services

Here citizens are considered customers with some limited choice, but little voice and no representation. They can choose between pre-existing packages or 'offers', but they have little influence on the content of the service or any of its features. Service quality is guaranteed through competition, where consumer choice determines the best quality.

New Public Governance is based on ideas of establishing a partnership between citizens and the government, where citizens are considered co-producers of public services. This not only gives them both choice and voice in service provision, but in some cases, even representation that gives them much greater direct influence than either traditional public administration or NPM. Here service quality is determined primarily by user participation, which allows them to observe service delivery on a weekly or even daily basis. This, in turn, promotes a dialog and mutual exchange between the professional providers and service users, among other things about service quality (Vamstad, 2012; Vidal, 2013).

Finally, in a *Communitarian regime* the role of service users is to provide many public services by and for themselves, with little or no public support, sometimes alongside, but often instead of the professionals. Here users and/ or their loved-ones and neighbors become informal caregivers or service providers, while professionals are transformed into 'back-up' agents who only intervene when the informal care provided proves insufficient. Determination of service quality becomes more like patchwork, because access depends on the availability, willingness and capacity of service providers or informal caregivers, which can vary considerably.

C.2 *The Role of Professionals in Determining Service Quality*

The role of professionals in guaranteeing service quality is contrasted in Figure 9.3.

In terms of service quality *Traditional public administration* relies heavily, if not exclusively, on training and professionalism to guarantee good service quality (Vamstad, 2012). Professionals in a hierarchal command and control system guarantee service quality through their training; thus, they alone decide on and prescribe appropriate measures, based on their professional knowledge, experience and insights. Collaboration, negotiations and competition are not normally taken into account in professional decisions. *New Public Management*, by contrast, places heavy emphasis on competition and consumer choice in relation to service quality, thus, leaving it to the market to provide a guarantee of service quality, rather than the activity or training of professional service providers or negotiations. NPM assumes that service quality is guaranteed by consumer choice, because better quality providers will attract more customers than inferior products or services. Professionals, regardless of whether public, private or nonprofit, will, therefore, focus strongly on competition between providers. Here, the mind set of professionals does not focus on either command and control or collaboration, but rather on competition between providers. Moreover, competition is necessary to attract new resources and expand operations.

New Public Governance emphasizes collaboration and negotiation between partners, regardless of whether public, private or nonprofit. Given this focus, user participation and mutual dialog between service users and the

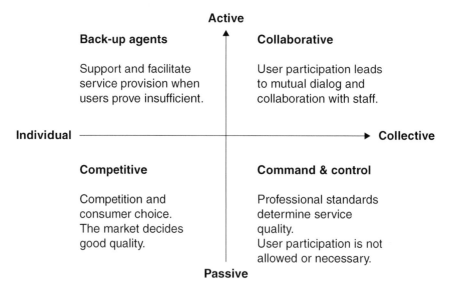

Figure 9.3 The Role of Professionals in Guaranteeing Service Quality

staff replaces professionalism or competition as the main guarantee of service quality (Vamstad, 2012; Vidal, 2013). Finally, the perspective of a *Communitarian regime* remains largely undeveloped in this respect, but professionals can complement informal care/service provision, by steering users/caregivers to available resources in the community or to voluntary organizations. However, the consequence of this for service quality or availability of services for different groups of users/caregivers remains to be seen.

C.3 The Role of the Third Sector as a Service Provider

The role of the third sector in delivering public funded services also varies considerably in these four public administration regimes. According to *traditional public administration*, third sector organizations are supposed to function as advocates of underprivileged citizens and/or providers of public financed services, for which they receive grants. By contrast, according to *NPM*, the third sector is expected to operate more or less like private firms do in the market. They are supposed to compensate for the loss of public funding by developing their commercial skills and functioning like 'social businesses'. Now they are expected to compete with other TSOs, often their previous partners, for public grants, as well as with private firms and multinational venture capitalists. When they are unable to win against such competitors, as research often shows is the case, they are advised to downplay their particular values, bridge their differences and amalgamate with other TSOs, or at least form consortia that can prepare more professional bids for public contracts.

New Public Governance governs through networks, in partnership with private service providers, including private for-profit firms and private nonprofit organizations. Here the third sector becomes the partner with the state, in collaboration with other service providers, where the 'rules of the game' are based on collaboration, rather than competition or simply following directives from their superiors. Finally, the role of TSOs remains unclear in a *Communitarian regime*, because they have no, or at best very limited, public funding. They are expected to help fill the gap left by sharp cutbacks in public services, but basically left to fend for themselves as service providers or to become 'social businesses' that can compete on the market with other consortia or private firms, in order to earn their income, rather than depending on grants from the state. They can only provide the services that their members are able to finance themselves or those that get funding from charitable donations. Critics from the UK voluntary sector lament that Big Society's objective to open up public services is "one of its greatest disappointments" (Independence Panel, 2015), while another states that "the biggest loser in Big Society has been the voluntary sector itself" (Slocock, 2015). In Japan, Integrated Community Care expects the community and third sector to provide services to the elderly and disabled persons instead of the public sector (Agenosono *et al.*, 2014; Tsutsui, 2014).

Thus, we find that each public administration regime has separate theoretical roots, value base, key concepts, as well as different roles for citizens, professionals and the third sector. Together they result in a unique constellation that helps distinguish one PAR from another. These differences have clear implications for co-production and the third sector. Co-production or citizen participation can, therefore, develop in different directions, with a different content and meaning in each PAR. Each of these directions implies different roles for service users and the professional staff. Historically, co-production doesn't appear to be a highly relevant concept for either traditional public administration or New Public Management, because both rely mainly on passive clients/customers, although both may pay lip service to active clients for strategic considerations. By contrast, a Communitarian regime and New Public Governance promote active users to a much greater extent, encouraging them to provide certain aspects of their own services, with or without public support and/or financing. In an NPG type of PAR, promotion of co-production will go hand in hand with a greater emphasis on citizens, democratic participation and the revitalization of democracy (Pestoff, 2009). In a Communitarian type of PAR, by contrast, efficiency and cutback in public spending will provide the main motive for promoting greater community and volunteer responsibility for service provision. It is natural, therefore, to expect that co-production will develop both in an individual or collective fashion and that it will involve more or less citizen participation, depending on the public administration regime. However, the mix of these two variables will be regime specific and service specific. These potential developments are shown in Figure 9.4.

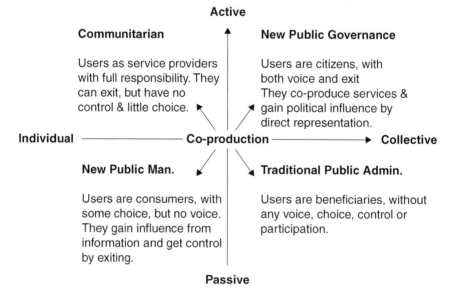

Figure 9.4 Co-Production at the Crossroads

This clearly poses challenges for the leaders of TSOs and complicates their situation. They need to understand these differences and what the implications of following one path of development means in relation to following another. Moreover, taken together, the growth of divergent PARs implies a more plural and pluralist world where TSOs and their leaders must learn to navigate between competing views and visions and choose to follow one that best encompasses values and aspirations for the future. These differences are discussed in greater detail in Chapter 10.

D. Summary and Conclusions

The roles of service users and professional service providers show similarities, but also some clear contrasts in different PARs, especially in terms of how they determine service quality. Also, the role of the third sector as a provider of public services is very different in different PARs. This analysis suggests that co-production appears very much at the crossroads today, with starkly different roles for its key actors, the users and professionals, and thus, it has a potential for developing in quite different directions. It will, therefore, take different meanings in different public administrative regimes. The role attributed or allowed to it will, however, depend in part on the level of activity ascribed to users and in part to the degree of individual or collective action necessary to achieve those goals or provide the service. However, each PAR not only implies different values, but also different roles for the public sector, as well as for professionals, users/citizen participation and for the third sector as a provider of public services. The way in which co-production develops depends, therefore, on the interplay of forces at the micro- and macro-levels of society that favor the development of one PAR rather than another. Obviously, the government alone can't dictate or decide to have more or less co-production; however, it can facilitate collective co-production or crowd it out.

Co-production is currently at the crossroads of major economic, social and political developments. This chapter argued that changes in public administration regimes not only set limits for citizen participation in the provision of public services and the focus of the professional service providers, but also set the parameters for activity of TSOs. One public administration regime may emphasize one set of competences, while another will give priority to another. Moreover, if TSOs leave the 'comfort zone' of a familiar public administration regime, the new 'rules of the game' in another PAR are often very complex and demanding. This can subject TSOs to new and sometimes contradictory logics, when they operate in uncharted waters, and where different professional competencies may be required to survive. This clearly poses challenges for the leaders of TSOs and complicates their situation; they must attempt to understand these differences and what the implications of following one path of development means in relation to another.

Moreover, people hold different theories and values that lead them, quite reasonably, to ascribe different contents to new concepts like co-production.

There are, in other words, multiple theories and multiple worlds of co-production, each with different implications for democracy. Historically and more so today, academic and practitioner discussions of co-production have underlined the risk of the concept being misused or misappropriated as a rationalization for cutting back funds for public services, requiring clients/citizens to bear more of the burden on an inadequate safety net and/or downsizing the public sector under the guise of empowerment. This makes it all the more important to specify in what context and for what purpose the concept of co-production is being employed.

10 Co-Production and Public Administration Regimes
Their Impact on Hybrid Organizations

A. Introduction

This chapter analyzes the impact of co-production and public administration regimes (PARs) on hybrid organizations. Both the study of PARs and co-production are relatively new academic fields, so there is still little systematic knowledge on how they impact hybridity, and in particular how they impact third sector organizations (TSOs). TSOs often work closely with public sector organizations, sometimes in partnership, so important changes in the way the public sector works have clear implications for TSOs and other hybrid organizations. For example, a major shift in the function and operation of traditional public administration in the early 1980s had clear and far-reaching ramifications for both the private sector and third sector. The growth and spread of a market ideology in the management of public services, later known as New Public Management (NPM), brought a new focus and mode of operating to public services, particularly for private and third sector providers. So, it is difficult to ignore such sweeping changes in the public sector when considering hybridity and the third sector.

The purpose of this chapter is to clarify the impact of public administration regimes (PARs) and co-production on hybridity in the third sector. This will be achieved, in part, by comparing and contrasting the values and goals of four PARs, with a focus on the role played by service users and professionals in the provision of public financed social services. The development of new PARs, like New Public Management, contributes significantly to the complexity and hybridity facing the leaders of third sector providers of public financed services. The concept of co-production furthers our study by focusing on the mix of activities that both public agents and citizens contribute to the provision of public services. It also adds to the complexity and hybridity facing the leaders of third sector providers of public financed services. How these two concepts interact with each other and with hybridity will also be explored below.

Hybridity is considered as the overlap between the third sector and other major social sectors, like the state, market and community, illustrated by the welfare triangle discussed below. Co-production is the mix of activities that both public service agents and citizens contribute to the provision of public services. Public administration regimes can be distinguished by a combination of elements, including their theoretical roots, value base and key concepts, as well as the role attributed to citizens, service professionals and the third sector in delivering services. Changes in public administration regimes help set the parameters for the activity and focus of third sector organizations and their leaders, as well as the limits for citizen participation and co-production. This, in turn, can determine the type of hybridity that develops in third sector organizations, i.e., 'shallow' or 'entrenched', and perhaps even an 'enforced' or coerced form of hybridity.

Elinor Ostrom (2009b) advised against promoting and pursuing overly simple models of human behavior, particularly ones that focus solely on self-interest. We need to embrace the challenge for the third sector and its leaders posed by the development of different public administration regimes, each with its own values and focus, and by the spread of co-production in the provision of public services. The complexity posed by public administration regimes and co-production has now become part of the contemporary environment of the third sector in most European countries, but it poses some new challenges for the leaders of TSOs. They will need to develop a better understanding of it in order to operate successfully and sustainably and to better achieve their goals. Thus, providing a better understanding of these new complexities is the main purpose of this chapter.

The chapter begins in Section B by employing a mixed sectoral approach to understanding the hybrid nature of study of many TSOs, particularly when they operate in the overlapping area with other major social sectors, like the state, market and community. It continues in Section C by introducing the ideas of public administration regimes (PARs) and briefly presents four of them. It argues that each of them is based on different values and they have different logics. PARs also attribute different roles to citizens, the professional staff and third sector organizations as providers of public financed services. This has some clear implications for the development of hybridity. Then it discusses the relationship between PARs and hybridity in Section D. After, it introduces the complexities of co-production in Section E, along with different levels of citizen participation in the provision of public services. It analyzes PARs, co-production and hybrid TSOs together in Section F. Finally, it presents a summary and reaches some conclusions about the impact of PARs and co-production on hybrid TSOs in Section G.

B. A Mixed Sectoral Approach to Understanding the Hybridity of the Third Sector

The Center for Social Investment defines hybrid organizations as entities that straddle the border between the public and private, as well as between the for-profit and nonprofit sectors. They often combine the logics of the seemingly distinct spheres of the market, state and civil society (Anheier,

2011). A mixed sectoral approach is used to explore the hybridity of the third sector and analyze the role of the third sector in the growing mix of service providers. It employs the welfare triangle to understand the relations between sectors (Evers, 1993, 1995; Laville, 1992, 1994; Evers & Laville, 2005; Pestoff, 1992, 1998, 2008a; Defourny *el al.*, 2014; Defourny & Pestoff, 2015).

The welfare mix approach utilized here can be considered from both a theoretical and empirical perspective. At the theoretical level, the idea of the welfare mix expresses variations in the importance attributed to the four major social sectors of community, market, state and associations, as well as the values associated with each of them (Streeck & Schmitter, 1995; Billis, 2010). However, sectoral divisions can shift over time and they also vary between countries. Thus, much of the debate in recent decades concerns the dividing line between the state and market, or the public and private sectors, and where the division between them goes or should go. By contrast, the third sector and households have received much less attention both in the public debate and academic discourse.

At the empirical level, the welfare triangle helps to emphasize the shifting role played by various sectors in delivering social welfare services and how this contributes to the current blurring of the third sector's borders (Brandsen *et al.*, 2003). Moreover, actors within the smaller inverted triangle at the center can express varying degrees of privateness/publicness, nonprofitness/for-profitness and formality/informality, placing them closer to one of the other three social sectors (Van Der Meer *et al.*, 2009). The circle that surrounds associations implies that many third sector organizations also overlap with the other social sectors. Thus, we should expect to find a higher degree of hybridity and clearer hybrid forms in the parts of the third sector circle that overlap with other social sectors in the pie shaped parts of Figure 10.1.

The overlap between (a) *the community and the third sector* provides numerous examples of hybrid organizations that operate with different logics. This includes self-help groups that provide mutual aid and comfort to their own members as well as support to others in the community, regardless of their formal membership status. For example, most HIV/AIDS groups serve both the interest of their members and of the community (Kenis & Marin, 1997; Walden-Laing & Pestoff, 1997). In the next area of the circle we find organizations in the overlap between (b) *the state and the third sector*. They comprise the increasingly important partnerships between TSOs and public authorities. This is illustrated by the growth of public-private partnerships (PPPs) in recent decades and third sector compacts in many European countries.

The final overlapping area between (c) *the market and the third sector* suggests that some third sector enterprises operate on the market and seek to earn a surplus from their commercial activities. But, they do not adopt all the rules that are typical of capitalist companies, i.e., shareholders only

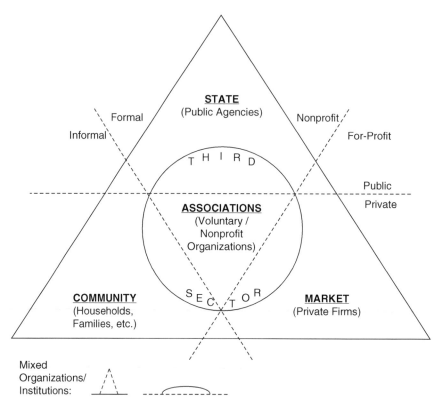

Figure 10.1 The Third Sector and the Welfare Triangle
Source: pestoff, 1998 & 2008.

receive a limited return on their capital and decision-making power can be distributed equally among members, often on the basis of one-member/one-vote (Defourny *et al.*, 2014). Anheier (2005) considers the overlap between the third sector and market an important source of hybridity that poses challenges to TSOs and their leaders. Accordingly, hybrid organizations attempt to combine business and nonprofit elements in relation to their objectives, orientation, outputs, etc. (*ibid.*: 184). Consumer and agricultural cooperatives constitute a classical example of this category, but they also illustrate the dangers inherent in such intermediary positions. They often face a serious challenge of goal displacement or organizational atrophy associated with pursuing multiple and sometimes conflicting goals (Pestoff, 1991). Their leaders must learn to balance the various conflicting stake-holder demands in order to survive and remain true to their original purpose (Pestoff, 2011b, 2012c; Pestoff *et al.*, 2016).

TSOs operating in these overlapping areas, in particular the one with the market, are subject to greater hybridity than those not doing so. However, in the long-run these hybrid areas can become their 'comfort zone', because TSOs and their leaders learn to adjust and accommodate themselves to a particular type of hybridity. However, if they leave one area of overlap and move to another they will expose themselves to a new type of hybridity, with new 'rules of the game' and new tensions stemming from such change.

Billis (2010) distinguished between 'shallow' and 'entrenched' hybridity in TSOs. The former is typically found when a TSO wants to expand its operations by engaging in commercial activities, sometimes referred to as 'social entrepreneurship', but more simply by using commercial means to promote its social mission. However, if the 'shallow' form of hybridity continues over time, it can eventually lead to 'entrenched' hybridity, which impacts both the governance and operational levels of a TSO (*ibid*.: 60). In the latter case, professionals become more dominant in managing the TSO and goal deflections can become a more serious challenge. Moreover, he argued that hybridity can either develop in an 'organic' or 'enacted' fashion. The former represents a more gradual development, while the latter expresses more sudden change found in today's 'frenzied' organizational experiments that result in greater hybridity (*ibid*.). The development of public administration regimes discussed below provide a good illustration of the latter type of development. However, it also suggests the existence of a new category, 'enforced' or 'coerced' hybridity, seen most clearly in New Public Management. The latter serves to illustrate one of the main theses of this chapter, i.e., PARs have a different focus and values that can impact the third sector, complicate their environment and increase their hybridity.

Co-production also bears important ramifications for understanding hybridity, because it opens new areas of collaboration between the public sector and third sector organizations as service providers. However, it not only involves third sector providers comprised of professionals and volunteers, but also includes service users as co-producers of services. So, a new kind of stakeholder is involved, once again resulting in greater complexity and more hybridity. Below, the co-production of public services will be considered in terms of its potential impact on the governance and leadership of hybrid organizations. It offers both new opportunities as well as challenges for collective solutions to growing problems with the provision of social services in Europe. However, greater citizen participation in and more third sector provision of social services can face hurdles both from traditional public administration and New Public Management (NPM), each based on a separate logic. Moreover, the extent to which greater citizen participation and co-production of public services poses new leadership challenges for TSOs also depends on the type of third sector provider, as noted in Section G below. Increased hybridity may seem inevitable given the growing complexity of today's societies. Yet, it is argued below that TSOs and their leaders can either orient themselves toward the type of hybridity represented by greater overlap between the third sector and market, under New Public Management that promotes 'entrenched' hybridity, or by pursuing the social values associated with co-production and New Public Governance (NPG) that represents 'shallow' hybridity.

C. Public Administration Regimes

This section introduces the concept of public administrations regimes (PARs) and then briefly presents four of them, i.e., traditional public administration, New Public Management (NPM), New Public Governance (NPG) and a Communitarian regime. Changes in public administration regimes can set the parameters for the activity of third sector organizations and the focus of their leaders, particularly those providing public funded services. They can also set limits for citizen participation and co-production of public services. It is therefore important to compare PARs and understand how they differ in terms of their values and focus. Such differences will help determine the type of hybridity that develops in third sector organizations, i.e., a 'shallow', 'entrenched', or perhaps even 'enforced' or coerced form of hybridity. The purpose of this section is to explore the possible ramifications of different public administration regimes, while the next section discusses the relationship between PARs and hybridity.

In the immediate post–World War II period, citizens faced a rapidly expanding, yet basically traditional public administration, with its hierarchical chain of command, where they were primarily viewed as passive clients or beneficiaries of mostly public services. Later, in the 1980s and 1990s, with the spread of New Public Management (NPM), citizens were expected to become consumers and exercise more choice between various providers of public financed services, either public, private for-profit or nonprofit. In NPM, the market replaces the state as the main mechanism for governing the expression of citizens' preferences. However, at the turn of the century we can witness the spread of network governance (Hartley, 2005) or New Public Governance (NPG) (Osborne, 2006, 2010). NPG implies a more plural and pluralist model of providing and governing welfare services, based on public-private networks. Citizens are expected to play a more active role as co-producers of some aspects of the services they demand and have come to depend upon in their daily life.

We need, therefore, to explore how changes in the public sector and the development of new public administration regimes impact on the relationship between the third sector and public sector in general. We need to ask how PARs impact the complexity facing the third sector and its leaders as a provider of public financed social services, and how they contribute to hybridity. Much more could, of course, be said about these four PARs, but, neither time nor space allow for that. Some of the core elements of each public administration regime are found in Figure 10.2. It summarizes some of the main points about PARs, including the theoretical roots, value base and some key concepts of each administrative regime.

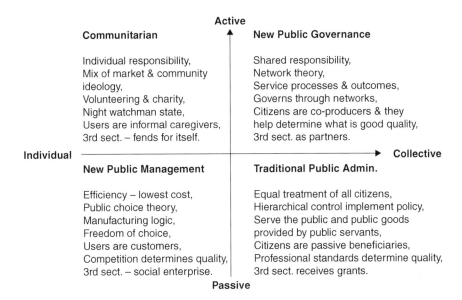

Figure 10.2 Public Administration Regimes: Citizen Participation and Responsibility

Figure 10.2 depicts these four PARs in terms of two important analytical dimensions that relate them to each other. They are the level of citizen participation in service delivery and the degree of individual or collective responsibility for the provision of such services. The first variable is rather straightforward and ranges from low to high, while the second is a bit more complex. It reflects the institutionalization of public vs. private responsibility for providing services to citizens. Health care or childcare can illustrate this. Is it a universal service provided to everyone in a given territory, or does it depend mainly on individual initiative, where access to service often relies on controlling various private assets? In the former case there is a collective responsibility for providing a service, with certain limits or eligibility criteria, while the responsibility for accessing services is primarily individual in the latter case. This variable ranges from individual to collective. Here, we can note some striking contrasts between different PARs.

Both Communitarian and New Public Governance regimes require a high degree of citizen participation in the provision of social services, but they are found at different ends of the continuum from individual to collective service provision. Similarly, neither traditional public administration or New Public Management provide much room for citizens to participate actively in service delivery, compared with NPG and Communitarian regimes, but they also reflect different degrees of individual and collective actions in the provision of public services.

From a historical perspective, we will begin our presentation of these four PARs with traditional public administration, as seen during most of the 20th century; followed by New Public Management (NPM), starting in the 1980s; and more recently the newly emerging paradigm of New Public Governance (NPG) at the turn of the century, based on ideas of network governance (Hartley, 2005; Osborne, 2006). We conclude this overview by presenting a potential new regime coalescing from ideas of Communitarianism/volunteerism in the United Kingdom, Japan and elsewhere. This brief summary also mentions some important features related to the principal agents in co-production, the users/citizens and the professional service providers, as well as the role of TSOs as service providers in each PAR. While these four regimes differ in many important aspects, they also share some common features with each other.

Although each PAR may be linked to a particular ideology or historical period, they can also be conceived as 'layered realities' that co-exist with each other (Hartley, 2005; Osborne, 2010). Thus, rather than one PAR simply replacing the other, more than one regime may be found at any given time, operating in different service sectors. One PAR may dominate in one sector, while another can do so in another. Moreover, they can shift over time, through the spread and ascent of a new public administration regime. Taken together these elements comprise crucial aspects of different PARs, similar to the idea of different welfare regimes (Esping-Andersen, 1990) and production regimes (Kitschelt *et al.*, 1999).

As noted, PARs also attribute quite different weight or importance to the role of citizens and the third sector in the provision of public services, and their perspective on the role of professionals in providing services also varies considerably, as too does their view on service quality guarantees. Therefore, Section E below returns to these differences in greater detail. It argues that co-production will develop in different directions in different PARs, with quite different roles attributed to its key actors, the users and professionals and to the third sector.

C.1 *Traditional Public Administration*

Traditional public administration has its theoretical roots in sociology, political science and public policy. It is based on a hierarchical model of command and control, stemming from ideas of Max Weber, with clear lines of vertical authority and responsibility. Weber's ideas were later developed and expanded by President Woodrow Wilson (Ostrom & Ostrom, 1971). The value base of traditional public administration is found in public sector ethos, or serving the public, and its key concept is public goods that are provided by the public sector or civil servants, who place a heavy emphasis on professional policy implementation and bureaucratic norms of equal treatment of all citizens.

C.2 New Public Management (NPM)

The theoretical roots of New Public Management (NPM) were found in growing criticism in the 1980s of the inefficiencies of traditional public administration, that were clearly articulated in 'public choice' theory and management studies. It promoted ideas of the marketization and commercialization of public services in order to rectify these shortcomings and improve the efficiency and productivity of public sector services. Its value base stems from industry and it promotes a manufacturing logic that emphasizes measuring service inputs and outputs, rather than a service logic that focuses on outcomes (Osborne *et al.*, 2013). Its key concepts are 'freedom of choice' for consumers and competition between various providers in order to insure better service quality.

C.3 New Public Governance (NPG)

The theoretical roots of New Public Governance (NPG) stem from sociology and network theory; its value base is considered as 'participatory democracy' by some (Pestoff, 2009) and 'neo-corporatist' by others (Osborne, 2010). NPG is based on a service logic of production that focuses on service processes and outcomes, where public value is a key concept (Denhardt & Denhardt, 2008). It governs through networks and partnerships, where the third sector and social enterprises can play an important role and citizens are active co-producers of public services.

C.4 A Communitarian Regime

The following is an early approximation at best, although some clues are gleaned from Brudney and England (1983), Horne and Shirley (2009), and Bovaird and Löffler (2012). The Coalition Government that ruled Britain after 2010 introduced a program called Big Society to promote community empowerment by reorganizing public services and facilitating social action (Hudson, 2011; Slocock, 2015). Its value base comes from volunteering, philanthropy and charity. During Cameron's reign this policy was reflected in massive budget cuts for public services, while encouraging families, communities and the third sector to fill the vacuum. How it will fare under Brexit remains to be seen. Similar policies are surfacing elsewhere: in Japan, under the guise of 'Integrated Community Care'; voluntarism in Thailand (Ungsuchaval, 2016); and in Europe, including Denmark (Politiken, 2015) and the Netherlands (Nederhand & Van Meerkerk, 2017), under the label of 'co-production and/ or co-creation' (*ibid.*). These diverse policy expressions are gathered under the heading 'Communitarian regime' herein. Government retains responsibility for design of service delivery, while citizens become co-producers, because they are now responsible for implementing public services, particularly welfare and care services (*ibid.*; Agenosono *et al.*, 2014; Tsutsui, 2014).

Thus, we find that each public administration regime has separate theoretical roots, value base, key concepts, as well as different roles for citizens, professionals and the third sector. Together they result in a unique constellation that helps distinguish one PAR from another. These differences have clear implications for hybridity, co-production and the third sector.

D. The Relationship between PARs and Hybridity

A new perspective can be found when hybridity is put into a political context of public sector reforms. Rapid change brought on by shifts in the macro-level political discourse can impact the possibility structures for TSOs and their leaders, opening new ones and constraining or closing old ones. They can also impact public administration by facilitating the development of a new public administration regime, seen in the growth and spread of New Public Management in the 1980s. This can result in a situation where TSOs that usually operate in one area of overlap in the welfare triangle, for example with the state, must shift rapidly or substantially to another area of overlap, like with the market. However, TSO leaders may be unprepared to cope with the challenges and demands of their new environment and the new 'rules of the game'. This can expose TSOs to increasing hybridity, and the uncertainty it implies. Thus, with the introduction of New Public Management across Europe, many TSOs lost their previously 'cozy relations' with public authorities that recognized their inherent social value added and financed their activities primarily through public grants. Once governments began to privatize the provision of public services, competition and efficiency became the principal criteria for distributing public funds and this cozy relationship ended. TSOs have to adapt to and operate in a new, highly competitive and insecure environment; moreover, one where many of their earlier partners or collaborators are now their competitors, along with many new entries in the form of private for-profit firms that may even include multinational companies and venture capitalists. This process of adaptation, however, takes time and requires resources, which can prove very challenging.

The development of a New Public Management regime forced many TSOs to change from being service providers in partnership with the government, often together with other TSOs as close allies, to preparing competitive tenders, where some of their previous collaborators were now their main competitor. Transitioning from an earlier situation under a traditional public administration regime was not necessarily an expression of their preference or something they chose to do of their own free will. Rather, it was something they felt that they had to do in order to survive. Hence it seems reasonable to refer to this as 'enforced' or 'coerced' hybridity' (cf. Fotaki, 2011). Today, TSOs' continued funding depends on winning a tender for providing services, but in order to succeed in this competitive environment they must become more 'professional'. In fact, their very survival in the competitive NPM environment demands greater 'professionalization', which, in turn, introduces a new stakeholder into the management of a TSO, i.e., the professional staff. The latter can develop separate and sometimes different interests than the board and/or the clients of a TSO, thereby increasing the risk of 'enacted' or 'entrenched' hybridity.

Moreover, there are different types or sets of professional competencies that can be promoted, including those that emphasize 'command and control', 'competition' or 'collaboration and negotiation'. One public administration regime may emphasize one set of competencies, while another will give priority to a different set of competencies. In addition, the new 'rules of the game' are often very complex and demanding, subjecting TSOs to new and sometimes contradictory logics, thereby increasing their hybridity. A more political perspective would, therefore, emphasize the potential status inconsistencies facing a TSO leaving its 'comfort zone' and shifting its operations to new and uncharted waters, where different professional competencies may be required to survive. Thus, a high degree of 'enforced' hybridity might imply more challenges and hurdles to overcome, diverting attention from the TSO's original mission that could have an impact on its ability to survive in a new and highly competitive environment.

Furthermore, recent developments in Europe and the USA suggest that TSOs often lose out to private for-profit actors that have more resources to promote their interests and understand the rules of the competitive game better. In fact, the preliminary evidence paints a bleak picture concerning ability of the third sector as a whole to adapt and adjust to this new competitive environment as providers of public funded social services. In Denmark, Germany, Sweden and the USA two trends are notable in the past decade: first, the dramatic growth of private for-profit providers of welfare services, and second, the marginalization of the third sector (Henriksen *et al.*, 2012; Shekarabi, 2012; Statistiska Meddelanden, 2012; Sivesind, 2016; Baturina *et al.*, 2016). This, in turn, reflects, to a large extent, the growing complexity of the bidding processes adopted by most New Public Management regimes, along with the heavy emphasis on competition and efficiency. Here, large actors, often international venture capitalists, appear to have a competitive advantage, particularly when strict financial criteria are applied to the bidding process and little, if any, consideration is given to social criteria and service quality (*ibid.*). Some will, of course, argue that TSOs must become more 'business-like' and make more professional bids in order to be more competitive; however, this may impact on, or even conflict with their social goals. Thus, the increasing overlap between the third sector and market logic, particularly in an NPM regime, will result in greater 'enforced' and 'entrenched' hybridity, complexity and both the internal and external tensions that many TSOs may find difficult to cope with.

E. Co-Production and Its Relation to Public Administration Regimes

The concept of co-production was developed by Nobel Laureate Elinor Ostrom and her colleagues in the 1970s to describe and delimit the involvement of ordinary citizens in the production of public services (Ostrom, 1996). This research led them to realize that the production of services, in contrast to goods, was difficult without the active participation of those persons receiving the service (*ibid.*). Thus, they developed the term 'co-production' to describe the potential relationship that could exist between the 'regular producer' (street-level police officers, schoolteachers or health workers) and their clients who wanted to be transformed by the service into safer, better-educated or healthier persons (see Parks *et al.*, 1981). Co-production is, therefore, noted by

> the mix of activities that both public service agents and citizens contribute to the provision of public services. The former are involved as professionals or 'regular producers', while 'citizen production' is based on voluntary efforts of individuals or groups to enhance the quality and/or quantity of services they receive.
>
> (*ibid.*)

Co-production was overshadowed in the 1980s and 1990s by NPM, but it gained renewed interest during the first decade of the 21st century, as seen in the growing number of academic conferences and publications devoted to this subject (Alford, 2002; Pestoff & Brandsen, 2006; Bovaird, 2007; Pestoff, 2009; Alford, 2009; Pestoff *et al.*, 2012). Studies of co-production have expanded rapidly among different disciplines, especially those focusing on public services and/or the third sector. For example, it has been used to analyze the role of voluntary and community organizations (VCOs) in the provision of public services in the UK (Osborne & McLaughlin, 2004) and in more mundane public services in Australia, the USA and UK (Alford, 2009), including the use of post or zip codes on letters and completing and returning annual income tax forms. We will now briefly summarize two studies of childcare in Europe that shed light on key aspects of co-production. This is important for understanding the role of the central actors in co-production, the users and professionals in different PARs, as well as the relation between co-production and PARs. Chapters 4 and 5 provide more details about these two studies of parent participation in childcare.

E.1 Central Aspects of Co-Production Found in Two Studies of Childcare in Europe

The TSFEPS Project studied parent participation in the provision and governance of childcare in eight EU countries (Pestoff, 2006). It found different levels of parent participation in different countries and in different forms of provision, i.e., public, private for-profit and third sector childcare. The highest levels of parent participation were found in third sector providers, like parent associations in France, parent initiatives in Germany and parent cooperatives in Sweden. It also noted the existence of different kinds of parent participation, i.e., economic, political and social. All three kinds of participation were readily evident in third sector providers of childcare services, while both economic and political participation were much more restricted in municipal and private for-profit services (*ibid.*). Vamstad's follow-up study (2007) compared parent and worker co-ops, municipal services and small for-profit firms providing childcare.

Turning to issues of parent and staff influence, Vamstad noted that parent influence was greatest in parent co-ops and least in small for-profit firms. Concerning their desire for more influence, he found that it inversely reflected how much influence they currently experienced. Very few parents in parent co-ops wanted more influence, while nearly three of five did so in small for-profit firms (*ibid.*). Shifting to the staff of these facilities, the staff in worker co-ops claimed the most influence and the staff in municipal facilities claimed the least influence. Once again, the proportion of the staff desiring more influence inversely reflected the proportion claiming much influence. Few wanted more influence in either the worker or parent co-ops, while the opposite was true of the staff in the other two types of childcare providers. Nearly three of five wanted more influence in municipal childcare and three of four did so in small for-profit firms (*ibid.*). Both studies demonstrate that parent co-ops in Sweden provided parents with unique possibilities for active participation in the management and running of their child(ren)'s childcare facility and for becoming active co-producers of high quality childcare services. Together, they also suggest the existence of a 'glass ceiling' in public and private for-profit childcare services. Chapters 4 and 5 provide more details. Moreover, public policies can either crowd-in or crowd-out desired behavior by citizens. Co-production is not an exception to this rule.

These findings lead to three clear conclusions about co-production. First, there are different forms of citizen participation in the provision of public financed social services like childcare, i.e., economic, social and political participation. Second, a higher level of citizen participation was noted for third sector providers of public financed social services, because they are based on collective action and direct client participation in service provision. Third, more limited citizen participation was noted for public provision of welfare services, where citizens were allowed to participate sporadically or in a limited fashion in municipal childcare. But, parents were seldom given the opportunity to play a major role in or to take charge of the service provision, or given decision-making rights and responsibilities for the economy of the service provider (Pestoff, 2009). This leads us to ask what role users and service professionals play in different PARs and in determining service quality.

E.2 The Role of Users and Service Quality

The role of users of public services varies considerably in different PARs, where they can either become beneficiaries, consumers, citizens or 'enforced agents' of such services, as noted earlier in Figure 10.2. Each of them will be commented on briefly below, followed by the role of service providers, which also varies notably between PARs.

Traditional public administration tends to be perceived as paternalistic by many because it is achieved through the 'professional gift' model of service provision. Here citizens are considered the beneficiaries of public services, but with a clearly passive role as recipients of services. Thus, there are no exit or voice options available to users. Their only recourse or channel of influence is found in the electoral system, which at best can provide indirect, intermittent representation of their interest, given the outcome of an election. In addition, service professionalism supposedly provides a guarantee of service quality in a command and control system, while third sector organizations are supposed to function as advocates and/or service providers, for which they receive public grants, but they seldom provide services.

New Public Management often attempts to achieve its goals by using a 'carrot and stick' approach to incentives designed to reward or discourage different behavior by the providers and users of services. Here citizens are considered clients or customers with some limited choice, but little voice and no representation. Users can choose between pre-existing packages or 'offers', but they have little influence on the content or features of such services. Service quality is guaranteed through competition, making the role of professionals highly competitive. Moreover, third sector organizations are expected to become 'social enterprises' that provide services in competition with each other and with private for profit firms, because they no longer qualify for public grants that have become a thing of the past.

New Public Governance is based on ideas of establishing a partnership between citizens and the government, where citizens are considered co-producers of public services. This not only gives them both choice and voice, but can even provide them with direct representation, giving users greater influence than in either traditional public administration or NPM. Service quality is guaranteed by user participation in the delivery of public services, while the role of professionals is collaborative. Here the third sector becomes a partner with the state, in collaboration with other providers of public services, including public bodies, TSOs, social enterprises and for-profit firms.

Finally, in a *Communitarian regime* the role of service users is to provide many public services by and for themselves, with little or no public support, sometimes alongside, but often instead of the professionals. Here users and/or their loved-ones and neighbors become informal caregivers or service providers, while professionals are transformed into 'back-up' agents who only intervene when the informal care provided proves insufficient.

Determination of service quality becomes more like patchwork, because access depends on the availability, willingness and capacity of informal caregivers or service providers, which can vary considerably. In addition, the role of the third sector is relegated to fend for itself by creating consortia or becoming social businesses that can compete on the market with other consortia or private firms, in order to earn their income, rather than depend on grants from the state.

E.3 The Role of Professionals in Determining Service Quality

Traditional public administration relies heavily, if not exclusively, on training and professionalism to guarantee service quality (Vamstad, 2012); thus, professionals alone decide on and prescribe appropriate measures for their clients, based on their professional knowledge, experience and insights. *New Public Management* places heavy emphasis on competition and consumer choice. It is therefore not surprising that professionals, regardless of whether they are public, private or nonprofit, should focus strongly on competition between providers. NPM assumes that service quality is guaranteed by consumer choice, where the best quality provider will attract more customers than those with inferior products or services. *New Public Governance*, by contrast, emphasizes collaboration and negotiation between various partners, public, private and/or nonprofit (Hartley, 2005; Osborne, 2006). Here greater user participation and mutual dialog between users and professionals (Vidal, 2013; Vamstad, 2012) replaces professionalism or competition as the main guarantee of service quality. The main focus of professionals is on promoting collaboration and negotiation, rather than on command and control or competition. Finally, the perspective of a *Communitarian regime* in terms of professionalism and service quality remain largely undeveloped in this respect, but professionals can complement informal care provision, mainly by steering users/caregivers to available resources in the community or voluntary organizations. However, the consequences of this for service quality or availability for different groups of users/caregivers remains to be seen.

Thus, co-production or citizen participation can develop in several different directions, with a different content and meaning in each PAR. Each of these directions implies different roles for service users and the professional staff. This clearly poses challenges for the leaders of TSOs, complicates their situation and increases their hybridity. They must understand these differences and what the implications of following one path of development means in relation to following another. Moreover, taken together, the growth of divergent PARs implies a more plural and pluralist world where TSOs and their leaders must learn to navigate between competing views and visions and choose to follow one that best encompasses their values and aspirations for the future.

E.4 Co-Production and Public Administration Regimes

Brandsen and Pestoff (2006) expanded the scope of co-production to explicitly include the third sector as a provider of public financed services and they proposed a rudimentary typology for studying this phenomenon, based on the existence of different venues for citizen participation in public policy-making. They suggested that direct citizen participation in the delivery of public services should be contrasted with co-management, or formalized coordination between public, private and third sector actors providing public services in a given territory, as well as with co-governance, or third sector participation in public policy-making (*ibid.*). Such a multi-level perspective provides a more nuanced understanding than a singular focus on co-production at the micro-level or using the same term for various phenomena at different levels. This multi-faceted approach encourages a more comprehensive view of the different roles the third sector may have within the complex structure of public service provision. Also, it promotes comparisons of the role of the third sector across the entire policy cycle, not just on advocacy or service provision, but on both the input and output sides of the political system (Easton, 1965). It should be noted, however, that these three concepts are not mutually exclusive. There are some potential trade-offs between co-production, co-management and co-governance (Pestoff *et al.*, 2006) that may contribute to greater hybridity.

It is also important to distinguish between individual and collective co-production (Pestoff, 2012a, 2012b). For example, Hudson (2012) sketches three phases in the shift from mass production to mass collaboration in the National Health Service (NHS). First, in mass production, professionals design and deliver services to their patients, who are passive recipients of health care. This corresponds with the traditional view of public administration. Then, in today's mass customization and personalization of services, professionals and patients may jointly design the services, but professionals take a clear lead in the implementation, by prescribing the appropriate treatments. Patients can become individual co-producers of such customized and personalized services, resulting in a patient-consumer model that fits well with a New Public Management perspective. By contrast, in mass collaboration and participatory health care patients, TSOs and communities are central in both the design and delivery of health services (*ibid.*), bringing it closer to ideas related to New Public Governance.

Moreover, issues of hybridity also become evident here. Co-governance can be seen as a core element for modernizing public services because it provides a means of bringing the views of TSOs and public service users into the design, management and delivery of welfare services, as promoted by NPG. A recent study of the challenges faced by one major TSO in the UK trying to facilitate more user influence in the National Health Service pilot program illustrated the tensions this created with its advocacy role (Martin, 2011). He concluded that sooner or later TSOs may discover that traditional management concerns outweigh those of newer participants in such public service networks. Rather than giving weight to TSO and user views, participation in these governance networks tended to co-opt them (*ibid.*). Furthermore, TSOs may experience a conflict of interest between divergent goals that can include: (a) increasing their own influence in a current project (co-management), (b) securing their role as a service provider in the next round of funding (co-production), and/or (c) promoting the development of institutions for greater user participation and influence (co-governance). Thus, TSOs often find their own values marginalized when governments compile lists of standard service providers that should compete with each other for funding (*ibid.*) according to the managerial and economic criteria used by NPM.

F. Discussion: Analyzing PARs, Co-Production and Hybrid TSOs

Starting with the relations between co-production and PARs, we saw in the TSFEPS study that co-production was clearly evident in childcare in France, Germany and Sweden, while co-management and co-governance were only found in France and Germany, but not in Sweden. Thus, parent participation was limited to the site of service delivery in Sweden, while French and German parents also had influence in the overall management of local childcare services and the development of childcare policy in general. Moreover, both of these studies of childcare also illustrate the co-existence of several different layers of public administration regimes in the same service sector and country, as suggested by Hartley (2005) and Osborne (2006). In Sweden, for example, most preschool services are provided by municipalities in a traditional top-down public administrative fashion, while private for-profit preschool services are inspired by ideas of greater consumer choice related to NPM. Parent co-ops contain some elements of NPG, like a work obligation for the parents who manage these facilities, making them active co-producers of their own childcare. This suggests that different public administration regimes produce different ideas of hybridity and a different mix of logics. Thus, a higher degree of citizen participation and co-production in third sector services appears more compatible with NPG than with NPM or traditional public administration.

Moreover, these three levels of TSO participation in delivering public services—co-production, co-management and co-governance—may result in competing expectations, both internally and externally, about the role of TSOs and what their distinctive contribution is, or should be. The professional staff may therefore argue for toning down traditional values, while emphasizing their professionalism or competitive advantage as service providers in order to gain continued funding. Such competing expectations and stakeholder conflicts need to be understood and balanced by the leaders of TSOs. Thus, coerced participation in competitive tenders and market-like arrangements will often result in greater 'enacted' or 'enforced' hybridity for TSOs and their leaders. Moreover, TSO participation in various aspects of co-production can augment such developments, leading to increased hybridity and goal conflict.

Furthermore, this introduces yet another dimension to our study of hybridity, namely that of internal decision-making in TSOs. Not all third sector providers of public financed services are able to facilitate client and/or staff participation to the same degree or in the same fashion. Some TSOs practice democracy in their internal affairs, while others depend on a more corporate governance model to lead their activities. Whether or not they can facilitate greater client and/or staff participation will depend, at least in part, on the degree of democracy in their own decision-making. Generally, those third sector organizations that are membership organizations and practice some form of democratic decision-making will probably facilitate and encourage greater citizen participation and more collective co-production of public services than those governed by a corporate model. By contrast, those TSOs that are not membership-based organizations may face clear difficulties participating in programs, services and/or networks based on greater citizen participation and co-production. They would have to introduce new, often foreign elements or structures in their organization. This can result in new challenges and will take time and effort. Moreover, the benefits of such changes may appear vague or elusive in relation to an organization's goals. Thus, whether or not NPG implies clear advantages for TSOs as service providers depends, in part, on the values and internal structures of the concerned TSO.

G. Summary and Conclusions

Hybridity was considered as the overlap between the third sector and other major social sectors, like the state, market and community. Co-production is the mix of activities that both public service agents and citizens contribute to the provision of public services. Public administration regimes can be distinguished by a combination of elements, including their theoretical roots, value base and key concepts, as well as the role attributed to citizens, service professionals and the third sector. Together they result in a unique constellation that distinguishes one PAR from another. These differences have clear implications for hybridity, co-production and the third sector. Therefore, major changes in PARs starting in the 1980s provide a political perspective on hybridity.

This chapter argued that changes in public administration regimes set the parameters for activity of TSOs and help determine the focus of their leaders. One public administration regime may emphasize one set of competences, while another will give priority to another. Moreover, the new 'rules of the game' are often very complex and demanding, subjecting TSOs to new and sometimes contradictory logics, thus increasing their hybridity. A political perspective, therefore, emphasizes the potential status inconsistencies facing a TSO leaving its 'comfort zone' and shifting its operations to new and uncharted waters, where different professional competencies may be required to survive.

This, in turn, is reflected in the growing complexity of the bidding processes adopted by most New Public Management regimes, along with the heavy emphasis on competition and efficiency. Here we noted that large actors, often international venture capitalists, appear to have a competitive advantage, particularly when strict financial criteria are applied to the bidding process and little, if any, consideration is given to social criteria and service quality. Some would therefore argue that TSOs must become more 'business-like' and make more professional bids in order to become or remain competitive. However, this may conflict with their social goals.

Changes between PARs will in turn help determine the type of hybridity that develops in third sector organizations, i.e., 'shallow' or 'entrenched', and perhaps even an 'enforced' or coerced form of hybridity. The rapid and sweeping changes under NPM seem more like 'enforced' or 'coerced' hybridity than the 'organic' or 'enacted' types suggested by Billis (2010). Thus, the increasing overlap between the third sector and market logic, particularly in an NPM regime, will probably result in greater 'enforced' and 'entrenched' hybridity, complexity and both internal and external tensions that many TSOs may find difficult to cope with.

PARs also have a clear impact on co-production and set limits for citizen participation. Two empirical studies reviewed here lead to three conclusions. First, citizen participation can take one or more forms, i.e., economic, social and political. Second, a higher level of citizen participation was noted for third sector providers of public financed social services. Third, more limited citizen participation was noted for public providers of welfare services, where citizens were only allowed to participate more sporadically or in a limited fashion.

Thus, co-production can also develop in several different directions, with a different content and meaning in each PAR. Moreover, each of these directions implies different roles for service users and the professional staff. This clearly poses challenges for the leaders of TSOs, complicates their situation and increases their hybridity. They must attempt to understand these differences and what the implications of following one path of development means in relation to another. Moreover, taken together, the growth of divergent PARs implies a more plural and pluralist world where TSOs and their leaders must learn to navigate between competing views and visions and choose to follow one that best encompasses their values and aspirations for the future.

The existence of layered or mixed reality, with different PARs in different social services suggest that hybridity will probably increase as the public service provision becomes more pluralistic and fragmented, as the difference between NPM and NPG develops and becomes clearer. This will contribute to the growing complexity facing TSOs and subject their leaders to greater challenges. A shift in PARs can either promote more competition and commercialization of the delivery of public financed services, in an NPM regime, or it will result in greater citizen involvement in the provision of public services, through co-production, co-management and co-governance, in an NPG regime.

The development of shallow hybridity will lead to fewer far-reaching changes in a TSO's structures and operations and can therefore be corrected and compensated more easily than entrenched hybridity. However, membership-based TSOs may adapt and adjust more easily to NPG and co-production than non-membership TSOs. Thus, the former TSOs will survive more readily in an NPG regime, while the latter will do so more easily in an NPM regime. So, different types of TSOs will probably orient themselves to different types of public administration regimes. Moreover, promoting co-production and new governance techniques can also pose some new challenges to the management of hybrid organizations in its own way. It can expose them to additional institutional and organizational forces and therefore increase the risks of failing to balance multiple goals and/or the interests of various stakeholders in a sustainable fashion (Pestoff *et al.*, 2016).

TSOs and their leaders can, therefore, choose which type of hybridity they want to operate and survive in, at least to some degree. Those TSOs that orient themselves toward greater market competition and NPM will have to learn to navigate both the pull and push from the overlapping and sometimes competing logics of the third sector and the market. In order to cope with this type of hybridity they will need to increase their professionalization, promote their competitive advantage(s) and improve their efficiency. This may, however, come at the price of their traditional values and goals, particularly if shallow hybridity is allowed to turn into entrenched hybridity. By contrast, those TSOs that want to retain more of their traditional social values and distinctiveness may opt to pursue an NPG vision by participating in service networks that emphasize co-production, co-management and co-governance. While this may promote a different kind of hybridity, one with greater overlap with both the public and community sectors, it too implies certain risks. However, these new roles imply other challenges, particularly under an NPM-dominated regime and/or service sector. It can also prove risky for some TSOs, particularly for those that lack well developed participatory institutions for democratic decision-making that provide them with legitimacy to embrace greater citizen participation or co-production of public services.

In order to more fully embrace the complexities posed by the spread of co-production and different public administration regimes for the third sector and its leaders, we should remember the conclusion of Elinor Ostrom's Nobel Prize speech in Stockholm. She emphasized the need to improve our frameworks and theories to be able to understand complexity and not simply reject it (2009b: 436). Including public administration regimes and co-production in our models of organizational behavior, particularly when studying third sector organizations and their leaders, is an important step for improving our framework and understanding the complexities facing TSOs in today's contemporary environment. These two concepts also go a long way in grasping the challenges that growing hybridity poses to third sector organizations and their leaders.

11 Reframing Co-Production
More Definitions or New Schools?

A. Introduction

A growing chorus of scholars and practitioners has called into question current attempts to define and delimit co-production. They argue that it is ill defined, poorly formulated or a muddled concept. Their solution is to propose a new definition that can hopefully encompass more elements and provide a more wholistic approach to the study of this phenomenon. However, the problem may not lay in definitions *per se*, but rather might be a question of different approaches, models or schools of study that color our understanding of this phenomenon.

The co-production of public services is a complex phenomenon that has attracted significant scholarly interest in recent years and gained adherents in several academic disciplines. They include, among others, business administration, economics, political science, policy studies, public administration and management, sociology and third sector studies. Similar to some other hot topics, like social enterprise or social innovation, this highly complex phenomenon involves multiple dimensions, e.g., economic, political and social, that require a truly multi-disciplinary approach (see Chapter 8). Yet, all academic disciplines have their own basic understanding or starting point, which can prove challenging in a multi-disciplinary endeavor. All of them should be reflected, to a greater or lesser extent, in attempts to promote a generic definition of co-production. However, this can result in growing confusion and a muddled concept that lacks a clear and consistent definition. In particular, many younger scholars may feel compelled to address different, and sometimes conflicting, perspectives of this phenomenon, without being able to reconcile or synthesize them. It is important, therefore, for scholars and practitioners to find better ways to explain and study co-production and its potential impacts. Failure to do so will not only result in growing ambiguity and further confusion about a complex phenomenon. It can also undermine efforts to evoke citizen engagement to improve public services and service quality.

Traditional definitions of co-production range from "the mix of activities that both public service agents and citizens contribute to the provision of public services" to "a partnership between citizens and public service providers". Here the service professionals collaborate with their clients, either as individuals or in groups, who want to enhance the quality and/or quantity of the services on which they depend. Ostrom and her colleagues coined the term 'co-production' in the early 1980s to capture the potential relationship between the 'regular producer', like street-level police officers, schoolteachers, or health workers, and their clients who wanted to be transformed by the service into safer, better-educated or healthier persons (Ostrom, 1996). But, she also noted that service professionals and users do not belong to or are not usually part of the same organization. Moreover, she maintained that the term 'client' is a passive term implying that citizens/ users are acted upon, while co-production is based on citizens playing an active role in producing public goods and services of consequence to them (*ibid.*: 1073).

Since then there have been repeated attempts to expand the study of co-production beyond the original focus on active citizen participation in the delivery of public services. To name only a few of these efforts, Brandsen and Pestoff (2006) extended citizen participation by distinguishing between co-governance, co-management and co-production of public services. Osborne and Strokosch (2013) called for integrating the service management and public administration perspectives, Alford (2014) discussed co-production's unexplored potential, Pestoff (2014a) focused on the role of the third sector in making co-production more sustainable, while Voorberg *et al.* (2015) suggest that co-production and co-creation are similar, if not interchangeable concepts. Other scholars have proposed various typologies of co-production. Bovaird and Löffler's (2012) proposal is based on co-commissioned and co-provided services where 'fully co-produced services' are high both in terms of commissioning and provision, while traditional services are low on both counts. Brandsen and Honingh (2015) distinguished between four different types of co-production in public services, based on citizen participation in the design and/or implementation of public services and whether it was undertaken in core or complementary tasks. Nabatchi *et al.* (2017) combine several aspects or dimensions of co-production in an ambitious effort to summarize and synthesize much of the recent debate on how to conceptualize co-production. However, this is not an easy task given the growing number of approaches to study this phenomenon today.

Furthermore, citizens have numerous roles in today's post-modern service societies, including several different ones vis-à-vis the public sector (Pestoff, 1998). Alford (2009) attributes four different roles to the clients of public sector services: paying customers, beneficiaries, obligates and citizens. Thomas (2012, 2013) distinguished between three principal roles played by the public vis-à-vis the professionals providing public services: citizens, customers and partners. Similarly, Nabatchi *et al.* refer to multiple roles of lay actors who interact with the state: citizens, clients and customers (2017: 770). The fact that citizens have multiple roles and a variety of interactions with the public sector should serve as a reminder that not all of them involve co-production.

Several of the pioneers warned against employing too broad a definition of co-production, where virtually any citizen activity direct or indirect connected with the public sector or public financed services was identified as co-production (Brudney, 1984). Therefore, Warren *et al.* (1982) and Rosentraub and Warren (1987) excluded certain types of activities from those considered as co-production. Ancillary actions are expected forms of behavior for citizens, such as obeying the law, paying taxes and following regulations or reporting crime. Parallel production involves services similar to those provided by public agencies, but produced by individuals or groups without any contact or cooperation with public agencies (*ibid.*). So, employing different terms, like ancillary and/or parallel production can help distinguish co-production from other forms of citizen interaction with the public sector in the design and delivery of public services.

B. The Purpose of This Study

There is a lively debate today about the concept of co-production. It is probably a healthy sign that we are still discovering new facets of this variegated phenomenon and also that there is still no consensus on a precise, generic definition of co-production. Nevertheless, questions about the 'true' nature of co-production often surface as interest in this relatively new field grows, i.e., questions about what it is and what it isn't, or perhaps what it should be. At a recent two-day seminar on co-production, every second or third author briefed his/her presentation with a comment to the effect "I wonder if this is really co-production?" but then continued to present her/his theories and data. One young scholar even asked if any kind of citizen participation except voting should be considered co-production. This clearly illustrates a conceptual risk—too broad a definition of a new phenomenon like co-production means that almost everything and anything can be included, but then there is nothing left to compare and contrast it with. Yet, too narrow a definition implies the opposite—almost nothing qualifies, and it becomes an empty or stand-alone phenomenon. In the first case, where anything goes, we are likely to end up with a broad, yet vague concept, while in the second case, where nothing qualifies, we are left with a feather rather than a chicken. In both cases meaningful academic pursuits become difficult, if not impossible.

Moreover, new academic concepts often gain inspiration from real life phenomenon that are not adequately covered or understood by existing concepts. So, quite naturally, there are different perspectives on similar phenomena in different countries, disciplines and sectors. This means that our understanding of a new concept, like co-production, is heavily influenced by its context, where discipline, service sector and even national setting can easily color it. Moreover, the same concept might be used quite differently in different public administration regimes. Co-production is a prime example of this and the role of the professional staff and their clients or users, is quite different in each public administration regime (see Chapter 9, Pestoff, 2018a). Therefore, it is important to make these different perspectives clear when presenting and discussing a new concept like co-production. Furthermore, there are several other challenging issues that need to be considered before any significant progress can be made in developing a third sector approach to co-production and the transformation of public service delivery. This suggests that the real problem is perhaps not so much one of definitions, but rather a question of different schools of or approaches to the study of co-production, much like the case with social enterprise (Defourny & Nyssens, 2017).

This chapter represents a growing concern that the possibility of finding or proposing a generic or unifying definition of this multi-faceted phenomenon is becoming more elusive as more scholars with different backgrounds and perspectives join this rapidly expanding field of study. Perhaps, we need, therefore, to shift focus a bit and consider identifying three or more schools of co-production. The purpose of this chapter is to briefly examine some of the differences between these perspectives and explore their implications for the potential of co-production to reform the public sector. Thus, the intention is neither to narrow the focus of the study of co-production nor to widen it, *per se*. Rather, it proposes that discussing certain key or core elements of co-production can help to illuminate different schools of co-production. The two main contenders today appear to be a classical political science/public administration input/output model that emphasizes citizen participation on the output side of the political system and the service management model that focuses on various stages in the value chain approach. Hopefully, juxtaposing them will serve to disentangle citizens' activities in the provision of public services and bring greater clarity to the debate among scholars and practitioners, in terms of the unique capacity of co-production to promote citizen/user participation in the delivery of public services of consequence to them (Ostrom, 1996). A third approach is seen with the growing interest in co-creation, while more recently there has been a call for developing a unique third sector approach to the study and practice of co-production. The first three approaches are more developed than the latter one. But, there is also some overlap between them, and they are not mutually exclusive. Following a brief introduction of these three approaches, some major challenges for developing a more coherent TSO model of co-production will be considered.

C. Three Schools of Co-Production: An Input-Output, a Value Chain and a Public Value Creation Model?

Whether we apply an input/output perspective, a value chain or a service management approach is crucial for our understanding of co-production and how it works, what it includes and excludes, etc. This is particularly relevant given the context and setting of the phenomenon at hand, i.e. reforming the public sector and the provision of public services by attributing citizens an active role in co-producing public goods and services of consequence to them. Mixing several perspectives, as is sometimes the case today, can unwittingly result in a state of confusion that can turn co-production into a 'fuzzy' concept that reflects a poorly formulated understanding of the phenomenon at hand.

C.1 An Input-Output Model

It is, therefore, important to underline a few of the basic features of public policy-making. Fundamental insights for understanding the public sector are found in the pioneering work of David Easton, *A Systems Analysis of Political Life* (1965). In particular, his input/output model is highly germane and provides a good starting point. He explicitly differentiates between the input and output sides of public policy-making, their different roles and functions. Traditionally, studies of citizen participation focus on the input side and include activities like voting, contacting elected representatives, demonstrations, etc. designed to influence politics and policy-making. The work of Elinor Ostrom and her colleagues helped to shift the focus of public administration to the output side of the political system by including citizen participation in the delivery of public services, not only making demands.

The distinction between citizen participation on the input or output sides of the political system is not a trivial matter, nor academic 'hair-splitting', as it might seem to scholars in other disciplines. The same individuals are not usually involved on both the input and output sides. The input side of policy-making is based on discrete activities that are usually limited in time, while the output side normally comprises continuous activities, where service users are often locked into service provision for several years (see Chapter 2, Pestoff, 1994). This also implies that participation on the input side is temporally more distant from the service actually provided as well as from the final outcome than participation on the output side. Moreover, citizens' daily activities in policy implementation usually become intertwined with or even part of the final outcome, and the collective process of achieving them can contribute added value to the outcome (Hirschman, 1982).

C.2 A Value Chain Model

Turning to the service management approach, Bovaird's prolific writings on co-production illustrates the importance of having a different starting point for research. He provided a robust definition of co-production (2007): "[u]ser and community co-production is the provision of services through regular, long-term relationships between professionalized service providers (in any sector) and service users and/or other members of the community, where all parties make substantial resource contributions" (*ibid*.: 847). But, it is based on the value chain perspective of service management; so, he argues that co-production is not only relevant to the "delivery phase of service management, but can also extend across the full value chain of service planning, design, commissioning, managing, delivering, monitoring and evaluations activities" (*ibid*.: 846), and he affixes a 'co' to each of the above terms. In more general terms, Bovaird and Löffler (2012) distinguish between four stages or types of citizen participation in public services: co-commissioning, co-design, co-delivery and co-evaluation of public services (*ibid*.). While a service management perspective does provide some valuable insights that enhance our understanding of co-production, it nevertheless appears to attribute equal importance to each link or stage in the value chain. It fails, therefore, to clarify if and how one link might prove more important than another for evoking their sustainable participation in co-production and, therefore, provides little guidance about what is most important for further studies of co-production.

C.3 Co-Creation: A Public Value Creation Model

Initially, Voorberg *et al.* (2015) seemed to use the terms 'co-creation' and 'co-production' interchangeably, but elsewhere they state that co-creation is limited to "the involvement of citizens in the initiation and design of public services" (Voorberg *et al.*, 2017: 366). Others consider co-production as part of the co-creation of public and social value for citizens and users. Osborne (2017) assumes that co-creation is based on an interactive dynamic relationship where value is created at the nexus of interaction between service users and public service organizations. However, similar to Grönross (1990), Osborne argues that public service organizations (PSOs) "*do not create value for citizens—they can only make a public service offering. It is how the citizen uses this offering and how it interacts with his/her own life experiences that creates value*" (2017: 4, italics in the original). He considers this very significant, because the discussion typically focuses on how public services could 'add in' the citizen or service user to enhance performance. But, by reversing the equation, the PSO becomes a facilitator, and "*it is the PSO that must be added to the equation as a co-creator of value, not the service user*" (*ibid*.: 5, italics in the original). This seems to eliminate the need to examine the actions of PSOs, whether they facilitate or hinder citizen participation. Rather, it puts the onus of successful co-production squarely in the hands of the individual citizen/user him/herself. While this seems to fly in the face of common sense and some recent research (Tortzen, 2016; Andersen & Espersen, 2017), it also begs the question about what co-creation research should study. Are customer surveys of citizens' willingness to co-create and focus group discussions sufficient to determine good co-creations policy?

Seen from a political science and public administration perspective, co-creation is similar to co-design and it is found primarily on the policy formulation or input side of public policy-making, while co-production refers to the implementation of a given policy and is particularly relevant for citizen participation at the micro-level or the site of service provision. Thus, clarifying differences between policy formulation and policy implementation, or the input and the output side of public policy-making, could help eliminate some unnecessary confusion between the concepts of co-creation and co-production. Moreover, designating the term co-creation to activities on the input side, while referring to those on the output side as co-production, might be a step in the right direction. Finally, given the significant differences in approach noted above, it seems more reasonable to study the development of different schools of co-production than to attempt to propose a definition that can satisfy most or all of these diverse approaches.

D. Some Critical Reflections on Volunteers in the Third Sector, Participation and Co-Production

De Tocqueville considered voluntary organizations as 'schools of democracy'. But, what role can voluntary organizations play today in the co-production of public services? There are three major challenges related to identifying a third sector model for citizen participation in the provision of public services and the ability of TSOs to facilitate co-production of public services: (i) the 'who, and what' of co-production and differences between professionals, co-producers and volunteers, and the tasks they perform, (ii) the 'where' of co-production and the role of third sector organizations in delivering public services and (iii) the contrast between an economic and social understanding of 'collective' co-production.

D.1 Reconfiguring Co-Production: Enter Volunteers or the 'Who and What' of Co-Production

An important issue for the role of TSOs is related to differences between volunteers and co-producers and the tasks they perform or the 'who and what' of co-production. Who are the main actors in co-production and what kinds of tasks do they perform? The classical stance is that citizens or service users and professional staff are the main actors in co-production (Ostrom, 1996; Parks *et al.*, 1981). However, the empirical question is what tasks citizens or users perform and what tasks the paid staff undertake. It has been suggested that they can either perform core or complementary tasks (Pestoff, 1998, 2006; Brandsen & Honingh, 2015). If citizens perform core tasks they will supplement the staff as service providers and this could pose a threat to the staff's job security. But, if users mainly perform complementary tasks they can augment service provision and/or improve the service quality (Ostrom, 1996). In the traditional configuration, the professional staff provides all the core tasks and users none. Facilitating co-production then becomes a question of evoking user participation in complementary tasks, without encroaching on the core ones. So, complementary tasks become a contested area, while the core ones remain the exclusive domain of the paid staff.

Recent research, however, suggests this relationship might be more complex than previously thought. For example, concerning the 'what' of co-production, it may prove necessary to go a step further by distinguishing between core, essential and complementary tasks, not simply core and complementary tasks. Core tasks are at the heart of the service provided, essential tasks are necessary, but not part of the core functions of a service, while complementary tasks are often tertiary ones that improve the quality of the service and give it a more personal touch. The importance assigned to these tasks may, however, shift with time and changing political preferences, as well as vary between service sectors.

Moreover, with the growth of different public administration regimes, especially those anchored in prolonged austerity of public finances, like NPM and Communitarian regimes, we can note the spread of volunteering in the provision of public services. For example, help in finding the right hospital clinic or ward is often provided today by volunteers, who guide patients and visitors both in public and private hospitals in many parts of the world. Another example is found in the growth of volunteers in fire departments, particularly in Europe. For example, local fire and rescue services in the UK now include volunteers who have job descriptions, work alongside the professional staff and wear the uniforms of firemen, but receive no pay (Schlappa & Imani, 2016). So, even the 'who' of co-production seems to be evolving, with the introduction of a third category of service providers, volunteers, in addition to the service users and paid staff. Thus, we note a new constellation of roles and tasks, with three main categories of providers and three kinds of tasks involved in many types of co-production, as seen in Figure 11.1.

The mix of actors and roles involved in citizen participation in the provision of public services is illustrated by some examples mentioned above. In firefighting services in the UK, paid staff provides the core services, but due to cutbacks in public funding, some essential services, like home safety inspections, are now provided by volunteers. In doing so, they also provide other services not normally associated with fire and safety services,

Roles/tasks:	Professional staff	Volunteers	Users
Core	M	N	N
Essential	C	C	C
Complementary	N	S	M

Figure 11.1 A New Configuration of the Roles and Tasks in Co-Producing Public Services
Key: M = main provider; S = secondary provider; N = none or few; C = contested tasks/roles.

like identifying socially isolated citizens, elders in need, etc. (*ibid*). Moreover, volunteers can provide all the firefighting services available in rural parts of some EU countries, like Estonia, thereby replacing the paid staff (Tönurist & Sruva, 2017). However, this type of volunteering should not be confused with co-production—there are no longer any public professionals with whom citizens can interact or co-produce. By contrast, in parent co-op childcare in Sweden, the staff provide the core pedagogical services, while parents provide both essential and complementary services, like the management and maintenance of the facility, arranging social events, etc. So, an approach that takes into account a more nuanced understanding than a dichotomy of actors and/or tasks seems appropriate in future research into co-production.

The above discussion of 'who' co-produces helps to identify a related consideration, i.e., the difference, if any, between volunteers and co-producers in the provision of public services. Some authors suggest volunteering and co-production are more or less the same thing, they use these concepts interchangeably and they take the recent expansion of volunteers in the provision of public services as a prime example of the growth of co-production (*ibid*.). Others argue that there are nevertheless some basic differences between them in terms of providing inputs to and/or consuming outputs from public goods and services (Alford, 2009). Yet, others warn about rushing to judgment and suggest more study and analysis is necessary. We will, therefore, briefly consider some similarities between volunteering and co-production, and then discuss the differences between them.

Volunteering and co-production often have a similar organizational base and their members may share similar values, although with a different emphasis (Pestoff, 1998, 2008a). Volunteers provide services to others without expecting a direct material reward for their efforts and without benefiting directly or personally from the services provided. They may, of course, receive indirect benefits, like job-training, skills development, social contacts and/or personal satisfaction, but volunteers are clearly not service recipients. Co-production, by contrast, is based on the participation of service users both in the provision and consumption of a service. Co-producers are, therefore, the direct beneficiaries of their own and others' activities in providing public services (Alford, 2009: 24).

How can these seemingly contrary perspectives on the relationship between volunteering and co-production be reconciled? One possible explanation for both volunteering and co-production being present and considered relevant concepts in public service provision is gleaned from the early findings of research on public administrations regimes (PARs) (see Chapter 9, Pestoff, 2018a). Volunteers only play a marginal role in traditional public administration and New Public Management (NPM). By contrast, New Public Governance (NPG) relies more heavily on citizen participation in the provision of public services and co-production is considered a key component or aspect of this PAR. Here it corresponds closely with the idea of dual roles of co-producers, who make unpaid inputs to public service provision by contributing their time and effort to improve the quality of public services and, at the same time, who receive or consume the same public services as service users. Finally, a Communitarian type of regime also calls for much greater citizen input to public service provision, primarily to compensate for public budget cutbacks, but here their role is mainly confined to being volunteers, rather than individual service users. (See Chapter 9 for details.)

So, the lack of clarity about the different role played by volunteers and co-producers stems, at least in part, from the institutional context of public sector reforms. Failing to distinguish between PARs and the role attributed to various actors, like volunteers and co-producers, by different PARs creates unnecessary confusion. Both NPG and a Communitarian type of regime call for more citizen participation in the provision of public services, but citizens participate in quite different ways. In NPG they participate as co-producers, while in a Communitarian type of regime they participate mainly as volunteers.

D.2 The 'Where' of Co-Production and the Role of TSOs

We also want to consider 'where' the co-production of public services takes place. Are public services provided in-house by a public agency or are they contracted out to a third sector organization (TSO)? The former implies a different set of relations with its main stakeholders than the latter, particularly from the perspective of co-production. Ostrom and her colleagues argued that co-production comprised lay activities by persons outside the public agencies delivering public services, i.e., they were not part of the public service providers (Ostrom, 1996: 1073). If so, then the role of professionals, volunteers and service users/citizens should be different in these organizations. This is illustrated in Figure 11.2.

Professionals are civil servants in public agencies delivering public services, while they are considered employees or staff in TSOs. Volunteers can contribute their time and effort for others either in public agencies or TSOs. But, if they do not consume the service, they are not considered co-producers of public or TSO services. Finally, service users are clients of public agencies that provide them with a service, while they are members of a TSO that

Service providers/service provision	Public agency (in-house service provision)	Services provision is contracted out to a TSO
Professionals	Civil servants	TSO employees
Volunteers	Public sector volunteers	TSO volunteers
Service users/citizens	Compliant clients	Members as co-producers

Figure 11.2 Service Providers and Service Provision—In-House or Contracted Out?

delivers public financed services to themselves and others. As clients they can choose to comply or not to comply with the advice and/or instructions provided by a public agency. For example, patients at the NHS can comply to a greater or lesser extent with their doctor's orders for reducing their daily sugar intake and getting more daily exercise to help stave off type 2 diabetes. While they can be more or less compliant, they do not belong to the NHS, so this is a purely individual act of co-production. By contrast, being a member of a diabetes association gives them both rights and responsibilities not afforded to individual clients. Co-producers both provide inputs to and receive outputs from their service organization. They also share in the outcomes of their engagement, often in the form of better quality services that depend in part on their contribution of time and effort as members. Members of a diabetes association that receives public funding for providing a public service clearly meet the criteria of being co-producers. For example, members of a local diabetes association that gets public support can help to co-produce a healthier lifestyle for themselves and their fellow members of the association (Söderholm Werkö, 2008). This clearly is beneficial for individual members and society-at-large, as well as for achieving public health goals related to promoting a healthy lifestyle among citizens.

Finally, two other key considerations for deciding what is and isn't co-production of a public service are related to the purpose of the public policy and whether outside activities to achieve public goals receive substantial public support. First, we need to ask whether a TSO attempts to fulfill public policy, either directly or indirectly, in a given area. Second, we should inquire whether its activities in delivering a service to the public and/or its members receives public financing or other kinds of public support. Figure 11.3 addresses this combination of factors.

A TSO can either attempt to fulfill public policy aims or not, with or without public support. TSOs that fulfill public aims, directly or indirectly, without public support are engaged in what is usually called 'parallel production' of services. These TSOs may provide various types of services

Fulfilling public policy aims and/or receiving public support	*Receives no public support for providing services*	*Receives public support for providing services*
TSO fulfills public policy aims	Parallel production of services by TSOs without public support.	Public supported co-production of services.
TSO does not fulfill public policy aims	TSOs provide various types of services to its members and/or the community, regardless of public policy	TSOs are financed for reasons other than providing public services.

Figure 11.3 TSOs Fulfilling Public Policy Aims and/or Receiving Public Support for Co-Production

to their members, based on their needs, and/or to the community regardless of public policy, without any public support. But, they are not attempting to co-produce public services. Similarly, TSOs that do receive public support may or may not attempt to fulfill public policy in a given area. Previously, many TSOs received general grants to cover a variety of civic activities deemed worthy by politicians and public authorities. However, with the advent of New Public Management, many general grants to TSOs were turned into contracts for service provision and became subject to public tender and competitive bidding. Today many TSOs receive funds for providing such services to their members. Parent-managed childcare services like those in France, Germany and Sweden that receive public funds, qualify as co-production, because most of their funds come from public sources. Yet, services that are not public policy specific, but nevertheless receive funds from public sources through general grants are not, therefore, considered co-production. Thus, only the service provision by TSOs that both fulfills public policy aims and receives substantial public support is considered co-production, according to this understanding. Other TSO services provided to members are either considered parallel production or independent provision and/or they are general grant financed services that either don't fulfill public policy and/or don't receive substantial public support.

D.3. Different Understandings of 'Collective' Co-Production

Finally, different approaches to 'collective' co-production are also found in the literature, and they have some implications for this discussion. Two main perspectives are considered herein: sociological and economic. Rich (1981) explored the interaction of the voluntary and governmental sectors in the USA in terms of co-production. He employed two dimensions to distinguish different types of co-production: the type of activity, passive or active, and its impact on the community, positive or negative. He also differentiated between individual and collective activities in terms of positive co-production (*ibid.*: 62). Taking home security measures or becoming a volunteer at a social service agency comprise a positive individual action, while joining a neighborhood watch or helping to arrange after school recreation activities for young people illustrate collective co-production (*ibid.*). From the perspective of sociology and social work, the main distinction between individual and collective volunteering is often related to informal and formal channels of engagement. Individual or informal volunteering to help friends and family is distinguished from formal or collective action through voluntary organizations to help persons in need. The latter puts greater emphasis on formal groups that attempt to promote the delivery of high quality, public financed social services for themselves and others. This approach reflects Olson's discussion of the 'logic of collective action' (1965, 1971), where the distinction between individual and collective co-production is based on formal membership in third sector organizations (Pestoff, 2014a).

By contrast, the classical economic understanding of 'collective' co-production focuses more on who benefits from a service than who produces it. Brudney and England (1983) proposed a typology based on three broad types of co-production: individual, group and collective. Individual co-production is self-explanatory, while group co-production involves voluntary, active participation by a number of citizens and often requires formal mechanisms between public service agents and citizen groups in order to facilitate their interaction, i.e., to coordinate the efforts of individuals and provide a liaison between them and public authorities. They use Neighborhood Watch activities as an illustration of group co-production (*ibid.*: 64), while Rich regarded it as collective co-production.

Turning to their 'collective' category, it has some unique features worth noting that are related to its origin and can, therefore, influence our understanding of co-production. It was primarily seen as a response to fiscal stringency in the early 1980s, particularly after Proposition 13 in California. Local authorities in many parts of the state sought new arrangements for service delivery that emphasized more direct citizen involvement (Ferris, 1984), but also eliminated many public sector jobs. For example, some or all library services could be provided by volunteers, so engaging residents as 'Friends of the Library' could relieve beleaguered municipal budgets from part or all of this burden. From an economic perspective they note that the benefits of such programs "may be enjoyed by the entire community and individuals cannot reasonably be excluded from enjoying them on the basis of their failure to contribute" (Brudney & England, 1983: 64). This comprises a classical example of an academic concept being (mis)appropriated by practitioners, who have other interests than scholars. Brudney and England wanted to identify/discuss co-production as a new approach/conceptualization of public service delivery, while many politicians and/or public sector administrators chose to interpret it as an appropriate response to fiscal concerns after Prop. 13.

Moreover, more affluent municipalities were clearly better prepared to promote this type of 'collective' co-production than less affluent ones. So, Friends of the Library in Palos Verdes Estates or Rolling Hills Estates can raise significant amounts of money from book donations by wealthy families to their weekly or monthly book sales, while this is not often possible in an urban ghetto like Watts. Furthermore, this 'collective' option pursued by many cities and counties after Prop. 13 lacks a genuine voluntary element on the part of many service users, who, in fact, appear to have little choice. Once the government cuts the funds for certain basic public services, citizens must either assume responsibility for providing it by themselves, without public funding, or they simply will have to go without. Thus, it seems more like 'coerced' co-production (Fotaki, 2011) than the "voluntary efforts by citizens to improve service quality", which was one of the five criteria of Brudney and England's much-cited definition (*ibid.*: 63). Rather, this is a classical 'public good' approach, and one that seems similar to policies currently pursued in Communitarian PARs in a variety of countries, like the Big Society program for reforming the public sector in Great Britain (Hudson, 2011; Slocock, 2015), 'integrated community care' that guides Japan's current eldercare reforms (Agenosono *et al.*, 2014; Tabata, 2014; Tsutsui, 2014) and similar public sector reforms in the Netherlands (Nederhand & Van Meerkerk, 2017) and Denmark (Politiken, 2015). Finally, it is worth remembering that when funding to public services is cut, there may no longer be any public servants with whom citizens can interact or co-produce.

E. Conclusions

A seminal OECD report (2011) on co-production calls for rethinking traditional public service delivery in a new socio-economic environment. It argues that existing models of public service provision are not only tenuous, but also not affordable in the long-run. This lends urgency to developing alternative models that focus on greater citizen participation on the output side of public service delivery, particularly in social services and health care. Co-production transforms the relationship between service users and providers, ensuring the former greater influence and ownership, by involving citizens/users in more systematic exchanges with the paid staff who create and deliver public services. Therefore, the OECD warns that co-production is more than consultations or simply giving citizens/users a say in and/or more responsibility for the design, provision or evaluation of public services (*ibid.*: 18). Providing citizens and users with more influence over public services, particularly about service quality, may prove crucial for evoking their participation as co-producers of enduring, labor intensive services like health care and social services. Herein lies both the challenges and opportunities posed by co-production.

Initially, co-production focused on the output side of the political system (Ostrom, 1996; Parks *et al.*, 1981), but the study of co-production expanded in scope, with the renewed interest in this phenomenon in the 21st century. While this favored a more encompassing or 'enhanced' approach to co-production, it came at the price of achieving clarity concerning what was included and what was not. However, this chapter represents a growing concern that the chance of finding or proposing a generic or unifying definition of this multi-faceted phenomenon is becoming more elusive as more scholars with different backgrounds and perspectives join this rapidly expanding field of study. Perhaps, we need, therefore, to shift focus a bit and consider identifying two or more schools of co-production. The purpose of this chapter was to briefly examine some differences between these different approaches to the study of co-production, and explore their implications for the potential of co-production to reform the public sector. The two main contenders as schools of co-production were an input/output model (Easton, 1965) that emphasizes citizen participation on the output side of the political system and a service management model that focuses on various stages in the value chain approach.

The input/output model emphasizes the basic features of the context in which co-production takes place, i.e., the political system and public policy-making. A service management approach views co-production from a value chain perspective that includes half a dozen different types of activities and appears to attribute them equal weight. Similarly, a co-creation approach embraces a service management's value chain perspective, but primarily seems to emphasize citizen participation in the design of public services. Hopefully, juxtaposing them can serve to disentangle citizens' activities in the provision of public services and bring greater clarity to the debate among scholars and practitioners, in terms of the unique capacity of co-production to promote citizen/user participation in the delivery of public services of consequence to them (Ostrom, 1996).

It continued by calling attention to the growing importance of volunteers and TCOs in the provision of public services. However, a voluntary sector management perspective faces a challenge from several issues related to distinguishing co-production from volunteering. So, it presented three key issues for the development of a coherent third sector model of co-production: (i) the difference between volunteers and co-producers or the 'who and what' of co-production; (ii) the 'where' of co-production and the role of TSOs; and (iii) the contrast between an economic and social perspective on 'collective' co-production. Therefore, this chapter proposed to reconfigure the concept co-production by expanding it to include three actors: paid staff, volunteers and users, as well as three types of tasks performed by these actors: core, essential and complementary. But, the intention was neither to narrow the focus of the study of co-production nor to widen it, *per se*. Rather, it maintained that the time is ripe to reconfigure our understanding of the actors, roles and tasks involved in co-producing public services, in order to better appreciate the realities facing citizens and practitioners today. Furthermore, given the clear difference in approaches noted earlier, it seems more reasonable to focus on mapping these diverse schools of co-production than attempting to provide yet another definition that cannot possibly encompass all these diverse approaches.

Volunteers can participate in the provision of public services, but they do not co-produce them. Moreover, citizen participation in co-production is very different from client compliance with a doctor's orders. Co-production, according to Ostrom, takes place outside public agencies, so TSOs can play a crucial role, when their members co-produce public services that are contracted out to them. However, only TSOs that both fulfill public policy aims and receive substantial public support for providing services are considered co-producers. Other TSOs engage in parallel production, provide various services to their members and/or to the community or subsist on public grants without fulfilling specific public policy aims, and without co-producing public services.

Finally, the distinction between economic or austerity measures initiated by the government and the voluntary promotion of collective citizen initiatives is important for policies designed to evoke greater citizen participation in co-production. A purely economic approach detracts attention from voluntary citizen participation in the provision of services of consequence to them. By contrast, collective co-production based on greater citizen/user participation in the implementation of public policies resembles a New Public Governance approach to reforming the public sector and provision of public services. The value chain approach and a co-creation perspective, combined with the growing use of volunteers to replace paid staff for providing public services, appears tied to a Communitarian type of public administration regime. Taken together, this can help to remind us that once co-production becomes equated with volunteering there will be little to compare it with or contrast it to.

The next chapter continues this discussion about rethinking traditional public service delivery in a new socio-economic and political environment. It does so by proposing new models of participatory democracy and democratic governance for the public sector, both at the micro- and macro-levels.

12 Co-Production and the Third Sector in the 21st Century

New Schools of Democracy and Participatory Public Service Management

A. Background

Today, leading scholars of international public management note that co-production has become one of the cornerstones of public policy reforms worldwide (Osborne, 2017). Earlier, a seminal OECD report (2011) on co-production called for rethinking traditional public service delivery in a new socio-economic environment. It argued that existing models of public service provision are not only tenuous, but also not affordable in the long-run. This lent greater urgency to developing alternative models that focus on citizen participation in the design and delivery of public services or co-production. But, it also noted that by involving citizens/users in more systematic exchanges with the paid staff who deliver public services, co-production transforms the relationship between service users and providers, ensuring the former greater influence and ownership. Thus, co-production is more than tokenism, occasional client consultation or focus group discussions. Providing citizens and users with more influence over public services, particularly about service quality, may prove crucial for evoking their participation as co-producers, particularly in enduring, labor intensive services like health care and social services. Herein lies both the challenges and opportunities posed by co-production, but the devil is often in the details.

Nobel Laureate Elinor Ostrom states that co-production is based on citizens playing an active role in producing public goods and services of consequence to them (1996: 1073). Co-production is considered a partnership between citizens and public service providers that is essential for meeting a growing number of economic, political and social challenges in the 21st century. These challenges include, among other things, improving the efficiency and effectiveness of public services in times of financial strain; increasing the legitimacy of the public sector after decades of questioning its ability with the spread of New Public Management; finding viable solutions for meeting the growing needs of aging populations in many parts of the world and facing the growing threat posed by populism in many advanced democracies today. Neither the government nor citizens can solve such issues on their own. Co-production can make an important contribution to the debate on public management because it goes to the heart of both effective public services delivery and the role of public services in achieving societal ends, like social integration and citizen engagement (Osborne *et al.*, 2013: 145).

Research on parent participation in European childcare and preschool services demonstrates arrangements that put the experiences and knowledge of the service user at the heart of public service design and delivery (Pestoff, 2006; Vamstad, 2007). For example, in France, Germany and Sweden, parent participation in public financed third sector childcare is manifested in their responsibility for the management and maintenance of these services. A work obligation for parents not only provides them with crucial insights into details related to the daily operation of services and their overall management, but also gives them a sense of belonging and 'ownership' of the services (Pestoff, 1998, 2006). Moreover, the boards of cooperative childcare facilities are comprised of parents who are responsible for the facility's economic stability and hiring the staff, as well as deciding important issues like its opening and closing hours, the availability of service on holidays and during summer vacations, etc. These issues not only concern individual parents, but they have important economic consequences for the viability of the social enterprises providing such services. Most important, these matters are no longer decided by distant politicians or bureaucrats, who are mainly interested in curtailing public expenses. Co-production allows service users and the front-line staff to gain more control over them, particularly over service quality, and, therefore, provides a good method for promoting democratic governance and participatory public management.

B. A Brief Summary of Previous Chapters

This book addressed a number of central topics related to the study of co-production, and it combined theoretical discussions and important conceptual issues with empirical research that corroborated these discussions and issues. Building on ideas of Hirschman, it maintained that co-production provides a strategy for moving beyond exit and voice, particularly in collective forms, for providing enduring public services. It confronted these ideas with unique empirical material from parents using various third sector providers of childcare in Sweden in the early 1990s, which by and large confirmed these theoretical considerations. Parents with experience of both public and third sector daycare overwhelmingly preferred the latter form of service provision. A second empirical study compared parent participation in preschool services in eight European countries. Parents with third sector providers participated more actively than they did in public or private for-profit services. These insights were also corroborated by a newer study that focused on different providers of these services in Sweden, parent and worker co-ops, public services and small for-profit providers (Vamstad, 2007).

These three studies suggest that public policies can either crowd-in or crowd-out desired behavior by citizens, and co-production is not an exception to this rule. This research on childcare and preschool services in Europe led to three main conclusions. First, there are different dimensions of citizen participation in the provision of public financed social services, namely economic, social, political and service specific participation. Second, a higher level of citizen participation on all dimensions is noted for third sector providers of public financed social services, because it is based on collective action and direct client participation. This was illustrated by parent co-op childcare in France, Germany and Sweden. Third, some limited citizen participation is also noted for public provision of childcare services, but parents are usually encouraged to contribute in more sporadic fashion, like helping with the Christmas or spring parties. However, they seldom have the opportunity to play a more active or significant role, like managing the services or having decision-making rights and responsibilities for the service provision. Thus, a 'glass ceiling' in public services limits citizens to playing a passive role as service users who can make demands on the public sector, but who do not participate in decisions nor take any responsibility for implementing public policy (Pestoff, 2008a, 2009).

This research also focused on crucial conceptual issues for understanding co-production of third sector social services and health care, particularly in relation to the facility and saliency of participating in such services. It also noted that in spite of some similarities between co-production and volunteering, there are nevertheless major differences between them. It continued by examining issues of small groups and collective action for the sustainability of co-production and noted the importance of more nuanced approaches by governments to promoting co-production. It turned to democratic innovations and underlined the synergy between the three key concepts, social enterprise, public sector innovation and co-production, for developing a more coherent post-NPM paradigm. It then argued that co-production is currently at the crossroads of four public administration regimes (PARs), i.e., traditional public administration, NPM, NPG and a Communitarian regime. The principal actors in co-production, the professional staff and citizens, play quite different roles in each of them, so citizen participation will mean different things in each of them. It continued by exploring the impact of public administration regimes and co-production on hybrid organizations. It noted that their impact will depend in part on the type of third sector organization and its internal decision-making rules. It considered the potential contribution of additional definitions and recognizing different schools of study to our understanding of this phenomenon. It also discussed the role of volunteers and third sector organizations to co-production. It argued that co-production now includes three main actors rather than two: the professional staff, volunteers and citizens/clients as well as three rather than two categories of tasks performed by them, core, essential and complementary.

Finally, this chapter reaches some conclusions about the contribution of co-production for managing public services, augmenting the legitimacy of the public sector and renewing democracy. It argues that co-production and the third sector together comprise a new model of democratic governance that can readily complement representative democracy rather than replace it by populism in the 21st century. It also considers the implications of participatory public service management.

C. A New School of Democracy?

The academic perspective on the role of third sector organizations has shifted radically in recent decades. De Tocqueville considered TSOs as 'schools of democracy' (1835), while Putnam argued more recently that TSOs could still 'make democracy work' (1993). However, society experienced massive changes that transformed it from rural and agrarian to urban and global, during the nearly 200 years since de Tocqueville. This has broad implications for citizen participation and democracy, where 'checkbook membership' seems to go hand in hand with 'bowling alone' today (2005).

Furthermore, it has been argued that co-production can eventually lead to a more democratic regime of governance (Pestoff, 1998, 2009; Becker *et al.*, 2017). But, we need to ask, what is democratic governance? Hirst defines governance as "a means by which an activity or ensemble of activities is controlled or directed, such that it delivers an acceptable range of outcomes according to some established social standards" (2000: 24). He argues that the concept of 'governance' points to the need to rethink democracy and find new methods of control and regulation of the big organizations that dominate both the public and private sectors (*ibid.*). Does the need to rethink democracy also imply greater citizen participation and influence in the provision of public services, particularly those services that directly impact their daily life and/or that of their loved-ones? Can co-production potentially provide a new method of control and regulation of big public organizations? We feel that it definitely can and does.

Held (1996) analyzed and contrasted classical and 20th century models of democracy. Participatory democracy is located in the lower right-hand corner of his scheme. According to this analysis, participatory democracy combines ideas of pluralism and direct democracy (*ibid.*). But, what do these traditional models of democracy say about future developments or newer models of democracy in the 21st century? Let's explore that question briefly. D. Easton's *Systems Analysis of Political Life* (1965) distinguished between the input and output sides of the political system, as well as its potential outcomes. The input side is related to decision-making, political parties, elections, legislatures, etc., while the output side implements decisions made on the input side and is comprised of the public administration and public services, etc. Democratic reforms traditionally focus on the input side, by mobilizing citizens, making their voice heard, giving them more influence, etc. E. Ostrom and her colleagues made a radical departure from this when they introduced the concept of co-production to analyze citizen participation in the provision of public financed services. Such a shift in focus opened entirely new possibilities for exploring democratic innovations in the provision of public services on the output side of public policy-making.

Returning briefly to the idea of voluntary associations as 'schools of democracy', they no longer appear to function as they were described by de Tocqueville and their decline was lamented by Putnam (2000). So, perhaps we need to consider other institutions and sites where citizens can learn democratic habits and develop democratic routines in their everyday life. One such institution or site in society could be membership in social enterprises and social co-ops that provide them with important social services of consequence to them and their daily life. Thus, such organizations have the potential to become new schools of democracy in the 21st century, when many of the older voluntary associations no longer seem to function as well as they once did. Herein lies one of the main challenges and opportunities posed by co-production that was explored from different perspectives in the chapters of this volume.

D. Participatory Public Service Management

In spite of its potential advantages, co-production will not occur spontaneously (Ostrom, 1996). Several prominent scholars have noted the need for co-production to be based on a complementary rather than a supplementary relation between service users and providers (Ostrom, 1996; Alford, 2009; Pestoff, 2008a; Brandsen & Honingh, 2016). About the same time as the renewed academic and professional interest in co-production, Peters (1994, 1996) discussed the emergence of four alternatives to the traditional model of public administration: the market model, the participatory state, flexible government and deregulated government. Given its affinity to co-production, we will focus on participatory public sector management. In a participatory state groups normally excluded under more hierarchical models are permitted greater involvement. This approach concentrates power in the lower echelons of the administration, the workers as well as the clients of the organization, rather than on the managers. It recognizes that the workers and clients found closest to the actual production of public goods and services have the greatest amount of information about these programs. If the energy, talents and ideas of those groups are harnessed government will work more efficiently and effectively. However, this calls for greater empowerment and self-governance for such groups, which has clear implications for managing the public sector as a whole. Both the staff and clients become more directly involved in managerial decisions and governance of the service (*ibid.*: 13), often through a greater dialog between them. Ostrom recognizes increased contacts between service users and providers as one of the conditions that can heighten the probability that co-production will lead to an improvement in public services (1996). A multi-stakeholder dialog between the front-line staff and service users helps to place the experience and knowledge of both groups at the heart of effective public service design and delivery (Osborne et al., 2013) and can promote collaboration between them.

The 'participatory state' model is still less familiar than the market approach in terms of its political ideology, but some of its recommendations, nevertheless, appear quite similar. Hierarchy is considered a severe impediment to effective public service management and governance. The participatory state proposes much flatter structures because better quality goods or services would require fewer controllers from above. A polycentric system allows both service users and providers more autonomy to make decisions about services on their own and to be able to follow through when implementing them (Ostrom, 1996: 1082). NPM focuses on the managers, while the participatory approach outlined by Peters concentrates on the lower echelons of workers, as well as on the clients of public service organizations to provide the solution (1994: 11). It also emphasizes the need for new structures to channel participation, especially for clients and front-line employees. This calls for the creation of a variety of councils, advisory groups, etc. to promote a dialog between front-line staff and their clients. This model enhances the role of the citizen and attempts to induce democratic participation into public management by means other than voting (*ibid.*: 13).

Moreover, the participatory state is dependent upon citizens themselves becoming involved in making some choices about policy, particularly its implementation, both in their role as users or clients and as providers of public financed services. It would give citizens more consumer choice and direct control over programs, similar to the market model. But, the manner in which consumer choices would be exercised in the participatory state would be through some sort of political process. Their participation might take the form of referenda on policy or it may be in local structures, like parent involvement in school committees, etc. (*ibid.*: 15). It could also include their direct participation, in collaboration with the professional staff, at the site of provision of a particular service, as noted earlier for parents in parent co-op preschool services in Europe.

Finally, although the prescriptions of neo-liberals and those proposing a participatory state may bear some similarities, they are definitely not the same. Rather than being a means for creating competition among service providers in order to facilitate the market, decentralization in the participatory model is intended primarily to channel control to a different set of bureaucrats, and/or to the clients (*ibid.*: 16), through new direct democratic or participatory institutions.

The chapters in this book have mainly focused on various aspects of increased citizen/user participation in the provision of public financed services of consequence to them and their loved-ones. They only referred occasionally to the other side of the coin, to the professional staff that provides these welfare services. However, the professional staff is not completely absent from this purview. Elsewhere in the course of this research on co-production and consumer influence, the focus has been on the work environment of the staff providing welfare services. The Karasek and Theorell model of demand, control and support (1990) has been employed to analyze work environment in the social enterprises providing preschool services in Sweden. The demand/control/support model posits that a high degree of both demands and control are necessary for a good work environment, while stress mainly occurs when demands are plentiful, but few possibilities exist for control. It is highly relevant for Peter's proposals for participatory public management reforms.

Corroboration for the idea of facilitating more participation both by front-line employees and their clients is found in Chapter 5 of this volume. Not only parents, but also the staff rated co-op preschools much better than municipal and for-profit services in terms of their influence. These social enterprises demonstrate that giving parents and staff more influence cannot only enrich the work environment (Pestoff, 2000; Pestoff & Vamstad, 2014), but also renew the public sector and improve service quality both in the eyes of users and the staff (Vamstad, 2012). This interpretation is premised on the assumption that service quality and work environment are closely related or linked to each other. An employee who feels tired and exhausted when she/he wakes up in the morning, who has tossed and turned all night worrying about work related problems, who dreads the idea of going to work because they have little or no control or influence on the what, when, why, where and how of their daily routines, who has little chance to learn new things or advance at work, such an employee will not provide as good quality service as one who has the opposite experience of their work. Likewise, a client who experiences an unhappy, stressed or disgruntled service professional will not experience as good service quality as one being served by an employee with the opposite feeling.

A second pillar in studies of social enterprises providing preschool services in Sweden was, therefore, the work environment of the staff providing such services. The empirical materials were obtained from two separate studies of work environment at Swedish preschool facilities, one from 1994–1995 and another from 2006–2007. These studies document that the work environment in the public sector deteriorated dramatically starting in the 1990s, with the ascendency of New Public Management and cutbacks in public budgets. However, small social enterprises that provide preschool services continued to offer a better work environment than public facilities (Pestoff, 1998, 2000; Pestoff & Vamstad, 2014). In the first study, the majority of the staff at social cooperatives had previously worked for municipal preschools and could therefore compare the work environment there, while the second study directly compared the staff attitudes in different organizations. The majority of the staff at all types of social enterprises preferred working for them compared to municipal preschools. In almost all respects, work life in the social enterprises was rated better or much better than municipal preschool services, and these differences remained stable over time (*ibid.*). In addition, the staff at social co-ops claim more freedom and responsibility to make decisions, i.e., they had more control according the Karasek-Theorell model. They also claim greater possibilities for self-development and more co-determination (*ibid.*), as might be expected according to a participatory public management model discussed by Peters.

In the terms of Karasek and Theorell, work in social enterprises in Sweden is psychologically demanding, but it provides high decision latitude and high social support for the workers. These work life attributes stood in sharp contrast with those found in the services provided by the large bureaucratic organizations often associated with public sector services in Sweden. This suggests that one of the best and most direct ways to enrich work life in the public sector, redesign the work organization and promote humane human resource management in the provision of welfare services in Sweden would be to decentralize the provision of social services by contracting them out to TSOs and letting social enterprises provide them, with continued public financing. Moreover, the loss of productivity, poor quality of services and the cost of treating stress related symptoms and absenteeism due to stress related sickness are widespread in the Swedish public sector, particularly in welfare services (Pestoff, 2008a). So, improving the work environment of public sector staff is, or should be considered, an important economic, political and social problem that requires immediate and sustained attention (Pestoff, 2000; Pestoff & Vamstad, 2014). Efforts to reform the public sector should, therefore, clearly take work environment into account. Enriching the work environment of front-line staff and facilitating the participation of citizens in the provision of services of consequence to them would help fulfill some of the goals indicated in the participatory public management model discussed by Peters. Furthermore, recognizing the interconnection between the two goals of co-production and participatory public management would be a step in the right direction for achieving a more participatory state and public management, because they don't conflict, but rather complement each other.

E. A Participatory State: Co-Production, Civil Democracy and Democratic Governance

Hirst (2002) states that the spread of the concept 'governance' underlines the need to rethink control and regulation in today's 'organizational society'. Big organizations on either side of the public/private divide in advanced industrial societies leave little room for citizen influence or democracy. Elsewhere, he argues in favor of 'associative democracy' that attributes citizens and civil society a greater role both in the production of goods and services as well as the decisions that govern such activities (1994). Civil democracy was defined as

> citizen empowerment through cooperative self-management of personal social services, where citizens become members of a social enterprise, where they participate directly in the production of local services they demand, as users and producers of such services, and where they therefore become co-producers of these services.
>
> (Pestoff, 1998: 25)

Democratic governance was defined as "a policy that promotes substantially greater citizen participation and third sector provision of welfare services, and thereby significantly greater welfare pluralism. At the micro-level, it involves significant users and staff participation and influence in the organizations providing welfare services" (Pestoff, 2009: 198). Chapter 5 suggested that they can both contribute to the development of a new paradigm of participatory democracy (*ibid.*).

Co-production is a central concept in New Public Governance and an essential part of a broader framework to provide a new theory for public service management. Therefore, it is a key concern for a participatory state and participatory democracy. As noted, the logic of providing services is very distinct from manufacturing in several ways. In particular, services are often co-produced by professional providers and the citizens/clients of the service. Moreover, co-production is central to effective public service delivery, because it helps to achieve societal goals, by placing the experience and knowledge of service users at the heart of effective public service design and delivery (Osborne *et al.*, 2013). A participatory state relies on democratic governance at the macro-level and significant user and staff participation and influence in the organization of welfare services. Taken together, the concepts of co-production, civil democracy and democratic governance can, therefore, make a significant contribution to developing a broader framework that can provide the base for a new theory, not only for public service management, but also participatory democracy and a participatory state. In order to more fully embrace the complexities posed by co-production, democratic governance and a participatory state, we should stop to ponder the concluding passage of Elinor Ostrom's Nobel Prize speech in Stockholm:

> Designing institutions to forge or nudge entirely self-interested individuals to achieve better outcomes has been a major policy prescription for more than half a century, yet it has failed miserably . . . When the world we are trying to explain and improve is not well described by a simple model, we must continue to improve our frameworks and theories to be able to understand complexity and not simply reject it.
>
> (2009b: 436)

The concepts of co-production, democratic governance and participatory public service management share the common vision of a new, more active, role for citizens in the provision of welfare services. They can make a major contribution to developing a more democratic framework and more nuanced theories necessary to challenge the dominance of New Public Management and the growing threat of populism facing many advanced democracies today.

References

Agenosono, Y., S. Kamozawa & T. Hori, 2014; Japan's Next Care System: How Do Communities Participate – a PowerPoint presentation; 3rd International Conf. on Evidence-Based Policy in Long-Term Care, London, 2 Sept. 2014.

Alcock, P., 2010; Building Big Society: A New Policy Environment for the Third Sector in England, *Voluntary Sector Review*, 1/3: 379–389.

Alford, J., 2002; Why Do Public Sector Clients Co-Produce? Towards a Contingency Theory, *Administration & Society*, 34/1: 32–56.

Alford, J., 2009; *Engaging Public Sector Clients: From Service Delivery to Co-Production*; Houndmills, Hamps., UK & New York, NY: Palgrave Macmillian.

Alford, J., 2014; The Multiple Facets of Co-Production: Building on the Work of Elinor Ostrom, *Public Management Review*, 16/3: 299–316.

Andersen, L.L. & H.H. Espersen, 2017; Samskabelse, samproduktion og partnerskaber—teoretiske perspektiver, *Partnerskaber og samarbejder mellem det offentlige og civil-samfundet*; Copenhagen: Socialstyrelsen.

Anheier, H., 2005; *Nonprofit Organizations: Theory, Management, Policy*; London & New York: Routledge.

Anheier, H., 2011; Governance and Leadership in Hybrid Organizations: Comparative and Interdisciplinary Perspectives; Heidelberg, Germany: University of Heidelberg, Centre for Social Investment, draft background paper.

Baglioni, S., 2017; A Remedy for All Sins? Introducing a Special Issue on Social Enterprise and Welfare Regimes in Europe, *Voluntas*, 28/6: 2325–2338.

Barber, B., 1984, 2003; *Strong Democracy: Participatory Politics for a New Age*; Berkeley, CA: University of California Press.

Baturina, D., T. Brandsen, R. Chaves Ávila, J. Matančević, J.B. Pahl, U. Pape, F. Petrella, B. Pieliński, C. Rentzsch, T. Savall Morera, R. Simsa & A. Zimmer, 2016; Transforming Policy Environments and Third Sector Development in Europe; ISTR Conference Paper, Stockholm.

Bauwens, M., 2005; The Political Economy of Peer Production, *1,000 Days of Theory*, A. Kroker & M. Kroker (eds.); www.etheory.net/articles.aspx?id=449.

Becker, S., M. Naumann & T. Moss, 2017; Between Coproduction and Commons: Understanding Initiatives to Reclaim Urban Energy Provision in Berlin and Hamburg, *Urban Research & Practice*, 10/1: 63–85.

Beckers, V., L. Tummers & Voorberg, W., 2013; *From Public Innovation to Social Innovation: A Literature Review of Relevant Drivers and Barriers*; Rotterdam: Erasmus University Rotterdam.

BEPA, 2010; *Empowering People, Driving Change: Social Innovation in the European Union*; Brussels: European Commission, Bureau of European Policy Advisers.

Billis, D., 2010; Towards a Theory of Hybrid Organizations, Ch. 3 in *Hybrid Organizations and the Third Sector: Challenges for Practice, Theory & Policy*, D. Billis (ed.); New York & London: Palgrave Macmillan.

Blomqvist, P., 2003; The Choice Revolution: Privatization of Swedish Welfare Services in the 1990s, *Social Policy & Administration*, 38/2: 139–155.

Blomqvist, P. & B. Rothstein, 2000; *Välfärdstatens nya ansikte*; Stockholm: Agora.

Borzaga, C. & J. Defourny, 2001; *The Emergence of Social Enterprise*; London & New York: Routledge.

Botero, A., A. Gryf Paterson & J. Saad-Sulomon, 2012; *Towards Peer Production in Public Services: Cases from Finland*; Helsinki: Aalto University.

Bovaird, T., 2007; Beyond Engagement and Participation: User and Community Co-Production of Public Services, *Public Administration Review*, 67/5: 846–860; DOI: 10.1111/j.1540-6210.2007.00773.x.

Bovaird, T. & E. Löffler, 2012; From Engagement to Co-Production: How Users and Communities Contribute to Public Services, Ch. 3 in *New Public Governance, the Third Sector and Co-Production*, V. Pestoff, T. Brandsen & B. Verschuere (eds.); London & New York: Routledge.

Brandsen, T., 2004; *Quasi-Market Governance: An Anatomy of Innovation*; Utretcht: Lemma Publ.

Brandsen, T., 2012; Social Innovation; PowerPoint presentation at the 3rd EMES Ph.D. Summer School, Trento.

Brandsen, T., 2014; *The Wilco Project: A Summary of the Findings, 2010–2014*; www.wilcoproject.eu, accessed 15 October 2015.

Brandsen, T., S. Cattacin, A. Evers & A. Zimmer (eds.), 2016; *Social Innovation in the Urban Context*; Heidelberg, New York & London: Springer Open.

Brandsen, T., A. Evers, S. Cattacin & A. Zimmer, 2016; Social Innovation: A Sympathetic and Critical Interpretation, Ch. 1 in *Social Innovation in the Urban Context*, T. Brandsen, S. Cattacin, A. Evers & A. Zimmer (eds.); Heidelberg, New York & London: Springer Open.

Brandsen, T. & M. Honingh, 2015; Distinguishing Different Types of Co-Production of Public Services: A Conceptual Analysis Based on Classical Definitions, *Public Management Review*, 76/3: 427–435.

Brandsen, T. & V. Pestoff, 2006; Co-Production, the Third Sector and the Delivery of Public Services: An Introduction, *Public Management Review*, 8/4: 503–520; reprinted as a hardback in 2006 and as a paperback in 2009, as *Co-Production: The Third Sector and the Delivery of Public Services*; V. Pestoff & T. Brandsen (eds.); London & New York: Routledge.

Brandsen, T., W. van der Donk & K. Putters, 2003; Griffins or Chameleons? Hybridity as a Permanent and Inevitable Characteristic of the Third Sector, *International Journal of Public Administration*, 28/9–10: 749–765.

Brandsen, T., T. Steen & B. Verschuere (eds.), 2018; *Co-Production and Co-Creation: Engaging Citizens in Public Service Delivery*; London & New York: Routledge.

Brudney, J., 1984; Local Coproduction of Services and the Analysis of Municipal Productivity, *Urban Affairs Quarterly*, 19/4: 465–484.

Brudney, J. & R. England, 1983; Towards a Definition of the Coproduction Concept, *Public Administration Review*, 43: 59–65.

Dahl, R. & E. Tufte, 1973; *Size and Democracy*; Stanford, CA: Stanford University Press.

Dahlberg, L., 2004; *Welfare Relationships: Voluntary Organizations and Local Authorities in Supporting Relatives of Older People in Sweden*; Stockholm: Studies in Politics, No. 101, Ph.D. dissertation.

Defourny, J., 2007; Concepts and Realities of Social Enterprise: A European Perspective; Conference Paper, Leuven, Belgium.

Defourny, J., L. Hulgård & V. Pestoff (eds.), 2014; *Social Enterprise and the Third Sector: Changing European Landscapes in a Comparative Perspective*; London & New York: Routledge.

Defourny, J. & M. Nyssens, 2006; Defining Social Enterprise, *Social Enterprise: At the Crossroads of Market, Public Policies & Civil Society*, M. Nyssens (ed.); London & New York: Routledge.

Defourny, J. & M. Nyssens, 2014; The EMES Approach of Social Enterprise in a Comparative Perspective; *Social Enterprise and the Third Sector: Changing European Landscapes in a Comparative Perspective*; J. Defourny, L. Hulgård & V. Pestoff (eds.); London & New York: Routledge.

Defourny, J. & M. Nyssens, 2017; Fundamentals for an International Typology of Social Enterprise Models, *Voluntas*, 28: 2469–2497.

Defourny, J. & V. Pestoff, 2015; Towards a European Conceptualization of the Third Sector, Ch. 1 in *Accountability and Social Accounting for NPOs, NGOs, Cooperatives and Social Enterprises*, M. Andreaus, E. Costa & L. Parker (eds.); London & New York: E. Elgar.

Denhardt, J. & R. Denhardt, 2008; *The New Public Service: Serving Not Steering*; Armonk, NY & London: M.E. Scharp.

De Tocqueville, A., 1835/1840, 2000; *On Democracy in America/Democracy in America*; Chicago: Chicago University Press.

Donati, P., 2011; *Relational Sociology: A New Paradigm for the Social Sciences*; London & New York: Routledge.

Donati, P., 2014; *The Ferment of a New Civil Society and Civil Democracy: New Insights into Relational Goods*, P. Donati & P. Calvo (eds.); Bologna: Dept. of Philosophy & Sociology, Recera Revista de Pensament i Analisi, 14. pp. 19–46.

Easton, D., 1965; *A Systems Analysis of Political Life*; New York: J. Wiley & Sons.

Elcock, H., 1993; What Price Citizenship? Public Management and the Citizen's Charter; *The Waves of Change: Strategic Management in the Public Services*; April, 1993: 5–6, Sheffield, UK.

EMES Research Network, www.emes.net; accessed 20 July 2012.

Esping-Andersen, G., 1990; *The Three Worlds of Welfare Capitalism*; Cambridge, UK: B. Blackwell & Polity Press.

Esping-Andersen, G. (ed.), 1996; *Welfare States in Transition: National Adaptations in Global Economics*; Thousand Oaks, CA: Sage Publications.

Evers, A., 1993; The Welfare Mix Approach: Understanding the Pluralism of Welfare Systems; CIES Conference Paper, Barcelona.

Evers, A., 1995; Part of the Welfare Mix? The Third Sector as an Intermediate Area, *Voluntas*, 6/2: 119–139.

Evers, A., 2006; Complementary and Conflicting: The Different Meaning of 'User Involvement' in Social Services, Ch. 7 in *Nordic Civic Society Organizations and the Future of Welfare Services: A Model for Europe?*, A.-L. Matthies (ed.); Copenhagen: Nordic Council of Ministers, Tema Nord. pp. 255–276.

Evers, A. & J.-L. Laville, 2005; Defining the Third Sector in Europe, *The Third Sector in Europe*, A. Evers & J.-L. Laville (eds.); Cheltenham, UK & Northampton, MA, USA: Edward Elgar Publisher.

Ferris, J., 1984; Coprovision: Citizen Time and Money Donations in Public Service Provision, *Public Administration Review*, 14: 324–333.

Fotaki, M., 2011; Towards Developing New Partnerships in Public Services: Users as Consumers, Citizens and/or Co-Producers Driving Improvements in Health and Social Care in the UK and Sweden, *Public Administration*, 89/3: 933–995.

Fulsang, L. & J. Sundbo, 2009; The Organizational Innovation System: Three Modes, *Journal of Change Management*, 5/3: 329–344.

Fung, A., 2004; *Empowered Participation: Reinventing Urban Democracy*; Princeton, NJ: Princeton University Press.

Galbraith, J.K., 1983; Power and Organization, *The Anatomy of Power*; Boston: Houghton Mifflin.

Galbraith, J.K., 1986; Power and Organization, *Power: A Radical View*, S. Lukes (ed.); London: Basil Blackwell.

Galera, G. & C. Borzaga, 2009; Social Enterprise: An International Overview of Its Conceptual Evolution and Legal Implication, *Social Enterprise Journal*, 5/3: 210–228.

Giddens, A., 1998; *The Third Way: The Renewal of Social Democracy*; Oxford: B. Blackwell & Polity Press.

Grönross, C., 1990; *Service Management and Marketing: Managing the Moments of Truth in Service Competition*; Lexington, MA & Toronto: Lexington Books.

Gross, K., 2008; Altruism and Ambivalence: How America Celebrates, Channels and Constrains Its Benevolent Spirit; plenary address at Conference on Contemporary European Perspectives on Volunteering; Ersta Sköndal University College, Stockholm.

Häggroth, S., 2005; *Staten och kommunerna*; Stockholm: SOU, Ansvarskommittén.

Hald Larsen, S., 2015; The Relatives as Co-Producers in the Danish Context of Eldercare; paper presented to the IIAS Study Group on Co-Production, Nijmegen, Holland.

Hartley, J., 2005; Innovation in Governance and Public Services: Past and Present, *Public Money & Management*, 25/1: 27–34.

Hartley, J. & J. Benington, 2006; Copy and Paste, or Graft and Transplant? Knowledge Sharing through Inter-Organizational Networks, *Public Money & Management*, 26/2: 101–108.

Held, D., 1996; *Models of Democracy*; Cambridge: Polity Press.

Henriksen, L.S., S. Rathgeb Smith & A. Zimmer, 2012; At the Eve of Convergence? Transformations of Social Service Provision in Denmark, Germany and the United States, *Voluntas*, 23: 458–501.

Hinz, V. & S. Ingerfurth, 2013; Does Ownership Matter under Challenging Conditions? On the Relationship between Organizational Entrepreneurship and Performance in the Health Care Sector, *Public Management Review*, 15/7: 969–991.

Hirschman, A.O., 1970; *Exit, Voice & Loyalty: Responses to Decline in the Performance of Firms, Organizations and States*; Cambridge, MA & London: Harvard University Press.

Hirschman, A.O., 1982; *Shifting Involvements*; Princeton, NJ: Princeton University Press.

Hirst, P., 1994; *Associative Democracy: New Forms of Economic and Social Governance*; Cambridge: Polity Press.

Hirst, P., 2000; Models of Democratic Governance in a Post-Liberal Society, *What Constitutes a Good Society?*, B. Greve (ed.); London & New York: Macmillan Press & St. Martins' Press.

Hirst, P., 2002; Democracy and Governance, *Debating Governance, Authority, Steering and Democracy*, J. Pierre (ed.); Oxford: Oxford University Press.

Horne, M. & T. Shirley, 2009; *Co-Production in Public Services: A New Partnership with Citizens*; Cabinet Office, the Strategy Unit; London: HM Government.

Hudson, B., 2011; Big Society: A Concept in Pursuit of a Definition, *Journal of Integrated Care*, 19/8: 17–24.

Hudson, B., 2012; Competition or Co-Production?, *Making Health and Social Care Personal and Local: Moving from Mass Production to Co-Production*, E. Loeffler, D. Taylor-Goodby, T. Bovaird, F. Hine-Hughes & L. Wilkes (eds.); London: Governance International & Local Government Information Unit. www.govint.org and www.lgiu.org.uk.

Hulgård, L., 2014; Social Enterprise and the Third Sector: Innovative Service Delivery or a Non-Capitalist Economy?, *Social Enterprise and the Third Sector: Changing European Landscapes in a Comparative Perspective*, J. Defourny, L. Hulgård & V. Pestoff (eds.); London & New York: Routledge.

Ilmonen, K., 2005; The Problem of Disinterestedness and Reciprocity in Gift Economy; Conference Paper, Helsinki.

Independence Panel, 2015; *An Independent Mission: The Voluntary Sector in 2015*; London: The Baring Foundation.

Johnson, S., 2010; *Where Good Ideas Come From: The Natural History of Innovation*; London & New York: Penguin.

Karasek, R. & T. Theorell, 1990; *Healthy Work: Stress, Productivity and the Reconstruction of Working Life*; New York, NY: Basic Books.

Karlsson, M., 2002; *Själv Men Inte Ensam. Om Självhjälpsgrupper i Sverige*; Stockholm: Stockholm University, Institution for Socialt Arbete, Ph.D. dissertation.

Kendall, J. & M. Knapp, 1995; A Loose & Baggy Monster: Boundaries, Definitions and Typologies, *An Introduction to the Voluntary Sector*, D.J. Smith, C. Rochester & R. Hedley (eds.); London & New York: Routledge.

Kenis, P. & B. Marin (eds.), 1997; *Managing AIDS: Organizational Responses in Six European Countries*; Aldershot, UK & Brookfield, NJ: Ashgate.

Kerlin, J., 2006; Social Enterprise in the United States and Abroad: Learning from Our Differences, *Research on Social Entrepreneurship*; R. Mosher-Williams (ed.); ARNOVA Occasional Paper Series, 1/3: 105–125.

Kitschelt, H., P. Lange, G. Marks & J.D. Stephens (eds.), 1999; *Continuity and Change in Contemporary Capitalism*; Cambridge & New York: Cambridge University Press.

Långtidsutredningen, 2003, 2004; Stockholm: Finansdepartmentet, SOU 2004:19.

Larsgaard, A.-K., H. Hauge & E. Ek, 2015; Improving Children's Participation in Child Welfare Services through Social Enterprise; paper presented at EMES Conference, Helsinki.

Laville, J.-L., 1992; *Les services de proximite en Europe*; Paris: Syros Alternative.

Laville, J.-L., 1994; *L'economie solidare Une perspective internationale*; Paris: Desclee de Bauwer.

Levander, U., 2011; *Utanförskap på entreprenad. Diskurser om sociala företag i Sverige*; Göteborg: Daidalos Förlag.

Martin, G., 2011; The Third Sector, User Involvement and Public Service Reform: A Case Study in the Co-Governance of Health Care Provision, *Public Administration*, 89/3: 909–932.

Meijer, A., 2012; Co-Production in an Information Age, *New Public Governance, the Third Sector and Co-Production*, V. Pestoff, T. Brandsen & V. Verschuere (eds.); London & New York: Routledge.

Möller, T., 1996; *Brukare och klienter i välfärdsstaten: om missnöje och påverkans möjligheter inom barn- och äldreomsorg*; Stockholm: Publica, Nordstedts juridik.

Moore, M. & J. Hartley, J., 2012; Innovations in Governance, Ch. 4 in *The New Public Governance? Emerging Perspectives on the Theory and Practice of Public Governance*, S.P. Osborne (ed.); London & New York: Routledge.

Moulaert, F., B. Jessop, L. Hulgård & A. Hamdouch, 2013; Social Innovation: A New Stage in Innovation Process Analysis?, *Handbook on Social Innovation: Collective Action, Social Learning and Transdisciplinary Research*, F. Moulaert, D. MacCallum, A. Mehmood & A. Hamdouch (eds.); Cheltenham, UK & Northampton, MA, USA: Edward Elgar Publisher.

Nabatchi, T., A. Sancino & M. Siclia, 2017; Varieties of Participation in Public Services: The Who, When and What of Coproduction, *Public Administration Review*, 77: 766–776.

Nederhand, M.J. & I.F. Van Meerkerk, 2017; Activating Citizens in Dutch Welfare Reforms: Framing New Co-Production Roles and Competencies for Citizens and Professionals, *Policy & Politics*; DOI: 10.1332/030557317X15035697297906.

North, D., 1990; *Institutions, Institutional Change and Economic Performance*; Cambridge & New York: Cambridge University Press.

OECD, 2011; *Together for Better Public Services: Partnering with Citizens and Civil Society*; Paris: OECD Public Governance Reviews.

Olson, M., 1965, 1971; *The Logic of Collective Action: Public Goods and the Theory of Groups*; Cambridge, MA & London: Harvard University Press.

Osborne, S.P., 2006; Editorial on 'the New Public Governance', *Public Management Review*, 8/3: 377–387.

Osborne, S.P., 2010; The (New) Public Governance: A Suitable Case for Treatment?, *The New Public Governance? Emerging Perspectives on the Theory and Practice of Public Governance*, S.P. Osborne (ed.); London & New York: Routledge.

Osborne, S.P., 2017; From Public Service Dominant Logic to Public Service Logic: Are Public Service Organizations Capable of Co-Production and Value Co-Creation?, *Public Management Review*, Editorial; DOI: 10.1080/1479037.2017.1350461.

Osborne, S.P. & K. McLaughlin, 2004; The Cross-Cutting Review of the Voluntary Sector: What Next for Local Government Voluntary Sector Relationships, *Regional Studies*, 38/5: 573–582.

Osborne, S.P., Z. Radnor & G. Nasi, 2013; A New Theory for Public Service Management? Towards a (Public) Service Dominant Approach, *American Review of Public Administration*, 43/2: 135–158.

Osborne, S.P., Z. Radnor & K. Strokosch, 2016; Co-Production and the Co-Creation of Value in Public Services: A Suitable Case for Treatment?, *Public Management Review*, 15/8: 639–653; DOI: 10.1080/14719037.2015.1111927.

Osborne, S.P. & K. Strokosch, 2013; It Takes Two to Tango? Understanding the Co-Production of Public Services by Integrating the Service Management and Public Administration Perspectives, *British Journal of Management*, 24: 31–47.

Ostrom, E., 1975; *The Delivery of Urban Services: Outcomes of Change*; Beverly Hills: Sage Publications.

Ostrom, E., 1996; Crossing the Great Divide: Coproduction, Synergy, and Development, *World Development*, 24/6: 1073–1087; reprinted in 1999 as Ch. 15, *Polycentric Governance and Development: Readings from the Workshop in Political Theory and Policy Analysis*, McGinnis, M.D. (ed.); Ann Arbor, MI: University of Michigan Press.

Ostrom, E., 2000a; Crowding out Citizenship, *Scandinavian Political Studies*, 23/1: 1–16.

Ostrom, E., 2000b; Collective Action and the Evolution of Social Norms, *Journal of Economic Perspectives*, 14/3: 137–158.

Ostrom, E., 2009a; Social Cooperation in Collective-Action Situations, *Neue Kölner Genossenschaftswissenschaft*, H.J. Rösner & F. Schulz-Nieswandt (eds.); Cologne: Work & Cooperative Sciences Institute, AGI Institute.

Ostrom, E., 2009b; Beyond Markets and States: Polycentric Governance of Complex Economic Systems; Nobel Prize Lecture December 8, 2009, Stockholm, Sweden, pp. 408–444.

Ostrom, E., 2012; Foreword to *New Public Governance, the Third Sector and Co-Production*, V. Pestoff, T. Brandsen & V. Verschuere (eds.); London & New York: Routledge.

Ostrom, E. & V. Ostrom, 1971; Public Choice: A Different Approach to the Study of Public Administration, *Public Admin. Review*, March/April: 203–216; reprinted in 1999 as Ch. 1 in *Polycentric Games and Institutions*, M. McGinnis (ed.); Ann Arbor, MI: University of Michigan Press.

Parks, R.B., P.C. Baker, L. Kiser, R. Oakerson, E. Ostrom, V. Ostrom, S.L. Perry, M.B. Vandivort & G.P. Whitaker, 1981; Consumers as Co-Producers of Public Services: Some Economic and Institutional Considerations, *Policy Studies Journal*, 9: 1001–1011; reprinted in 1999 as Ch. 17 *in Local Public Economies: Readings from the Workshop in Political Theory and Policy Analysis*, M.D. McGinnis (ed.); Ann Arbor, MI: University of Michigan Press.

Pekkola, E., S. Tuurnas, J. Stenvall & K. Hakari, 2015; Implementing Top-Down Localization Policies: Creation of Local Public Value?; paper presented at IIAS Study Group on Co-Production, Nijmegen.

Percy, S., 1984; Citizen Participation in the Co-Production of Urban Services, *Urban Affairs Quarterly*, 19/4: 431–446.

Pestoff, V., 1977; *Voluntary Associations and Nordic Party Systems: A Study of Overlapping Memberships and Cross-Pressures in Finland, Norway and Sweden*; Stockholm: Dept. of Political Science, Studies in Politics, No. 10, Ph.D. dissertation.

Pestoff, V., 1984; *Konsumentinflytande och kosumentorganisering—den svenska modellen*; Stockholm: Swedish Ministry of Finance, Ds 1984:15.

Pestoff, V., 1988; Exit, Voice and Collective Action in Swedish Consumer Policy, *Journal of Consumer Policy*, 11: 1–27.

Pestoff, V., 1989; *Näringslivsorganisationer och politiken i Sverige*; Stockholm: TCO Info, Data, Dokument, Debatt.

Pestoff, V., 1990; Nonprofit Organizations and Consumer Policy: The Swedish Model, *The Third Sector: Comparative Studies of Non-Profit Organizations*, H. Anheier & W. Seibel (eds.); Berlin & New York: Walter de Gruyter.

Pestoff, V., 1991; *Between Markets and Politics: Cooperatives in Sweden*; Frankfurt & Bolder: Campus Verlag & Westview Press.

Pestoff, V., 1992; Third Sector and Cooperative Social Services: An Alternative to Privatization, *Journal of Consumer Policy*, 15/1: 27–45.

Pestoff, V., 1994; Beyond Exit & Voice in Social Services: Citizens as Co-Producers, *Delivering Welfare: Repositioning Non-Profit and Co-operative Action in Western European Welfare States*, I. Vidal (ed.); Barcelona: CIES & Autonomous University of Barcelona. p. 6.

Pestoff, V., 1998; *Beyond the Market & State: Social Enterprises and Civil Democracy in a Welfare Society*; Aldershot, UK & Brookfield, NJ: Ashgate.

Pestoff, V., 2000; Enriching Swedish Women's Work Environment: The Case of Social Enterprises in Day Care, *Economic & Industrial Democracy*, 21/1: 39–70.

Pestoff, V., 2005; Globalization and Swedish Business Interests Associations in the 21st Century, *Governing Interests: Business Associations; Facing Internationalization*, W. Streeck, J. Grote, V. Schneider & J. Visser (eds.); London & New York: Routledge.

Pestoff, V., 2006; Citizens as Co-Producers of Welfare Services: Preschool Services in Eight European Countries, *Public Management Review*, 8/4: 503–520; reprinted in 2006 as a hardback and 2009 as a paperback, *Co-Production: The Third Sector and the Delivery of Public Services*; V. Pestoff & T. Brandsen (eds.); London & New York: Routledge.

Pestoff, V., 2008a; *A Democratic Architecture for the Welfare State: Promoting Citizen Participation, the Third Sector and Co-Production*; London & New York: Routledge.

Pestoff, V., 2008b; Co-Production, the Third Sector and Functional Representation, *The Third Sector in Europe: Prospects and Challenges*, S. Osborne (ed.); London & New York: Routledge.

Pestoff, V., 2009; Towards a Paradigm of Democratic Governance: Citizen Participation and Co-Production of Personal Social Services in Sweden, *Annals of Public and Cooperative Economy*, 80/2: 197–224.

Pestoff, V., 2011a; Lost in Translation or What's Not Included in the Polish Social Economy?; paper presented at the ISTR International Conference, Siena, Italy.

Pestoff, V., 2011b; Cooperatives and Democracy in Scandinavia: The Swedish Case, *Nordic Civil Society at a Cross-Roads: Transforming the Popular Movement Tradition*, F. Wijkstrom & A. Zimmer (eds.); Baden-Baden: Nomos.

Pestoff, V., 2012a; Co-Production and Third Sector Social Services in Europe: Some Concepts and Evidence, *Voluntas*, 23: 1102–1118.

Pestoff, V., 2012b; Co-Production and Third Sector Social Services in Europe: Some Crucial Conceptual Issues, Ch. 2 in *New Public Governance, the Third Sector and Co-Production*, V. Pestoff, T. Brandsen & B. Verschuere (eds.); London & New York: Routledge.

Pestoff, V., 2012c; Hybrid Tendencies in Consumer Cooperatives: The Case of Sweden, Ch. 9 in *The Co-operative Model in Practice: International Perspectives*, D. McDonnell & E. Macknight (eds.); Aberdeen: University of Aberdeen & Co-Operative Educational Trust Scotland.

Pestoff, V., 2014a; Collective Action and the Sustainability of Co-Production, *Public Management Review*, 16/3: 383–401.

Pestoff, V., 2014b; Hybridity, Co-Production and Third Sector Social Services in Europe, *American Behavioral Scientists*, 58/11: 1412–1424.

Pestoff, V., 2016; Democratic Innovations: Exploring Synergies between Three Key Post: NPM Concepts in Public Sector Reforms, Ch. 15 in *Social Entrepreneurship and Social Enterprises: Nordic Perspectives*, L. Lundgaard Andersen, M. Gawell & R. Spear (eds.); London & New York: Routledge; eISBN: 9781315621982.

Pestoff, V., 2018a; Co-Production at the Crossroads of Public Administration Regimes, Ch. 4 in *Co-Production and Co-Creation: Engaging Citizens in Public Service Delivery*, T. Brandsen, T. Steen & B. Verschuere (eds.); London & New York: Routledge.

Pestoff, V., 2018b; The Impact of Public Administration Regimes and Co-Production on Hybrid Organizations, forthcoming as Chap. 4 in *Handbook on Hybrid Organizations*, D. Billis & C. Rochester (eds.); Cheltenham, UK & Northampton, MA: Edward Elgar Publisher.

Pestoff, V. & T. Brandsen (eds.), 2006; Co-Production: The Third Sector and the Delivery of Public Services, Special Issue of *Public Management Review*; reprinted in 2008 as a hardback and in 2009 as a paperback; London & New York: Routledge.

Pestoff, V., T. Brandsen & S. Osborne, 2006; Patterns of Co-Production in Public Services: Some Concluding Thoughts, *Public Management Review*, 8/4: 591–595; reprinted in 2009 in *Co-Production: The Third Sector and the Delivery of Public Services*; V. Pestoff & T. Brandsen (eds.); London & New York: Routledge.

Pestoff, V., T. Brandsen & B. Verschuere, (eds.), 2012; *New Public Governance, the Third Sector and Co-Production*; London & New York: Routledge.

Pestoff, V. & L. Hulgård, 2016; Participatory Governance in Social Enterprise, *Voluntas*, 27/4: 1742–1759; DOI: 10.1007/s11266-1015-99962-3.

Pestoff, V., A. Kurimoto, C. Gijselinckx, A. Hoyt & M. Vuotto, 2016; Volunteering in Consumer and Service Cooperatives, Ch. 21 in *The Palgrave Handbook of Volunteering, Civic Participation, and Nonprofit Associations*, D. Horton Smith, R.A. Stebbings & J. Grotz (eds.); Houndmills, Hamps & New York, NY: Palgrave Macmillian.

Pestoff, V., Y. Saito & J. Vamstad, 2016; *Co-Production in Health and Elder Care: The Japanese Model for Better Service Quality: A Project Description*; Stockholm & Osaka: Ersta Sköndal University College and Osaka University.

Pestoff, V. & J. Vamstad, 2014; Enriching Work Environment in the Welfare Service Sector: The Case of Social Enterprises in Swedish Childcare, *Annals of Public and Co-Operative Economics*, 85/3: 353–370.

Peters, G., 1994; Alternative Models of Governance: The Changing State of Public Service; IPSA Congress paper, RC27, Berlin.

Peters, G., 1996; *The Future of Governing: Four Emerging Models*; Lawrence, KS: University Press of Kansas.

Politiken; 25 October, 2015; Copenhagen, Denmark.

Porter, D., 2012; Co-Production and Network Structures in Public Education, *New Public Governance, the Third Sector and Co-Production*, V. Pestoff, T. Brandsen & B. Verschuere (eds.); London & New York: Routledge.

Putnam, R., 1993; *Making Democracy Work: Civic Traditions in Modern Italy*; Princeton, NJ: Princeton University Press.

Putnam, R., 2005; *Bowling Alone: The Collapse and Revival of American Community*; New York: Simon & Schuster.

Rich, R.C., 1981; Interaction of the Voluntary & Governmental Sectors: Towards an Understanding of the Coproduction of Municipal Services, *Administration & Society*, 13/1: 59–76.

Rogers, E.M., 1995; *Diffusion of Innovation*; New York: Free Press.

Rosentraub, M. & R. Warren, 1987; Citizen Participation in the Production of Urban Services, *Public Productivity Review*, 41: 75–89.

Salge, T. & A. Vera, 2009; Hospital Innovativeness and Organizational Performance: Evidence from English Public Acute Care, *Health Care Management Review*, 34/1: 54–67.

Schlappa, H. & Y. Imani, 2016; Leading Service Co-Production: Preliminary Findings from a Study of the Hertfordshire Fire and Rescue Service; Tampere: IIAS Study Group on Co-Production.

Sharp, E.B., 1980; Towards a New Understanding of Urban Services and Citizen Participation: The Co-Production Concept, *Midwest Review of Public Administration*, 14/June: 105–118.

Shekarabi, A., 2012; *Vinst och den offentliga tjänstemarknad*; Stockholm: Arena ide, Ny Tid Rapport 15.

Sivesind, K.-H., 2016; *The Changing Role of For-Profit and Nonprofit Welfare Provision in Norway, Sweden and Denmark and Consequences for the Scandinavian Model*; Oslo: Institute for Social Research.

Slocock, S., 2015; *Whose Society? The Final Big Society Audit*; London: Civil Change.

Socialstyrelsen, 2014; *Flere og stærkere socialøkonomiske virksomheder i Danmark*; Copenhagen: Ministeriet for børn, ligestilling, integration og sociale forhold & Socialstyrelsen.

Söderholm Werkö, S., 2008; *Patient Patients? Achieving Patient Empowerment through Active Participation, Increasing Knowledge and Organization*; Stockholm: Stockholm University, Doctoral Dissertation in Business Administration.

Statistiska Meddelanden, 2012; *Finansiärer och utförare inom vård och omsorg 2010*; Stockholm: SCB, Sveriges Officiella Statistik, OE 29 SM 1201.

Strandbrink, P. & V. Pestoff, 2006; *Small Scale Welfare on a Large Scale: Social Cohesion and the Politics of Swedish Childcare*; Huddinge: Södertörns högskola, Research Report 2006: 5.

Streeck, W. & P. Schmitter, 1995; Community, Market, State: And Associations?, *Private Interest Government: Beyond Market and State*; Beverly Hills & London: Sage Publications.

Stryjan, Y., 1989; *Impossible Organizations: Self-Management and Organizational Reproduction*; Westport, CT: Greenwood Press.

Tabata, K., 2014; Health and Welfare Policy in Japan: Toward the Establishment of 'Integrated Community Care System'; paper presented at the CIREC 30th Congress, Buenos Aires.

Taylor, M., 2011; Community Organizing and the Big Society: Is Saul Alinisky Turning in His Grave?, *Voluntary Sector Review*, 3/3: 299–328.

Thomas, J.C., 2012; *Citizen, Customer and Partner: Engaging the Public in Public Management*; Armonk, NY: M.E. Scharp.

Thomas, J.C., 2013; Citizens, Customers, Partners: Rethinking the Place of the Public in Public Management, *Public Administration Review*, 73: 786–796.

Thomsen, M. K. & M. Jakobsen, 2015; Influencing Citizens: Co-Production by Sending Encouragement and Advice: A Field Experiment, *International Public Management Journal*, 18/2: 286–303.

Tönurist, P. & L. Sruva, 2017; Is Volunteering Always Voluntary? Between Compulsion and Coercion in Co-Production, *Voluntas*, 28: 223–247.

Tortzen, A., 2016; *Samskabelse i kommunale rammer—hvordan kan ledelse understötte samskabelse?*; Roskilde: Institut for Samfundsvidenskab og Erhverv, Ph.D. dissertation.

Tsutsui, T., 2014; Implementation Process and Challenges for the Community-Based Integrated Care System in Japan, *International Journal of Integrated Care*; Jan–Mar, 14, e002, on line, PMID: 24478614.

Tuurnas, S., 2015; Learning to Co-produce? The Perspective of Public Service Professionals; *International Journal of Public Sector Management*, 28/7: 786–796.

Ungsuchaval, T., 2016; NGOization of Civil Society as Unintended Consequence? Premises on the Thai Health Promotion Foundation and Its Pressures toward NGOs in Thailand; ISTR Conference Paper, Stockholm.

Vamstad, J., 2007; *Governing Welfare: The Third Sector and the Challenges to the Swedish Welfare State*; Östersund: Mid-Sweden University, No. 37, Ph.D. thesis.

Vamstad, J., 2012; Co-Production and Service Quality: A New Perspective for the Swedish Welfare State, *New Public Governance, the Third Sector and Co-Production*, V. Pestoff, T. Brandsen & B. Verschuere (eds.); London & New York: Routledge.

Van Der Meer, T., M. Te Grotenhuis & P. Scheelers, 2009; Three Types of Voluntary Associations in Comparative Perspective: The Importance of Studying Associational Involvement through a Typology of Associations in 21 European Countries, *Journal of Civil Society*, 5/3: 227–242.

Van Kersbergen, K. & F. Van Waarden, 2004; Governance as a Bridge between Disciplines: Cross-Disciplinary Inspiration Regarding Shifts in Governance and Problems of Governability, Accountability and Legitimacy, *European Journal of Political Research*, 43/2: 143–171.

Verschuere, B., T. Brandsen & V. Pestoff, 2012; Co-Production: The State of the Art in Research and the Future Agenda, *Voluntas*, 23/4: 1083–1101.

Vidal, I., 2008; Should Social Enterprise Be a Core Element in the Provision of Public Services or Is It a Distraction?, *The Third Sector in Europe: Prospects and Challenges*, S. Osborne (ed.); London & New York.: Routledge.

Vidal, I., 2013; Governance of Social Enterprises as Producers of Public Services, Ch. 10 in *Organisational Innovation in Public Services: Forms and Governance*, P. Valkama, S. Bailey & A.-V. Anttiroiko (eds.); New York & London: Palgrave Macmillian.

Villancourt, Y., Social economy in the co-construction of public policy, *Annals of Public and Co-operative Economy*, 82/2: 275–313.

Voorberg, W.H., V.J.J.M. Bekkers, S. Flemig, K. Timeus, P. Tönurist & L. Tummers, 2017; Does Co-Creation Impact Service Delivery?, *Public Money & Management*, 37/5: 365–373.

Voorberg, W.H., V.J.J.M. Bekkers & L.G. Tummers, 2015; A Systematic Review of Co-Creation and Co-Production: Embarking on the Social Innovation Journey, *Public Management Review*, 17/9: 1333–1357; DOI: 10.1080/14719037.2014.930505.

Wahlgren, I., 1996; *Vem tröstar Ruth? En studie av alternativa driftsformer i hemtjänsten*; Stockholm: Stockholm University, School of Business, Ph.D. dissertation.

Walden-Laing, D., 2001; *HIV/AIDS in Sweden and the United Kingdom Policy Networks 1982–1992*; Stockholm: Stockholm University, Studies in Politics, No. 81, Ph.D. dissertation.

Walden-Laing, D. & V. Pestoff, 1997; The Role of Nonprofit Organizations in Managing HIV/AIDS in Sweden, in *Managing AIDS: Organizational Responses in Six European Countries*, P. Kenis & B. Marin (eds.); Aldershot, UK & Brookfield, NJ: Ashgate.

Walker, R.M., 2014; Internal and External Antecedents of Process Innovation: A Review and Extension, *Public Management Review*, 16/1: 21–44.

Walzer, M., 1988; Socializing the Welfare State, *Democracy and the Welfare State*, A. Gutmann (ed.); Princeton, NJ: Princeton University Press.

Warren, R., K. Harlow & M. Rosentraub, 1982; Citizen Participation in the Production of Services: Methodological and Policy Issues in Coproduction Research, *Southwestern Review of Management and Economics*, 2: 41–55.

Westin, A., 2006; Med rätt att bestämma själv; Östersund: Mid-Sweden University, Master's thesis.

Whitaker, G., 1980; Co-Production: Citizen Participation in Service Delivery, *Public Administration Review*, May/June: 240–246.

Wikström, S., 1993; The Customer as Co-Producer, *Studies in Action and Enterprise*; Stockholm: Stockholm University, Department of Business Administration.

Wikström, S., 1996; Value Creation by Company: Consumer Interaction, *Journal of Marketing Management*, 12: 259–274.

Williamson, O.E., 1985; *The Economic Institutions of Capitalism: Firms, Markets and Relational Contracting*; New York: The Free Press.

Williamson, O.E., 1992; Institutional Aspects of Economic Reform: The Transaction Cost Economic Perspective; Transformation Processes in Eastern Europe: Challenges for Socio-Economic Theory, Cracow Academy of Economics, Krakow, sem. paper, no. 19.

Wood, V.R., S. Bhuian & P. Kiecker, 2000; Market Orientation and Organizational Performance in Not-for-Profit Hospitals, *Journal of Business Research*, 48/3: 213–226.

Young, D., 2008; Alternative Perspectives on Social Enterprise, *Nonprofits & Business*, J.J. Cordes & C.E. Steuerle (eds.); Washington, DC: The Urban Institute. pp. 21–46.

Young, D., 2009; A Unified Theory of Social Enterprise, *Non-Market Entrepreneurship: Interdisciplinary Approaches*, G.E. Shockley, G.P. Frank & R. Stough (eds.); Cheltenham, UK & Northampton, MA, USA: Edward Elgar Publisher.

6, P. & I. Vidal, (eds.) 1994; *Delivering Welfare – repositioning non-profit and co-operative action in western European welfare states*. Barcelona: CIES.

TSFEPS Reports

The TSFEPS Project, Changing Family Structures and Social Policy: Childcare Services as Sources of Social Cohesion, took place in eight European countries between 2002 and 2004. They were Belgium, Bulgaria, England, France, Germany, Italy, Spain and Sweden. See www.emes.net for more details and the reports listed below.

Dandalova, I., 2003; *Transformations des familles et modes d'accueil à la petite enfance: politiques, services et cohésion sociale*; Sofia: Bulgarian Academy of Sciences, Housing & Urban Research Assoc.

Evers, A. & B. Riedel, 2003; *Governance and Social Cohesion in Childcare: The Example of Frankfurt and München*; Giessen: Justus-Liebig-Universität.

Fraisse, L. & E. Bucolo, 2003; *TSFEPS Etude de Cas—France*; Paris: CRIDA.

Lewis, J., et al., 2003; *TSFEPS: UK Case Study Report*; Oxford: University of Oxford, Dept. of Social Policy & Social Work.

Lhuillier, V., 2003; *TSFEPS—Études de Cas: Bruxelles—Schaerbeek et Ottignies—Louvain la Neuve*; Louvin: CERISIS, Universite Catholique de Louvain.

Mingione, E., et al., 2003; TSFEPS: WP4, Italian Case studies report; Dept. of Sociology & Social Research, Milan: Università Degli Studi di of Milano—Bicocca.

Strandbrink, P. & V. Pestoff, 2003; *Small Children in a Big System: A Case Study of Childcare in Stockholm & Östersund*; Huddinge & Östersund: Södertörns högskola & Mid-Sweden University.

Vidal, I. & N. Claver, 2003; *TSFEPS, Spain: Case Study*; Barcelona: CIES & Autonomous University of Barcelona.

Index

Page numbers in italic indicate a figure and page numbers in bold indicate a table on the corresponding page.

Printed in the United States
By Bookmasters